If You Seduce a Straight Person, Can You Make Them Gay?
Issues in Biological Essentialism versus Social Constructionism in Gay and Lesbian Identities

John P. De Cecco, PhD
John P. Elia, PhD (cand.)
Editors

If You Seduce a Straight Person, Can You Make Them Gay? Issues in Biological Essentialism versus Social Constructionism in Gay and Lesbian Identities, edited by John P. De Cecco and John P. Elia, was simultaneously issued by The Haworth Press, Inc., under the same title, as a special issue of *Journal of Homosexuality,* Volume 24, Numbers 3/4, 1993. John P. DeCecco, Editor.

Harrington Park Press
An Imprint of
The Haworth Press, Inc.
New York • London • Norwood (Australia)

353727

ISBN 1-56023-034-7

Published by

Harrington Park Press, 10 Alice Street, Binghamton, NY 13904-1580 USA

Harrington Park Press is an imprint of The Haworth Press, Inc., 10 Alice Street, Binghamton, NY 13904-1580 USA.

If You Seduce a Straight Person, Can You Make Them Gay? Issues in Biological Essentialism versus Social Constructionism in Gay and Lesbian Identities was originally published as *Journal of Homosexuality,* Volume 24, Numbers 3/4 1993.

Library of Congress Cataloging-in-Publication Data

If you seduce a straight person, can you make them gay? issues in biological essentialism versus social constructionism in gay and lesbian identities / John P. De Cecco, John P. Elia, editors.
    p. cm.
    Includes bibliographical references and index.
    ISBN 1-56024-386-4 (alk. paper).–ISBN 1-56023-034-7 (pbk. : alk. paper)
    1. Homosexuality. 2. Gays–Identity. I. De Cecco, John P. II. Elia, John P.
HQ76.25.I38 1993
306.76'6–dc20
                           92-39461
                            CIP

If You Seduce a Straight Person, Can You Make Them Gay?
Issues in Biological Essentialism versus Social Constructionism in Gay and Lesbian Identities

CONTENTS

ALL HARRINGTON PARK PRESS BOOKS
ARE PRINTED ON CERTIFIED
ACID-FREE PAPER

If You Seduce a Straight Person, Can You Make Them Gay?
Issues in Biological Essentialism versus Social Constructionism in Gay and Lesbian Identities

ABOUT THE EDITORS

John P. De Cecco, PhD, has been editor of the *Journal of Homosexuality* since 1977. He is presently the director of the interdisciplinary program in human sexuality studies at San Francisco State University, where he has been Professor of Psychology since 1960. He is now editor-in-chief of The Haworth Press Gay and Lesbian Study booklist.

John P. Elia received two Bachelor of Arts degrees in history and physical education and a Master of Arts degree in history from San Francisco State University, where he has been teaching health education, human sexuality, and psychology courses for the past five years. He is currently a doctoral student in education at the University of California, Davis. He is the author of *Human Sexuality: Instructor's Manual* (second edition, Mosby-Yearbook Publishers, 1992). In addition, he has published articles on the history of sexuality. Also, he serves as assistant editor and book review editor for the *Journal of Homosexuality* as well as being a research associate in the Center for Research and Education in Sexuality (CERES) at San Francisco State University.

Preface

In their original form, the papers published in this volume, with two exceptions, were among those presented in the social studies section of the last international conference on lesbian, gay, and bisexual studies, *Homosexuality, Which Homosexuality?* held in 1987 at the Free University in Amsterdam. Most of the papers have been updated and revised. The publication of some of the historical papers presented at the conference is planned for future issues of *Journal of Homosexuality.*

The conference was organized by a group of Dutch scholars who, in collaboration with English-language researchers, were interested in creating a broad interdisciplinary forum for research and theoretical speculation on homosexuality. The conference was specifically designed to introduce "social constructionist" views of sexuality and gender as a challenge to the "essentialist" approaches that had dominated the research of the preceding decade. These two perspectives are described later.

The HWH conference, as it came to be known, followed on the heels of another, *Homosexuality Beyond Disease,* hastily assembled by former members of the Gay and Lesbian Studies program at Utrecht University, which was then known as the home of Dutch essentialism. The almost simultaneous occurrence of the two conferences was Janus-like, one face looking back to the so-called essentialist research of the seventies, with its heated quest for the hidden history of gay men and lesbians, and the other looking forward to what has become the scholarship of the late eighties and nineties, now collectively characterized as social constructionist.

Among the many intellectual progenitors of the HWH conference were scholars who had examined the meanings of sexuality and gender to show how they varied with their historical and cultural contexts. They included feminists such as Carole Vance and Martha Vicinus; the sociologists such as John Gagnon, Mary McIntosh, Kenneth Plummer, and Jeffrey Weeks; the historians of early modern Europe, such as Alan Bray, Randolph Trumbach, and Theo van der Meer; and the ranking French intellectual of the era, Michel Foucault. What had begun in the seventies and early eighties as a modest effort to chronicle and universalize homosexuality as a unitary biological phenomenon that transcended its historical and cultural contexts, unwittingly led such scholars to challenge the view of sexuality and gender generally held by the public, which we are calling *biological essentialism.*

There are many persons we wish to thank for their contributions to this collection. First of all there are the authors who warmly responded to our invitation to include their papers and patiently revised their manuscripts. We are indebted to our faithful research assistants, Linda Heidenreich and Alan Wolf who, over a period of several months, diligently edited the papers, which was a demanding task for both them and the authors since English was not the native tongue of several contributors. Linda deserves our special thanks for her expert word-processing of the edited papers.

We are grateful to the many organizers of the HWH conference, particularly Anna van Kooten-Niekerk and Theo van der Meer, who encouraged us to undertake this project, provided us the means of contacting contributors, and, in innumerable ways, made the senior editor's sabbatical year in Amsterdam a very special intellectual and pleasurable sojourn.

John P. De Cecco
San Francisco State University

John P. Elia
San Francisco State University
and University of California, Davis

I. INTRODUCTION

A Critique and Synthesis of Biological Essentialism and Social Constructionist Views of Sexuality and Gender

John P. De Cecco, PhD
John P. Elia, MA, PhD (cand.)

SUMMARY. To say that a person is homosexual is a statement about an individual in a particular social context and at a particular point in that person's life. Homosexuality is an aspect of sexual and gender expression that profoundly reflects contemporary social and cultural values. The essay is critical of both biological essentialist and social constructionist views. Biological essentialism depicts a process in which biological influences precede cultural influences and set predetermined limits to the effects of culture. In effect, it submerges sexual preference, a human process, into sexual orientation, a biological mechanism. Social constructionism tends to depict the individual as an empty organism that is filled and shaped by culture and society and is devoid of consciousness and intention. An alternative view is proposed that views sexual and gender expression as a product of complementary biological, personal, and cultural influences.

THE BIOLOGICAL ESSENTIALIST VIEW
OF SEXUALITY AND GENDER

Biological essentialism is an academic version of conventional beliefs about sexuality and gender that had their origins in the eighteenth and nineteenth centuries. The conventional view reduces sexuality to sex. To maintain the distinction between biological and social levels of discourse, we shall use *sex* to refer to the physical and material ingredients that make up the actors and their behaviors, and *sexuality* to embrace the interpretations or meanings assigned to the body, behavior, and desire in various individual, historical, and cultural contexts. From the public perspective sexuality is collapsed into sex as a palpable *thing* of nature, a biological given, lodged in the body and concentrated in the genitals, everywhere and at all times the same basic thing.

The conventional view, in effect, anchors sexual and gender expression in anatomy. Anatomy (along with physiology) becomes destiny. Although its adherents are not troubled by the possibility that sexual experience includes pleasure and bonding, it is popularly believed that "nature" intended sexuality as a biological imperative for reproduction. In this conception, the physical structures of ovaries, uterus, and vagina are believed to be the essential elements of female sexuality; for males there is a complementary structure consisting of a penis and testicles. As behavior, sexuality is essentially an act of copulation, fucking, a physical act that fits together the divinely, or naturally, matched penis and vagina of the "opposite" sexes.

The motive power for the sexual act, in the popular imagination, lies within the physical recesses of the body, particularly the genitals. Sexual attraction is believed first of all to be a physical attraction–the overwrought working of a sexual instinct, drive, proclivity, tendency, impulse or body chemistry–that irresistibly propels each sex toward the other and resolutely and triumphantly toward the performance of the great primal act. The motor of sex is believed to be assembled before birth and steers us through a lifetime of sexual experience. When operating according to its pre-ordained biological norms, it leads individuals to the fulfillment of their heterosexual reproductive destinies.

The emotional properties of sexual and gender expression are conceived as physical derivatives. With the penis leading the way, men are the active principle in their sexual congress with women–the pursuers, the initiators, the penetrators, and the controlling tops. Women, with swollen breasts and outstretched arms, are the receptors, yielding bottoms, more interested in love and pleasing their men than in their own physical gratification. In the twentieth century update of the conventional view, it is believed that is how nature intended it to be when men were designed to be driven by testosterone, the "male" hormone, and women governed by estrogen, the "female" hormone, which is popularly associated more with fertilization and pregnancy than sexual arousal.

This popular view of sexuality and gender is grafted on to homosexuality with three transformations that leave the parent view fully intact. First, the idea of sexual drive, which propels people to have sex, is transformed into the idea of "sexual orientation" that includes both the original, independent biological motive power but now adds the possibility of attraction to people of one's own gender. Second, to preserve the notion of opposite-sex attraction, the genders are inverted so that men engaging in homosexual behavior are seen as behaving as women, with penises, and the women so engaged as behaving as men, with vaginas. Third, the *act* of having sex with a partner of one's own gender becomes the *actor,* so that we end up with "homosexuals" who represent a biological, psychological, and social curiosity, a "sport" of nature, that keeps them distinct from "heterosexuals."

The history of early modern northern Europe shows that a reconceptualization of gender occurred in the eighteenth century and a thorough medicalization of gender followed in the nineteenth century. In the eighteenth century two genders, male and female, became four when it was believed that there could be a heterosexual or homosexual version of each gender. The homosexual gender in men became associated with femininity; in women it was associated with masculinity (Trumbach, 1991).

Under the panoply of science, it was medicine, in the nineteenth and twentieth centuries, that took over the popular view of sexuality and gender. In the nineteenth century it pathologized the two homosexual genders and the associated sexual behavior. In the twentieth century, medicine, now in the scientific garb of sexology, has attempted to quantify the older qualitative division of heterosexual vs. homosexual while retaining the notion of the heterosexual-homosexual dichotomy.

This quantification has occurred in several ways. First, since the medical invention of homosexuality as a mental and physical condition, there had always been the distinction between "inherited" (sometimes called "obligatory") and acquired (also called "facultative") homosexuality. It was assumed that those born homosexuals were more homosexual than those who merely succumbed to the temptations of the moment or lack a heterosexual outlet. Secondly, the Kinsey scale, along which ratings could vary from 0 (an unblemished heterosexual record) to 6 (a perfect homosexual record), intended by Kinsey and his associates to identify behavior, was used to identify the degree to which a person was homosexual. Third, particularly with the discovery of the hormones, a person could be more or less heterosexual or homosexual, depending upon her or his pre-natal or current hormonal status (itself determined by genes) and the relative absence or presence of specific tissue in one region of the brain. Although current research on the "causes" of homosexuality use quantitative measures of sexuality, both research reports and press reports of the research continue to label their subjects categorically as either homosexuals or heterosexuals, with some reluctant allusions to bisexuals who perversely make their presence known, it would appear, only to muddy the otherwise tidy conceptual waters.

SOCIAL CONSTRUCTIONIST VIEW OF SEXUALITY AND GENDER

We will use two of the HWH conference papers, one by Carole Vance (1988) and the other by Jeffrey Weeks (1988), to outline the social constructionist view. Their adumbration of this position presents it both as a critique of biological essentialism and as an independent set of principles.

It appears that their most basic tenet is that what has been popularly regarded as a fixed biological reality is malleable. Vance (1988, p.13) states, "Social construction theory in the field of sexuality proposed an extremely outrageous idea. It suggested that one of the last remaining outposts of the 'natural' in our thinking was fluid and changeable, the product of human action and history rather than the invariant result of the body, biology, or innate sex drive." In fact, Weeks (1988) entitled his conference paper "Against Nature." Both Vance and Weeks point to the human contribution to sexuality. Although both believe that history bequeaths or confronts us with social circumstances not of our own choosing, it is society and culture that construct new sexualities.

Although Vance and Weeks would agree that human sexuality is constructed, they appear to conceive the results somewhat differently. In the tradition of the social sciences, Vance (1988, p. 23) favors a behavioral definition. She writes of "core behaviors and physical relations [that] are reliably understood as sexual, even though they occur in diverse cultures and historical periods." In a more literary tradition, Weeks focuses more on what people think or feel than what they do. He refers to collective or personal "subjectivities" (i.e., sexual identities such as gay, lesbian, sadomasochist). A sexual subjectivity, in his words (p. 207), is "not inborn, pregiven or 'natural'. It is striven for, contested, negotiated, and achieved often in the struggles of the subordinate to the dominate." Therefore, he regards the gay identity as an historical achievement even though it may represent a biological fiction.

Weeks' position has been that homosexuals are not a natural biological species but an invention (i.e., construction) of a biological species by nineteenth century medicine and sexology, the conversion of an act or behavior, previously called sodomy, into a psychobiological *condition*. Still later, in the twentieth century, the condition was depathologized and converted into a sexual identity by the homophile and gay liberation movements.

As this example demonstrates, what changes most strikingly, according to Weeks, are the meanings and categories that deal with gender and sexuality in various historical periods and in various types of writing or "languages" such as medical reports, religious treatises, romantic novels, and political tracts. The meanings or categories that are employed in such discussions of sexuality become its regulators. The languages of sexuality, Weeks asserts (1988, p. 208), "tell us what sex is, what it ought to be, and what it could be." Because of the multiplicity of languages, he points out, the sexual messages put forth at a given historical moment can be contradictory.

Vance is also concerned with changes in subjectivity and meaning. She focuses on the contrasting conceptions of sexual functioning and pleasure that we encounter in moving from one culture to another. In North American sexology, for example, female orgasm is often conceived as centered in the clitoris and experienced as the pinnacle of sexual pleasure. Vance ponders such questions as the following: Can sexual pleasure be experienced by women who have undergone a culturally ordained clitoral circumcision, which occurs in parts of Africa, without orgasm as a physiological response to coitus? Is female orgasm itself socially constructed? Is it possible to construct women's sexual pleasure without including orgasm?

In the eyes of Vance and Weeks, because the gay or lesbian identities rest on interpretations of sexuality and gender rather than on biology does not make them trivial or whimsical. Since interpretations of sexuality and gender are institutionalized, Vance believes they are perceived by those who subscribe to them as social and cultural realities. Individuals, therefore, are not able to change at will since any change must adapt to the historical constraints under which it is contemplated. Taking a more political stance, Weeks (p. 207) believes that, although new interpretations of sexuality and gender are historically molded, they are of major importance "in challenging the imposition of arbitrary social norms" and should be defended with passion and commitment.

How do their social constructionist views of sexuality and gender accommodate the body? The body appears to be a more explicit concern for Vance than for Weeks. Vance (p. 26) asks how the body can be a part of social constructionism without the theory reverting to biological essentialism: "Are there ways to integrate the bodily sensation and function into a social constructionist frame, while still acknowledging that human experience of the body is always mediated by culture and subjectivity?" Vance believes that social constructionists who deny any innate, undifferentiated sexual impulse or drive have taken a radical position that may cause the body to slip out of theoretical sight. Vance is willing to concede that the direction it takes but not the sexual impulse itself is socially determined.

Weeks (p. 211) asserts that he does not want to deny the importance of biology, "let alone deny the body." Rather than postulating an independent sexual impulse, he states that "we can only fully understand our needs and desires when we grasp the historical forces, the unconscious motivations, and the personal and collective responses that shape our sexualities." Weeks appears to be asserting that our sexual needs and desires are products of history and culture apart from biology.

We have now briefly sketched some biological essentialist and social constructionist views of human sexuality and, in particular, of homosexuality. In the section that follows, we wish to outline a position that avoids elements of determinism and reductionism that appear to be integral to both views and use this position as the basis for our critiques of biological essentialism and social constructionism.

A SYNTHESIS OF BIOLOGY, THE INDIVIDUAL, AND CULTURE

To provide a basis for our critique of biological essentialism and social constructionism, we will outline a view of sexuality and gender based on our interpretation of a book by R.C. Lewontin, Steven Rose, and Leon J. Kamin, entitled *Not in Our Genes* (1984). Lewontin is an evolutionary geneticist, Rose a neurobiologist, and Kamin a psychologist. First we shall briefly outline their approach, which they call "dialectical," and then apply it to the discussion of sexual preference.

Deterministic and reductionist views assume the existence of two distinct types of phenomena variously called heredity and environment, nature and nurture, body and mind, biology and culture, and so on. Although both essentialists and constructionists concede an "interaction" between the two types in shaping human thought and expression, each assigns primacy and agency either to the biological or to the cultural. In the view of these authors (p. 75), to understand the human condition (we include human sexuality):

> demands an integration of the biological and social in which neither is given primacy nor ontological [i.e., as a state of being] priority over the other but in which they are seen to be related in a dialectical [i.e., interpenetrative] manner, a manner that distinguishes epistomologically [i.e., as forms of knowledge] between levels of explanation relating to the individual and levels relating to the social without collapsing one into the other or denying the existence of either.

Applied to homosexuality, as an example of a human phenomenon, the authors would assert that it is simultaneously biological and social: "The biological and social are neither separable, nor antithetical, nor alternatives, but complementary" (p. 75). The sociobiological assertion that homosexuality is caused by selfish or altruistic genes is mixing levels of discourse. Genes can be described in physical, chemical, or biological language. Such attributes as selfishness and altruism and, indeed, homosexuality, are attributes of wholes, in this case human beings, who are much more complex than genes. To attribute personality characteristics or preference to genes is an egregious use of the social level of discourse to describe a physical, bio-chemical phenomenon.

According to Lewontin and his colleagues (p. 11), "the properties of parts and wholes co-determine each other." Personal sexual preferences, for example, do not exist apart from society; instead, they emerge from social interaction. Yet our social life is the result of our being human instead of being animals or plants. As individual beings we are composed of various characteristics which can be described singly. The combination and interpenetration of these characteristics with each other and with the social environment, however, results in a complex personality and character that is qualitatively different than its parts.

In the case of all organisms not only is the whole greater than the sum of its parts, but also the parts as ingredients are qualitatively different. To illustrate this point the authors use the example of baking and tasting a cake. There are ingredients, including butter, flour, sugar, and baking soda, which are combined in certain amounts and then baked at a particular temperature. The taste of the cake cannot be reduced to percents of butter, flour, and so on, although each ingredient makes its contribution to the final product. Applied to sexual preference or taste, we can assert that genes, hormones and brain tissue all contribute to heterosexual or homosexual preference but we cannot reduce such a preference to any single ingredient or to various quantities of these ingredients which in themselves have undergone transformations in the process of human experience. The cake is not just butter nor, after baking, is the butter present in its original form.

Since this interpenetration among ingredients occurs over time, both history and biography are of overriding importance. According to these authors (p. 11) "Where and how an organism is now is not merely dependent upon its composition at this time, but upon a past that imposes contingencies on the present and future interaction of its components." They continue (p. 13):

> All organisms bequeath to their successors when they die a slightly changed environment; humans, above all, are constantly and profoundly making over their environment in such a way that each generation is presented with quite novel sets of problems to explain and choices to make; we make our own history, though in circumstances not of our own choosing.

In their view human beings are both the cause and result of their environments rather than the product of two sets of fixed, independent phenomena, biology and culture. They write (p. 275): "The relation between organism and environment is not simply one of interaction of internal and external factors, but of a dialectical [i.e., interpenetrative] development of organism and milieu in response to each other."

How does this apply to mental development? The mind, in this formulation, is a product of the sequence of past experiences and of internal biological conditions. The authors remind us that the human cortex is composed of billions of cells and hundreds of thousands of possible interconnections. Both our internal biology and our experience shape the interpretations of reality upon which we act (p. 276): "The mental world, the world of perceptions, to which the mind reacts, . . . at the same time is a world created by our mind." By acting on our perceptions of the objective world we recreate it. If we perceive others of our own gender to be interested in us as sexual partners, we behave toward them as if they are interested and thus transform the perception into reality. If their interest is reciprocated by our own, we have created an environment for a possible pleasurable sexual encounter. An adult's interest in making sexual contact with individuals of her or his own gender is then the result of perceiving and treating them as possible sexual partners.

Ruth Doell, a biologist, and Helen Longino, a philosopher (Doell and Longino, 1988), distinguish between the stereotyped, reflexive behaviors of sub-human animals and what they call the *intentional* behaviors of human beings. They define intentional behavior as (p. 57) "that which requires at a minimum the ability to represent to oneself one's actions in the world along with some of their possible consequences." Unlike reflexive behaviors like eye blinking in response to an unexpected exposure to a bright light and withdrawing one's hand from a hot stove, intentional behavior to some degree can be controlled by the individual. Intentional behaviors are mediated by higher mental processes which endow humans with the capacity for consciousness and purpose. Such mental states, Doell and Longino make clear, do not introduce into the explanation of human behavior non-material entities or a mind/body dualism nor do they deny the biological contribution to human behavior.

Doell and Longino go on to argue that the more complex behaviors of humans, like the choice of sexual partners, must be treated in their entirety. To explain sexual preference, for example, requires that we include, along with biological capacity, how the person perceives herself or himself and the cultural influences on sexual and gender behavior. Regarding the biological models of sexual preference, they write (pp. 59-60): "Until we have a satisfactory model of the role of the human brain in human behavior (including developmental aspects), it is simply not possible to know how biology interacts with environment in general or to assess, in particular, the contribution of prenatal hormones to later behavior."

Historical and cultural studies of homosexuality show that the patterns of homosexual behavior have changed as individuals and societies have changed their interpretations of sexuality and gender. With some tribal inhabitants of Melanesia, older adolescents and young unmarried men inseminated boys because they believed this was a way to masculinize the boys and prepare them for tribal warfare. In classical Greece adult citizens formed relationships with the sons of other citizens in a system of personal and cultural mentorship called pederasty. Trumbach (1988, 1991) has sketched the pattern of homosexual relationships in pre-modern Europe. From the eleventh to eighteenth centuries in Western Europe men who had sex with other males chose adolescent boys as partners. The act involved the adult male anally fucking the boy. The act was probably not regarded as "homosexual" since the boy was conceived as a female substitute. The men also fucked women–both those they married and others, including prostitutes. The boys, when they became adults, also married, and fucked boys and other women. Since the adult male played the role of the top, the homosexual act was no threat to his dominance in the gender hierarchy. And since the boys became tops in adulthood, their manhood remained unflawed.

It was in the eighteenth century, in such countries as England, Holland, and France, that male homosexuality became associated with effeminacy, so that those who engaged in homosexual acts were considered to belong to a "third sex" or gender. Today, in northern Europe and North America, partners are chosen from among age peers for relationships that involve sexual gratification and bonding. Modern practitioners of homosexual behavior eschew any sexual relationships with the opposite sex when they view homosexuality and heterosexuality as dichotomous biological and mental states in which male homosexuality is associated with femininity and female homosexuality with masculinity.

We have no reason to believe that the discrete biological ingredients that contribute to homosexual behavior are not identical in Greek, premodern, and modern North European and American men. However, when these ingredients are baked in quite different historical, individual, and cultural ovens, they appear as contrasting forms of sexual and gender expressions.

What then is homosexuality if we follow the view of Lewontin, Rose, and Kamin and Doell and Longino? To say that a person is homosexual is a statement about an individual in a particular social context at a particular point in that person's life. There is no biological basis for dividing individuals into two dichotomous groups, heterosexual vs. homosexual. The individual does have a sexual urge. But that urge can be renounced and suppressed, it can be channeled exclusively into procreation, it can be directed toward humans, animals, and inanimate objects, it can become the central focus of one's life and identity, it can be sublimated, and so on. As an isolated biological phenomenon it sets no specific, preordained limits or direction for sexual and gender expression. Unlike the sexual urge, homosexuality is not a material aspect of an individual. It is, in the words of Lewontin and his colleagues (p. 261), "an aspect of sexual expression that is profoundly reflective of contemporary social and cultural mores."

This is one of the things that SC challenges, by not thinking this way they are being more inhumi to people.

A CRITIQUE OF BIOLOGICAL ESSENTIALISM

Our critique of biological essentialism will be brief since much of our criticism is implicit in our presentation of the social constructionist position and in the synthesis of the two positions that has been proposed. Biological essentialism depicts a process in which the biological influences precede the cultural influences and set pre-determined biological limits to the effects culture can have in shaping sexual and gender expression. It assumes that each biological ingredient (i.e., genes, hormones, and brain tissue) is an independent agent that, in some additive and sequential fashion, exerts its influence without itself undergoing change. Since the ingredients are conceived as fixed entities, they result in fixed products. Hence, on the one hand, biological determinists and reductionists believe that "you can't change human nature" since the basic ingredients, as they conceive them, never change. We, on the other hand, are maintaining that all the ingredients, biological, individual, and social, co-determine the effects that each has on the other and on the shaping of human preference.

We have asserted that biological essentialism is both reductionist and deterministic. When applied to homosexuality, the reductionism is most clearly seen in terminology. The idea of *sexual preference,* with its connotations of consciousness, intention, and choice occurring under unpredictable circumstances, is reduced to *sexual orientation,* a concept which asserts the presence of a single, fixed, independent biological mechanism that steers individual desire or behavior either toward men or toward women irrespective of circumstances and experience. As a reductionist concept, sexual orientation, a biological given, transcends biography and history. This biological reification of sexual preference is a prime example of how reductionists collapse one level of discourse into another–in this case, the social level into the biological. Partner options can be conceived and exercised only in a social context where the language of biological mechanisms is an inappropriate level of discourse.

language

From the determinist point of view what happens before birth (i.e., genetic endowment, hormonal environment during pregnancy, and brain differentiation) determines whether or not the sexual orientation manifested in the adult years after birth will be either heterosexual or homosexual. Although determinists do grant that this innate directional mechanism in post-natal life can be blocked or facilitated by cultural circumstances, they contend that the core attraction itself is precoded in the genes and brain and as biological essences cannot be changed by experience. Such an assertion ignores the fact that most of human brain development occurs *after* birth and that genes are unspecified potentialities, active agencies, the effects of which are manifested only in some environmental context.

Even the research design, which Doell and Longino (1988, p. 58) call "linear analytic" and upon which the biological essentialists rest their claims, is inappropriate for explaining sexual preference. Such a design assumes a one-way causation (e.g., biology affects the individual but the individual does not affect biology). It also involves a series of steps in which new factors are added to those preceding them to produce a particular effect. In the case of "sexual orientation" the effects of genes are added to hormonal effects during pregnancy and these latter effects are then added to events occurring in the lower brain. Such a sequence of effects is then assumed to cause adult homosexuality. The linear-analytic model fails in two respects. First, it rules out the influence that factors later in the sequence have on the earlier ones. Second, it fails to explain the whole phenomenon as a human experience. The biology of human sexual and gender expression is part of a larger whole that, as we have seen, includes individual self-perception and intention as well as social, historical, and cultural contexts.

A CRITIQUE OF THE SOCIAL CONSTRUCTIONIST VIEW

The essentialist view of sexuality and gender is flawed chiefly by the submersion of the individual and culture into "nature," what we have called its biological determinism and reductionism. It is to the great credit of social constructionists that they have shown how changing social meanings and concepts of sexuality and gender have had a formative influence on sexual and gender expression. However, their historical and cultural accounts of sexual and gender concepts of categories, when divorced from biology and personal consciousness, seem to suspend a disembodied individual in a sea of categories. In effect, social constructionism, when it attempts to provide a comprehensive account of sexual and gender expression exclusively at the level of historical and social analysis, submerges biology and the individual in society, thereby displaying its own reductionism.

Lewontin, Rose, and Kamin identify two forms of cultural reductionism, both of which are evident in some versions of social constructionism. The first gives primacy to the social over the individual. It is the mirror image of biological reductionism. Social reductionism "holds that individuals are shaped in all but the most trivial ways by their social circumstances'' (p. 76). Although the discourse aims to explain sexual and gender expression at an individual level, the categories it employs are more appropriate for a social level of analysis. To the extent that the social constructionist view has been shaped by labeling and deviancy theory, it has shown strong tendencies toward this form of cultural reductionism. The concept of "homosexual role," which we will critique below, illustrates this form of reductionism.

The second form of cultural reductionism identified by Lewontin and his colleagues is that which purports to explain phenomena at an individual level but treats the individual as a *tabula rasa,* devoid of consciousness and intention, an empty organism and therefore infinitely malleable from the outside. In its most blatant form, psychological behaviorism, particularly in its Skinnerian avatar, holds that individual behavior is shaped by rewards and that those behaviors reinforced later in life are contingent upon the person's early reward history. In its liberal form, cultural reductionism assumes the presence of ethnic, class, sexual, and gender subcultures that are passed from one generation to another as purely cultural phenomena. The various subgroups are assigned characteristics that are represented as cultural but still conceived as entrenched and immutable, e.g., the rich as the great benefactors of the arts, the poor as impulsive spenders, the Japanese as wiley business people, and gay men and lesbians as heirs to artistic sensitivity. Change is possible through education, what our authors call, "changing their heads," which is advocated as the means of changing the political and economic system. A narrowly conceived gay and lesbian studies is devoted to searching out and establishing these cultural strands and markers.

The first form of cultural reductionism appears frequently in sociology and cultural anthropology when the individual is subsumed under sexual and gender labels, scripts, and roles. Such categories purport an explanatory independence of their own. Thus, Mary McIntosh (1968) has proposed that the emergence of the "homosexual role" at the end of the seventeenth century in England channeled the sexual desire of groups of men exclusively toward members of their own gender and led them to engage in cross-gender behavior. Although she acknowledges that not all men, then as now, who have engaged in homosexual behavior have subscribed to the "homosexual role," we are not told how the men who did take on the role differed in mentality from those who did not and how the latter group viewed homosexual and cross-gender behavior.

Without arguing the influence of social categories in shaping sexual and gender expression, attributing change to a "role" is based on three *they still assume a great deal!*

untenable assumptions about human beings: (a) they are passive recipients of social categories such as the idea of roles; (b) they lack their own perceptions and interpretations of society; and (c) they lack purpose and intention of their own that can result in their changing social conditions (and categories) with which they are confronted.

By adding human consciousness and intentionality to the idea of the homosexual role, the dynamic relationship of the biological and the social are preserved. It was in the interpenetration of (a) the sexual urge as it was perceived and directed by the individual, (b) the individual perception that sexual partners could be persons of one's own gender and age and that gender expression could cross conventional boundaries, (c) the personal encounter with a set of historical circumstances that loosened the ties of sexuality to the family and made possible homosexuality as an exclusive practice, and (d) the formulation of the idea of the homosexual role–all occurring at the same point in time and each influencing the other–that led to the association of male homosexuality with femininity and the adoption of homosexuality by some men as an exclusive form of sexual expression. This conceptualization includes biology, the individual, and society but avoids assigning primacy or immutability to one of these to the exclusion of others. When the biographical and historical evidence is fragmentary, as it often is, and fails to meet the requirements for a full explanation that includes all the relevant levels of analysis, we would do well to acknowledge that our accounts of sexuality and gender expression are unavoidably schematic and provisional.

Neither Vance's nor Weeks's social constructionism presents a unified view of biology, individuality, and culture, although none of these elements is completely missing from their accounts of sexuality and gender. It is to their credit that they both emphasize the collective contributions that society and culture make to constructions of sexuality and gender and that these contributions can change from one historical period to another and vary from one culture to another and that the changes are contingent upon the forms that preceded them. It appears, however, that biology and individuality are often treated as separate, autonomous spheres that interact with society but are left unchanged by the interaction.

Regarding biology and the individual, Vance grants the presence of the sexual impulse in the body. In asserting that sexuality is "fluid and changeable," she is asserting that biology is not a natural given, the raw materials of our sexuality and gender. It is not clear, however, whether or not she is subsuming the biology of sexuality under its history, which would be one form of cultural reductionism. The biology of human sexuality is not fluid and changeable in the abstract but only as ingredients of a human life and then only in relation to individual awareness of the body and the formulation of intentions to direct its impulses and uses in a particular historical context.

Weeks's social constructionism seems almost completely culturally determined; body and individual consciousness and inventiveness seem to be captives of sexual and gender categories. What he calls sexual "subjectivities" are not so much personal perceptions of sexuality and gender, but social classifications to which individuals may subscribe. Categories such as the gay or lesbian identity and sadomasochism, in his system, are primarily political inventions designed to resist heterosexist domination. Weeks insists that he does not want to deny the importance of biology and he refers often to unconscious motivations and personal responses. Still, it is difficult to discern how the body and personal consciousness interpenetrate and transform a given set of sexual and gender categories. It appears that in rejecting the conventional categories the remaining option for the individual is to subscribe to another set that is also supplied, now by a new sexual-gender ideology. Weeks correctly criticizes the notion of (p. 206) "the individual as a reconstituted, unified whole." He goes on, however, to endorse the reductionist idea of the individual as *only* an assemblage of social relations. By pairing these assertions he seems to be eliminating individuals along with their biology, including cortical consciousness, as making any contribution to sexual and gender expression and to an integrated and comprehensive understanding of it.

Weeks's radical cultural determinism follows in the footsteps of Michel Foucault (1976), who believed that the category of sexuality itself was a modern invention of sexology. Sexology, he believed, paved the way for medicine and, through medicine, the government and other institutions, to gain power over the most intimate details of an individual's life. Foucauldian thought is an extreme form of cultural reductionism, in which such phenomena as madness, sexual desire, and gender are "problematized," that is, reduced to the disembodied and decorticated status of social and political inventions. According to Foucault, medical categories of sexuality and gender have been invented (1976, p. 36) "to constitute a sexuality that is economically useful and politically conservative."

THE POLITICS OF SEXUALITY AND GENDER

We have already referred to the Utrecht school and its sponsorship of the competing conference in Amsterdam in 1987. Utrecht scholars chose as their major research effort the documentation of discrimination against homosexuals that had historically occurred in Dutch society and persisted to the present day. Their research program was based on the assumption that "homosexuals" have existed as an identifiable group throughout history. In effect, the Utrecht group had adopted the medical model of homosexuality that had originated in the nineteenth century and the ethnic model that became popular in Europe and the United States as a result of the holocaust and the black civil rights struggle that followed World War II. Gays and lesbians, in effect, became a minority group, among a number of persecuted minorities, with their own biological markers.

The model of an oppressed minority has conveniently meshed with the essentialist model of homosexuality. First, by transforming homosexual acts into homosexual persons, membership was created for a political group to advocate legal reform and social tolerance. Second, to the extent that this group could lay claim to biological origins, it would resemble ethnic groups, especially those identified by such characteristics as darker hues of skin, coarser hair texture, and high-slung buttocks, "obvious" products of genetic endowment. Third, the model of oppression fitted *par excellence* with the transformation of homosexual acts into persons, since it was then possible to show that there have been centuries of oppression targeted against gays and lesbians. Finally, there was the gay liberation movement, now a century old, which based its campaign for equality on the premise that homosexuals were discriminated against, denied their legal rights as persons and a group, and defenseless against bigots, baiters, and even bashers. Since the biological markers were not visible, participants in the movement made homosexuality the core ingredient of their personal and social identity in the public ritual of "coming out."

A main current of the feminist movement, the battle to win social, economic, and political equality between men and women, has been to "deconstruct" gender, to show that inequality of opportunity, status, achievement, and reward is *not* an inevitable product of women's biology. In this view, women are not biologically mandated to be only nurturers of men and the sole emotional guardians of human relationships.

Whereas feminists have challenged the biologization of gender, leaders of the gay liberation movement have endorsed the biologization of homosexuality and the heterosexual-homosexual dichotomy. The political merit of basing the battle against homophobia on essentialist notions of homosexuality is extremely dubious for several reasons. First, if we define homophobia as the fear and hatred of homosexual expression (along with its imputed cross-gender peculiarities) and if we assume that one form, either homosexual or heterosexual, of expression over a lifetime does not preclude the other, then the freedom of individuals to retain a homosexual preference or, to change preferences, or to exercise both preferences is recognized. If, however, homophobia is defined as fear and hatred of homosexuals as persons, conceived as creatures of biological or historical determinism, then one form of sexual expression precludes the other and the freedom to change is diminished.

Second, on the basis of a heterosexual-homosexual dichotomy, almost everyone will identify with the heterosexuals, including many individuals with a homosexual preference. This leaves the homosexuals as a relatively tiny group fighting for equality and freedom from the margins of the society and faced with a Sisyphean struggle to dismantle heterosexual privilege brick by brick. Although some mainstream acceptance of gay and lesbian people can be won under the banner of pluralism and diversity, the responsibility for fighting for freedom of sexual and gender expression falls upon the heads and shoulders of those who are least powerful to make change.

Third, those people who make the heterosexual-homosexual dichotomy, conceived as an incontrovertible biological, individual, or social division of the human race, the central focus of their lives end up living in communities that endorse one preference to the exclusion of the other. The price of community membership is the surrender of the freedom to change one's mind and behavior and to participate broadly in society. The tests of community allegiance may include subscribing to the belief that the in-group is oppressed or threatened by the outside group and that the in-group is the heir of a particular folk wisdom and sensibility denied the other group.

Finally, since it is only the homosexual component of the heterosexual-homosexual dichotomy that is medicalized and the question regarding the causes of heterosexuality considered to be merely rhetorical, the political threat of medical intervention to prevent the birth of a homosexual child or to change an adult homosexual preference to heterosexual, persists. Medical efforts to localize the homosexual preference in either the body or early childhood experience and thereby modify or eradicate it, as thoroughly determinist and reductionist as they are, pervade the twentieth century.

Although social constructionists have been willing to cast the struggle for freedom of homosexual expression in broader terms than the biological essentialists–as the freedom for many forms of sexual and gender expression–they have often subscribed to gay and lesbian essentialist politics. We believe this political alliance stems from the determinism and reductionism that both points of view embrace. The gay and lesbian politics of biological essentialists is intended to protect a minority species of the human race from the ignorance and intolerance of the heterosexual majority. In the case of the social constructionists the struggle is conceived as the efforts of the gay and lesbian community to resist heterosexual domination. For the constructionists, community becomes reified and confers personal identity. Identity begets ideology which, in turn, dictates individual decision.

There may be good reasons for bridging the heterosexual-homosexual dichotomy. These have to do with gender stereotypes, which have become stumbling blocks in the road to social progress and personal happiness. The gender stereotype of heterosexual men is characterized by dominance, aggression, and rivalry. The gender stereotype of homosexual men and women are simple inversions of those for the so-called heterosexuals.

To the extent that stereotypes faithfully describe the behavior and attitudes of those to whom they are applied, much is to be learned by stepping outside of them. In a world of growing mutual dependence, any propensity toward aggressiveness, competition, and self-interest can be disruptive when cooperation and altruism are the crucial ingredients for resolving conflict and solving problems. Submissiveness can perpetuate a course of male-dominated action that is destructive and unreasonable for one that requires a defter, more intuitive, and steadier hand. Surely some "straight" men can learn about emotional bonding from some "gay" men and some "straight" women about appropriate assertion from some "lesbians."

On the homosexual side of the dichotomy is the problem of gay men and lesbians living their lives in monosexual societies, which in many ways perpetuate the very gender stereotypes and gender inequalities they encounter in mainstream society. Both at the personal and social levels much is lost for the individual and the community.

By bridging the heterosexual-homosexual and gender dichotomies we can view the heterosexual and homosexual gender stereotypes as a crude representation of the array of options generally available to men and women. No longer do the stereotypes need to be viewed as biologically or socially mandated. Selecting from these crudely defined options, individuals can form relationships with either gender that meet personal and social needs while retaining the fluidity of relationships necessary in a rapidly changing world.

Between community obligation and biological mandate little room is left for individual perception and choice. Experience for those who seek it on both sides of the heterosexual-homosexual dichotomy is ideologically precluded. Yet, it is often from the breadth and commonality of experience of those who dare trespass over established boundaries that social understanding and acceptance emerge.

CONTRIBUTIONS OF THE ARTICLES

The articles in this volume reflect an interdisciplinary approach to the study of the origins of homosexuality and shed light on an age-old debate, which has been called–depending on the historical period in which it occurred–the debate over nature vs. nurture, biology vs. environment, and essentialism vs. social constructionism. While many scholars and non-scholars alike contend that the debate is over, resolved, or worthless, there are nonetheless myriad radio and television shows, scholarly and popular articles, and courses in higher education that continue to struggle with the issues.

Unlike many books on the essentialist and social constructionist debate, this volume: (1) does not pretend or propose to provide the definitive word on the subject; (2) examines both the theoretical and practical aspects of both sides; and (3) explores the issues not only from the perspectives of several disciplines, viz., anthropology, biology, history, psychology, and sociology, but also by examining how the debate has had and continues to have an impact on the lives of many gays and lesbians.

The volume begins with a collection of articles that focus on the biological and medical aspects of homosexuality. The first article in this collection is by Sarah Franklin, who addresses the issue of how the new bio-technologies of reproduction such as genetic screening, artificial insemination, *in-vitro* fertilization (IVF), and pre-natal diagnosis have theoretically provided reproductive options for those who do not fit the mold of the traditional heterosexual couple. Franklin points out, however, that the well-established heterosexual essentialism has precluded gays and lesbians from taking advantage of the newly and widely available reproductive technologies.

In the following article, Jay Paul examines how the research on the etiology of homosexuality treats it as a disturbed gender identity or gender role. Paul focuses heavily on the biological research and does a thorough job of criticizing it. In keeping with the general tone of this volume, he stresses the fact that biological factors contribute to sexual preference but must be considered along with the experience of the individual and the social context. Paul makes it quite clear that the "hard line" essentialists, who only consider a simple physiological explanation for the cause of homosexuality–whether it be genetic, hormonal, or neurological–are setting themselves up for empirical failure. Paul's article also discusses both childhood cross-gender behavior and adult homosexuality and the problems of using retrospective self-report data.

In the next article, Mildred Dickemann, like Paul, argues that the causes of homosexuality cannot be explained by genetic theories. Dickemann asserts that such theories, based on sociobiological speculations, are historically inadequate. However, Dickemann does believe that homosexuality can be explained by a transhistorical, neo-Darwinian theory called "life history theory." This theory suggests that parents are extremely influential with their children in order to secure "maximal reproductive gain." The author uses social phenomena such as the "eronemos" of ancient Athens, the medieval "cadet sons," and the "spinsters" of early modern Europe to support this theory. Dickemann ends up asserting that the influx of homosexuality in modern industrial nations can be attributed to economic conditions, which ultimately allow for many sexual and gender options.

While at first glance Dickemann's analysis appears to be anti-biological, one must focus more on the evolutionary theory she espouses. Here, we see how a scholar applies a theory born essentially out of the natural sciences, viz., biology and applies it to history and various societies to explain many forms of homosexuality and the rise of homosexuality in the modern industrial world.

The final article in the biology section is by Jörg Hutter. Unlike the previous articles, he traces the biologization of homosexuality to the nineteenth century. This article, more specifically, deals with psychiatry and forensic medicine. His main point is that the bio-medical research done during the nineteenth century influenced sexual legislation in Germany during that time. To support his thesis, Hutter explores such issues as the social construction of knowledge, sexual theories, the penal code, and the medicalization, and criminalization of sexual acts, through forensic psychiatry. Hutter makes it quite clear that bio-medical research alone attempted to answer the questions regarding sexuality and excluded other disciplines. Furthermore, the scientific research was intimately linked to law enforcement.

These articles on the biological and medical aspects of homosexuality show quite clearly that the research has had and continues to have far reaching influences upon gays and lesbians. In addition, it should be noted that our contributors are neither biology bashers nor cultural and social determinists. Rather, all of the contributions place the biological contributions to the study of homosexuality in broader focus. Paul and

Dickemann are very critical of the research that is biologically determin-istic. They do a solid job of exploring how historical, cultural, psycho-logical, and social factors also play a role. Along the same lines, but with a slightly different focus, Franklin's and Hutter point to the control legal agencies and government exercise in the interest of heterosexual essential-ism. Again, Franklin's and Hutter's articles force the reader to under-stand the implications that bio-medical technology and the medicalization of homosexuality have had on gays and lesbians.

Leaving behind the discussion of the biologization of homosexuality, the next three articles explore social and political aspects of homosexuali-ty with regard to professional life and "coming out," marital status, and parenting. These articles focus on the social and political pressure that surrounds those issues. The first article, by Peter Dankmeijer, discusses at the most general level, the requirement of gays and lesbians to "come out" in public, which he sees as a central demand of those who endorse and are a part of the gay liberation ideology. The author focuses on teachers and the gay political pressure to "come out," despite the teach-ers' professional survival and their broader political and professional concerns. Dankmeijer's study shows that many of the teachers he studied have various lifestyles. Those teachers who espoused "coming out" were strong proponents of gay liberation. The women teachers were often not too concerned with this because they were more strongly identified as feminists than as lesbians. Additionally, men for whom homosexuality was not a major component of their lifestyles did not feel compelled to step out of the proverbial closet. One of the major issues Dankmeijer raises is that more attention ought to be given to the homophobic condi-tions under which teachers have to work, rather than the demand that teachers "come out."

The article by Hans van der Geest looks at marital partners who occa-sionally wander from the blessed bed of marital fidelity. Van der Geest believes that fidelity is not necessarily broken just because of incidental homosexual activity. He stresses that modern fidelity can be viewed with more flexibility than the traditional construct. According to the author, individuals can construct their own relationships, such as a homosexual man who couples with a heterosexual woman. Fidelity for these "new couples" is not dependent on whether or not one of them has sexual encounters outside of the relationship. Furthermore, van der Geest asserts that deception about one's homosexuality violates fidelity and ultimately undermines the marriage.

In the following article, about gay parenting, Gerd Büntzly discusses anecdotal evidence gathered from one-hundred gay fathers in Germany.

First, Büntzly shows how their ties to religion and the family often hinder these fathers from exploring the various components and dynamics of their homosexuality. In sum, this article discusses the often unworkable relationships gay fathers find themselves in with their wives and lovers, each wanting one-hundred percent of their beloved. Finally, the author discusses the unfortunate political stance of the gay male community, which not only excludes females, but also puts enormous pressure on gay fathers and husbands to choose between marriage and parenthood and participation in the community.

In reading Dankmeijer, van der Geest, and Büntzly, it is abundantly clear that being gay and lesbian can be and often is more complicated than most people realize. All three authors emphasize how gays and lesbians socially construct their own lives. Perhaps the most important point of these articles, however, is how lifestyles of the individuals mentioned in these articles would be viewed as politically incorrect, as if there is a single set of standards and requirements one must follow in order to be considered truly gay or lesbian. These articles shatter the myth that there is a single truth or monolithic model that must be sought after and followed.

The next two articles by Herman Meijer and Eric de Kuyper, discuss the fluidity of sexual identity; they both stress that sexual preference is a choice. For instance, Meijer's work is about three men who, before their first homosexual relationships, identified as exclusively heterosexual. Meijer's main point is that sexual preference can change and is not an innate biological predisposition. He credits this sexual fluidity to the gay liberation movement, which depathologized homosexual desire. The author contends that the choice of heterosexuality or homosexuality depends on personal experience and social context. In order to avoid falling into the chasm of labeling oneself as either heterosexual or homosexual (Which am I?), Meijer suggests that we examine what we like sexually (What do I like?). He avers that if we decide to answer these questions about ourselves in the order that he suggests, this will put us on the road to sexual freedom.

Eric de Kuyper examines homosexuality in terms of Freudian theory. The author states early in this work that Freud considered neither heterosexual nor homosexual desire to be innate. In fact, de Kuyper argues along with Laplanche, that there is an unavoidable homosexual component in the heterosexual resolution of the Oedipal complex. The author points out that in the resolution of the Oedipal complex, boys can choose either the father or mother as a love object or as persons with whom to identify. De Kuyper also maintains that homophobia is the residue of the heterosexual resolution of the Oedipal conflict. The reading of Meijer's and de Kuyper's articles undoubtedly confronts one with the lability of sexual preference: there is a choice to be made regarding the form(s) of sexual expression.

The next segment of this volume deals exclusively with homosexuality in non-Industrial/Third World societies. The first article in this section is by Gloria Wekker. It deals with the institution of *Mati-ism* and *Black Lesbianism.* The author maintains that these two forms of sexual expression can only be understood by using the social constructionist view of homosexuality. She explains how black women in the Diaspora express their erotic fascination with other women. It is clear that many *Mati* (the Sranan Tongo word that refers to women who in addition to their sexual relations with other women, continue to maintain sexual relationships with men) often have children. When exploring the history of Surinam, it is obvious that female forms of homosexuality in the Diaspora are anything but uniform. This point is illustrated by examining the lives of two eminent women poets, who, in fact, have two different cosmologies for female homosexuality in black communities.

Arslan Yuzgun writes about how Turkish gay men continue to suffer due to a shift in religious practices. The author asserts that during the early periods of Turkish history, when the religion was Shamanism, homosexuality was not only accepted, but even widely embraced. However, with Turkey's shift to Islamism, homosexual behavior became unacceptable. The author maintains that while Turkey is constantly endeavoring to become "westernized" and that steps are being taken to provide those who participate in homosexual activity their rights, there is nevertheless much brutalizing and torture of homosexuals by Turkish police. According to documented evidence presented in this article, gays are fighting this oppression on the federal level, even by launching hunger strikes. These struggles represent significant steps to change the political and moral history of Turkey.

In keeping with the cross-cultural pieces, Barry Adam explores male homosexuality in Nicaragua of the late 1980s. Homosexuality, as experienced in Nicaragua, was different than the type of male to male sexual relations in the United States and Europe. The author offers several explanations for this. First, the political economy of the nation was subjected to a devastating revolution and created conditions in which sexual relations among men could not become organized into a gay world that is familiar to North Americans and Europeans. The author also believes that the emphasis on *activos* and *passivos* and the treatment of individuals in these sexual categories also played a role, yet there was little by way of research literature on homosexuality to support this conclusion. The only connection to an outside organized gay world came via foreigners. Perhaps the most significant factor was that homosexually-inclined men remained fully integrated into family and neighborhood life where they were often "known about" but not "recognized," a condition that not only dissolved separateness but also suppressed the development of a gay culture.

In the final article of this section, Daniel Bao takes on the formidable task of examining the construction of Argentinean homosexuality during the beginning of the twentieth century. While undertaking this task, Bao also thoroughly examines early European sexologists' works regarding sexual "inverts," and then goes on to discuss the theories advocated by Argentinean doctors regarding congenital and acquired homosexuality. Bao paints a vivid picture of how the "inverts" resisted the medical and legal establishments. The author also describes the stereotypes, the sense of community, and the activities of female and male "inverts," noting the similarities between Buenos Aires and large European cities in the construction of sexual inversion.

What is the purpose of including the four above-mentioned articles in this volume? While they are not similar in terms of content, they all attempt to illustrate how each of the societies socially constructs its own realities regarding the expression of same-sex relations. Most scholarly works focus on the highly developed industrialized nations of the Western world. We thought that it is crucial to include these works in order to link the debate to the non-industrialized world. Although all of the articles in this section are social constructionist in their claims and emphases, they do not push cultural determinism to the point of eliminating the possibility of biological and personal influences on sexual preference.

The final two articles, by John Lauritsen and Joel Brodsky, explore the economic factors at work in the development of the gay male identity of the 1970s and early 1980s in the United States. Lauritsen asserts that the concept of social construction is inadequate in many ways and has little applicability when it comes to issues of the real world. The author devotes much attention to the lifestyle of the gay male clone, including the use of amyl nitrate (or "poppers"). The major thrust of the article, however, is to elaborate on how the lifestyle of the gay male clone is neither created by gay men nor in their interest. Essentially, it is argued that this lifestyle was politically and economically constructed. Lauritsen even goes so far as to assert that the gay lifestyle was largely founded and fostered, not because of any deep moral or socio-political convictions, but rather because of the potential profit to be made from a flourishing part of the sex-industry.

Much like Lauritsen's contribution, Joel Brodsky does a retrospective ethnography of the Mineshaft, a sadomasochistic sex club for gay men in New York City, and discusses the economics of such a club. In examining the Mineshaft from the patrons' perspective, other gay bars are studied in the context of gay male urban life circa-1980 in North America. However, specifically at the Mineshaft, the gay male clientele was able to socially construct their sense of "real brotherhood" despite the stereotypical notion that gay males are effeminate. In addition, sadomasochism is thoroughly defined and examined in both anthropological and sociological contexts. Following the exploration of sadomasochism, the article shows how the "set up" and atmosphere of the Mineshaft was conducive to have the customers socially create their reality. The power of culture and social organization are emphasized in this article.

A close examination of Lauritsen's and Brodsky's contributions reveals that even though the profit motive played an extremely important role in operating a sex club such the Mineshaft or by catering to the gay male clone lifestyle as Lauritsen proposes, other socio-cultural influences cannot be denied. Such enterprises create a conducive atmosphere where gay men can realize their fantasies and feel comfortable in the process. The articles discuss the creation of a sub-culture in which self-exploration and comradeship can occur in a secure environment despite economic motives.

As Robert Padgug states so eloquently, "[h]uman biology and culture are both necessary for the creation of human society. It is as important to avoid rigid separation of 'Nature' and 'Culture' as it is to avoid reducing one to the other, or simply uniting them as an undifferentiated reality" (Padgug, 1990, p. 52). Many scholars staunchly endorse either the essentialist view or the strict social constructionist position. As pointed out earlier, these positions are both deterministic–either biologically or culturally–and fail to acknowledge that biology and culture together could possibly play a role in forming one's sexual preference. It is our hope that this introduction and ensuing articles help to clarify the debate.

REFERENCES

Doell, R.G., & Longino, H.E. (1988). Sex hormones and human behavior: A critique of the linear model. *Journal of Homosexuality, 15* (3/4), 55-78.

Foucault, M. (1976). *La volenté de savoir*. Paris: Editions Gallimard. [Trans. R. Hurley, *The history of sexuality: Volume I: Introduction*. New York: Vintage, 1978].

Lewontin, R.C., Rose, S., & Kamin, L.J. (1984). *Not in our genes: Biology, ideology, and human nature*. New York: Pantheon.

McIntosh, M. (1968). The homosexual role. *Social Problems, 16,* 182-192.

Padgug, R. (1990). Sexual matters: On conceptualizing sexuality in history. In E. Stein (Ed.), *Forms of desire: Sexual orientation and the social constructionist controversy* (pp. 43-67). New York & London: Garland Publishing.

Trumbach, R. (1988). Gender and the homosexual role in modern western culture: The eighteenth and nineteenth centuries compared. In A. van Kooten Niekerk & T. van der Meer (Eds.), *Homosexuality, which homosexuality?* (pp. 149-169). Amsterdam: Jhr. Mr. J.A. Schorerstichting.

Trumbach, R. (1991). London's sapphist: From three sexes to four genders in the making of modern culture. In J. Epstein & K. Straub (Eds.), *Body guards: The culture and politics of gender ambiguity* (pp. 112-141). London: Routledge.

Vance, C.S. (1988). Social construction theory: Problems in the history of sexuality. In A. van Kooten Niekerk & T. van der Meer (Eds.), *Homosexuality, which homosexuality?* (pp. 13-34). Amsterdam: Jhr. Mr. J.A. Schorerstichting.

Weeks, J. (1988). Against nature. In A. van Kooten Niekerk & T. van der Meer (Eds.), *Homosexuality, which homosexuality?* (pp. 199-214). Amsterdam: Jhr. Mr. J.A. Schorerstichting.

II. BIOLOGICAL ISSUES IN GENDER AND SEXUAL IDENTITY

Essentialism, Which Essentialism? Some Implications of Reproductive and Genetic Techno-Science

Sarah Franklin, PhD

Lancaster University

SUMMARY. New technologies, such as genetic screening, artificial insemination, *in vitro* fertilization, and pre-natal diagnosis, have given new meaning to human reproduction. Such innovations make clear that marriage, procreation, and the biological family are not the sole "natural" means of perpetuating the human race. One would have hoped that these inventions would eventually have raised in public regard the gay/lesbian family to the same level as heterosexuality and the biological family. Franklin shows, however, that the old heterosexual essentialism is preserved by government restricting the use of the new technologies to two-parent families consisting of both mother and father. What should have resulted in the erosion of heterosexual privilege has, instead, led to its reinforcement. Franklin draws a parallel with the AIDS epidemic which could have been the opportunity to spread knowledge and acceptance of varied forms of sexuality but has instead been used to shore up a traditional sexual morality and a renewed vilification of homosexuality.

Sarah Franklin is a lecturer in cultural anthropology and women's studies in the Department of Sociology at Lancaster University, England.

INTRODUCTION

Embryo research, fetal surgery, in vitro fertilization, genetic screening, pre-natal diagnosis–the late twentieth century is witnessing dramatic transformations in the technological, discursive and political construction of human reproduction. These changes are linked to a "knowledge explosion" in the biological sciences, particularly concerning reproduction and genetics, which are expected to provide new medical therapies, new industrial processes, new commercial products and a new resource base for free market capitalism. [1] These developments have been widely hailed by the media as the beneficial results of scientific progress which will improve the quality of human life by alleviating human suffering and increasing "man's" ability to control "nature."

Feminists and socialists alike have been slow to acknowledge the politics at stake in these recent and fast-paced "advances" at the frontiers of reproductive and genetic techno-science. Indeed, some feminists and socialists have been eager to welcome these new developments as progressive–offering greater reproductive "choice" for women, and new industrial possibilities for workers. [2] What could possibly be wrong with the attempt to provide children for the infertile, to eliminate genetic diseases or the use of biotechnology for industry, agriculture or manufacturing? It is difficult to challenge the very powerful desire to believe in scientific knowledge/power/progress that saturates the cultures of post-industrial societies. It is, however, important for us to consider what is at stake, both culturally and politically, in the domain of reproductive and genetic techno-science. [3]

It is important for us to think about the position of gay and lesbian people in relation to these technologies, for it is not at all self evident. In this brief article I hope to be able to address this question from two different, but related, perspectives: what is the position of lesbian and gay people in relation to the technologies themselves; and what is the place of these technologies in relation to the essentialism/constructionism debates?

THE SEPARATION OF PROCREATION
FROM SEXUALITY–
DECONSTRUCTING ESSENTIALISM?

Given that the new reproductive technologies such as gamete intra-fallopian transfer [GIFT], or in vitro fertilization [IVF] clinically require a separation of reproductive activity from heterosexual activity, it is tempting to imagine they might increasingly unsettle the conflation of the two which guarantees the "naturalness" of heterosexuality, marriage and the patriarchal nuclear family. Indeed the test-tube baby could easily be interpreted as "proof" that even something as "natural" as pregnancy can be artificially produced, socially constructed, literally pieced together in the laboratory. Certainly the Pope is worried; perhaps this is a happy indication? Similarly, the commercialization of parenthood and procreative products evident in artificial insemination and the burgeoning industry of "surrogate" motherhood clearly undermines traditional assumptions about the inviolability of the mother-child bond–that most natural of natural ties–and of biological paternity, the pillar of patrilineage.

Given these auspicious signs, it is tempting to hope that these shifts in traditional procreative arrangements will give rise to a more diversified, more encompassing and more admittedly artificial and socially constructed kinship system, thus allowing more space for non-traditional sexual, procreative and familial arrangements. But will surrogacy and in vitro fertilization make lesbian motherhood and gay fatherhood look more acceptable? Less unnatural? Will these techniques make them more feasible? Will they eventually destabilize certain forms of sexual and reproductive essentialism at the heart of heterosexism and homophobia?

Certainly they will to a degree, and all of these techniques have precipitated busy controversy, even moral panic in some quarters. However it is tempting to overestimate to what extent they will bring about or enable progressive social change. As I intend to argue, these techniques have created the basis for a new moralism, linked to new forms of essentialism, which deserve our attention precisely because they deploy very familiar prescriptions under increasingly unfamiliar guises. It must be remembered that there is a danger in assuming that scientific and technological change can bring about what years of social activism and political struggle have failed to achieve. There is also a danger in the assumption that "in the right hands" these technologies could achieve something other than what they were designed for.

THE RECONSTRUCTION OF ESSENTIALISM–PART ONE

The paradox of reproductive technology is not dissimilar to the paradox of the AIDS crisis. While AIDS has forced homosexuality and explicit discussion of all forms of sexual practice out into the open to an unprecedented extent, the degree of increased public tolerance or understanding of homosexuality has been vastly overshadowed by the backlash of reactionary sexual ethics. This is reflected in a stigmatization of promiscuity, a renewed and vigorous homophobia, a retrenchment of conservative family morality and a re-establishment of marriage, fidelity and monogamy as the only legitimate or acceptable context for sexual pleasure. Likewise with reproductive technology, what might have been (or is to a limited extent) a disruption of the so-called "natural" basis for the nuclear family and heterosexual marriage *has instead provided the occasion for reconsolidating them.*

It is important here for us to consider the relationship between ideas about "the natural," essentialism and morality. The clearest way to illustrate this is to look at the organization of kinship in western societies. Because kinship is a fundamental source of social identities and cohesion in any culture, it is inevitably central to any cultural expression of morality. In western societies, kinship can be seen to be organized according to two systems–"the order of nature and the order of law."[4] We are related to people either "by blood" as in nature, or "in law" as through marriage. Morality in western cultures is dependent upon precisely the same cultural "orders" of law and nature. Thus, what is unnatural or illegal (criminal) is also immoral.

The enforcement of a certain construction of the "natural," and a reliance upon it to justify discrimination against what is said to be "unnatural" (and therefore criminal and immoral) is, of course, one of the main issues at stake in the radical critique of essentialism. The obvious example is the age-old persecution of lesbianism and homosexuality as "crimes against nature." What is "essentialist" about this claim is, of course, the assumption that there is one essential form of human sexuality which is the only acceptable form of sexuality because it is the only *natural* expression of it. What is argued against this view is that human sexuality is not based on a "natural" essence (e.g., biologically determined) but is instead *socially constructed,* taking different formations in different cultural and historical contexts.

In the case of reproductive technology, it might seem that the disruption of the so-called "naturalness" underlying the moral imperative to preserve the "unity of the sexual and procreative function" might lead to a weakening of certain key essentialist beliefs. I will argue however, that what we see actually happening is not quite exactly this.

In fact, the threat to essentialism has provided a basis for reconstructing it, thus allowing us a very good look into the social construction of essentialism itself. This is clearly evident in the response of the State to new reproductive technologies. So far, committees have been commissioned by Governments to propose statutory legislation in Great Britain, Australia, Canada, the United States and many countries in western Europe. None of these committees have recommended that lesbians and gay men, or, for that matter, even single parents, should have equal access to the new reproductive technologies. To the contrary, the attitude uniformly has been that the larger the role of the State in the production of a child, the greater the responsibility of the State for the welfare of that child. In other words, in the words of Patrick Steptoe, the "father" of in vitro fertilization himself, "It would be unthinkable to willingly create a child to be born into an unnatural situation such as a gay or lesbian relationship."

LEGISLATION OF THE NEW REPRODUCTIVE TECHNOLOGIES IN THE UNITED KINGDOM

Great Britain, where IVF was originally developed and where Louise Brown, the first test-tube baby was born in 1978, has so far produced the most comprehensive legislation in the form of the Human Fertilization and Embryology Act, passed in 1990. It is useful to consider this example in evaluating the probable legal and social position of lesbians and gay men in relation to the new reproductive technologies. It also demonstrates how the essentialist base of family ideology is being reconstructed and maintained to compensate for the loss of its "natural" foundation.

In 1982 the British Parliament commissioned a committee of inquiry into human fertilization and embryology chaired by Mary Warnock, an existential philosopher at Oxford and eminent elder British citizen. Like all committees of inquiry commissioned to propose legislation, the Warnock Committee requested public input from both individuals and organizations on the questions at issue. The Campaign For Homosexual Equality and Action for Lesbian Parents both submitted statements. Neither were invited to present evidence before the Committee, nor were any of the women's groups who submitted statements. After deliberating upon the rights of lesbians and gay men in their report, the Warnock Committee concluded "that as a general rule it is better for children to be born into a two parent family with both father and mother." (Warnock, 1985:11). No explanation was offered for why this should be so.

In addition to the use of the "in the best interests of the children" argument, which is the perennial excuse for homophobic prejudice against gay and lesbian parenthood, this section of the Warnock Report is also significant in terms of its conflation of lesbian and gay parenthood with single parenthood. This is evident in its conflation of a heterosexual couple with a "family": if a child is born into a heterosexual couple it is born into a "family," whereas if it is born into a lesbian or homosexual couple it is not. This both demonstrates the centrality of marriage and heterosexuality to the definition of parenting and how these assumptions can be made into statutory requirements. These requirements would potentially subject gay and lesbian parents to the threat of criminal prosecution, were this statutory precedent to be used in a prescriptive rather than a preventative manner.

The intersection of statutory legislation with the family, long a problematic area for the law, as a result of the need to regulate the new reproductive technologies could easily provide a number of legal precedents restricting access of gay and lesbian parents to children. If legal and social policy regarding adoption and fosterage by gay or lesbian couples is any indication, we can expect this area to be a stronghold of homophobic prejudice. Currently it is not even possible for lesbian or gay couples to foster lesbian or gay teenagers! What the "logic" of the Warnock Report demonstrates is, among other things, that where the "natural" basis for certain forms of essentialist moralism has been eroded it can easily be reconstructed through other channels, such as the law. The threat to essentialism is thus recuperated *in order to reestablish it*. In other words, because reproductive technologies threaten the "natural" basis of the family, the State is justified in strengthening its *legal* foundations in order to promote the same essentialist ideologies.

This process is quite explicit in the Warnock Report. Early on the Committee emphatically pointed out that they were unhappy with the use of the concept of the "natural" in arguments regarding so-called "treatments" for infertility: "in view of the ambiguity of the concepts 'natural' and 'unnatural'" [ibid, p. 9]. Nonetheless, the unsubstantiated assumption, only pages later, that it is "better" for a child to be born into a heterosexual "family" clearly reflects the kind of common sense social prejudice that is usually expressed in terms of what is considered to be "unnatural" and therefore criminal and immoral. Given that many of the "experts" who testified before the Committee were known to be opposed to lesbian or gay parenthood because it is unnatural, and that there was a tremendous response from religious organizations to the Committee, I believe ideas of the natural played a far greater role at the level of common sense assumptions than the Warnock Committee was willing to admit.

However worrisome this sort of "reasoning" may be, in its explicit and all too familiar heterosexism, it is notable that the proposals of the

Warnock Committee did not become law for several years following the publication of their report, due to the politically volatile nature of legislation in this area.[5] Moreover, even following the enactment of this legislation, it remains evident there are many contradictions within the law and there will undoubtedly arise many disjunctures between the letter of the law and its interpretation in the courts.

For example, precisely because they are neither hightech or new reproductive options, the law has always shied away from attempts to legally restrict the practice of surrogacy or artificial insemination. In England, the first recommendation of the Warnock Report to be made statutorily binding was the Surrogacy Arrangements Act, which made *third party* participation in surrogacy arrangements a criminal offence. The law did *not* prohibit informal surrogacy contracts between the commissioning parent/s and the surrogate, only the commercial participation of outsiders. This is, in part, because it is undermining to the authority of the Law to establish unenforceable statutes. Since informal surrogacy arrangements or the use of artificial insemination would be almost impossible to legally substantiate and prosecute, they are unlikely to be made criminal offenses.

Although the Warnock Committee attempted to prescribe a form of essentialist procreative morality, this is not fully established in recent legislation. Despite a proviso in the Act requiring clinicians before providing treatment to consider as part of the child's best interests the child's "need" for a father this is hardly a Draconian measure. Hence, though many commentators have described the task of the Warnock Committee as one of making new reproductive technologies safe for the traditional heterosexual family, this has proved more difficult to accomplish than was perhaps first hoped. Nonetheless, it is clear that maintenance of privileged heterosexual access to parenthood is on the agenda for future legislation in this and related areas.

THE RECONSTRUCTION OF ESSENTIALISM–PART TWO

There is, on the other hand, a far more insidious and worrisome form of essentialism emerging as a result of the new reproductive technologies, particularly as a result of their close relationship to new forms of genetic engineering.[6] For the purpose of this brief discussion I will refer to this as *the new genetic essentialism,* the return of the "it's all in your genes" mentality that flourished under the name of eugenics before WWII and has reappeared under various guises since, most notably in the form of sociobiology.

What is evident in the new genetic essentialism is very Foucaultian. There is the emergence of a scientific discourse and a corresponding technology, with the potential to establish social categories based on an essential truth about the body. This provides the basis for surveillance, prohibition and control of subjects through various channels including the medical profession and the apparatuses of the State. For example, "DNA fingerprinting" has for some years now been widely used in England by the police to investigate crimes. Genetic screening is also said to offer benefits for employers and insurance companies to provide "bio-data" on their employees/clients. Medically these techniques are intended to eradicate genetic "defects" and "abnormalities."

There are many other parallels between the emergence of this new discourse of genetic essentialism and the emergence of the discourses described by Foucault. Just as the drive to elicit the "truth" of sex prefigured the emergence and deployment of a scientific discourse intended to name, to classify and to control the hidden secrets of sexual pleasure/desire/practice; so the current fascination in the biological sciences with reproductive and genetic processes reflects a desire to name, to classify and to control the "facts of life," the "secret of life" and "the mysteries of creation" by forcing the body to confess its truths to science. Just as the discourse of sexology created the sexed subject, so the discourse of genetic essentialism creates a genetic subject, and, correspondingly, the reproductive subject as well.

There are many links between the historical debates about sexuality and debates about genetic inheritance, of which the current essentialist-constructionist debates are only one example. Most importantly, both sets of debates have concerned the idea of an individual essence at the root of certain "deviant" behaviors, be they sexual, criminal, psychological or all of the above. This idea of an individual essence is described in the language of a pathology. Thus originated the debates in sexology about whether or not homosexuality is an inherited trait–a condition lesbians and homosexuals are born with. These debates reflect the influence of the biological in producing a particular social construction of the body, of pathological identity, and thus of subjectivity, in western culture.

The predominance of the biological world view has long been evident in western cultural constructions of conception and procreation. It is said in anthropology that what a culture believes about conception can be read as a condensation of a peoples' beliefs about many other aspects of their lives, from gender and sexuality to cosmology and politics. This culture is no exception. The western procreation story is a strictly bio-genetic one: sperm meets egg. Its origin myth is also a bio-genetic one, about "man's" evolution through the bio-genetic law of survival of the fittest. These two stories are two variations on a bio-genetic theme. Procreation is seen as the result of biological drives and selfish genes. Conception occurs when sperm meets egg, when Xs meet Ys, and a new, "genetically unique," individual is created.

Even the simple story about sperm and egg contains an easily recognizable condensation of popular beliefs about gender and masculine and feminine sexuality. The active sperm burst into the dark tunnel of the vagina, furiously competing against each other in an obstacle race against time to reach the enormous, passive egg and be the first to penetrate it, fertilize it, and thus ensure the perpetuity of its genes. That this is also a story about cosmology and politics becomes evident in its myriad fetishized retellings.

What is occurring at the moment is a massive discursive/scientific elaboration of this bio-genetic event, which is, inevitably, a social reconstruction of it as well. Now that conception and fertilization have been extracted from the "dark continent" of the woman's body, they can be subjected to scientific scrutiny, "improved," illuminated, redefined and, most importantly, controlled. Simultaneously, a global scientific project to "map the human genome" is underway, and tests are being developed so that the genetic composition of embryos can be determined "pre-implantation." The development of DNA fabrication, splicing, replication and synthesis techniques have also introduced many possibilities of genetic manipulation for commercial, medical, military and scientific exploitation. Approximately 10% of Star Wars funding, for example, has been spent on genetic research.

It is enough to give the barest of outlines to this emerging techno-science, popularly known as the biotechnological revolution, to appreciate its scope. Reproductive technology, the so-called "treatments for infertility" are central to this emerging field.[7] Human genetic research means embryo research, and embryos come from in vitro research and clinical practice–the linkages are direct. Thus, the new reproductive technologies are only a very small part of a much broader picture which must be taken into account in any attempt to evaluate them.

This is especially important when we consider the politics at stake in the emergence of this latest biogenetic discourse. Like eugenics, the new genetic essentialism and the construction of the genetic subject, *homo geneticus*, is about genetic fitness, about good genes and bad genes. This introduces a whole new language about genetic defects, abnormal genes, genetic predispositions, genetic selection, genetic screening, genetic therapy, genetic counselling, etc. This is a language about the surveillance of individual pathology. It is a powerful and privileged language, produced and guaranteed by the authority of science and the expertise of the medical profession. It is important to realize that we are being asked to have a great deal of faith in their ability.

POST-MODERN PROCREATION

As Lyotard has argued, the late twentieth century is witnessing the demise of certain privileged post Enlightenment orthodoxies, such as the belief in a unified human subject, a universal human truth, a rational teleology of history, and a law-abiding language. The evidently chronic fragmentation, and corresponding impotence of these sustaining orthodoxies of rational humanism and the western belief in progress have, according to Lyotard, produced a crisis–a crisis of what he calls the Great Narratives (*grands recits*) which have legitimated western culture's definition of itself. Science, he argues, plays a central role in this post-modern dissipation of identity and purpose [Lyotard, 1984].

Several feminists who have speculated on the relationship of feminist to post-modern theories note the importance of a changing cultural consciousness about reproduction. [8] Barbara Creed, for example, has argued recently that the current proliferation of popular films which represent "alien" forms of reproduction are symptomatic of the cultural crises identified in both feminist and post-modernist debates.

> The sci-fi horror film's current interest in the maternal body and processes of birth points to changes taking place on several fronts. Among the most important of these are the developments taking place in reproductive technology which have put into crisis questions of the subject, the body and the unconscious. . . . In more recent years, as experiments with reproductive technology have begun to make enormous headway, the sci-fi horror film has become increasingly preoccupied with alternative forms of the conception-gestation-birth process. . . . [Creed, 1987: 56-7]

Creed argues this preoccupation reflects several post-modern anxieties, the "loss of the body as a site of resistance," the "uncertainty of the future," the "'disappearance of that first dwelling'," and the threat of techno-science literally penetrating into the body [ibid, 56-7].

Thinking about the cultural significance of the new reproductive technologies at this level gives rise to many questions. It is worth considering, for example, what role the disruptions of traditional patriarchal sexual and procreative arrangements brought about by feminist, lesbian and gay activism play in this post-modern procreation panic. Is the post-modern anxiety about the loss of the paternal signifier, the symbolic guardian of phallocentrism, in any way related to the anxiety generated by the increasing ambiguity about the paternal role in procreation? Has the emergence of a new symbolic father, the laboratory scientist, who now performs the acts of penetration and insemination, threatened a replacement of the penis with the petri dish? Surely there are multiple symbolic crises and contradictions here that merit our attention.

SUMMARY

Thus far, I have attempted to present some of the many questions that need to be asked about the implications of the new reproductive technologies for lesbians and gay men. I have stressed that we should be wary of expecting either social or scientific "progress" from these techniques, and that we should beware of their potential to be used as an occasion to re-consolidate the status quo. I have also argued that there is a danger of a new genetic essentialism through which individual pathologies may be subjected to vetting, on the basis of whether they are genetically "fit." It is unnecessary to elaborate upon the implications of such an eventuality in the present context of increasing social inequality, particularly in terms of sex and race, which are both "genetically determined."

At a more cultural level, I have tried to show how the emergence of both the new reproductive technologies and the bio-genetic discourses of which they are a part can be analyzed in terms of feminist, post-structuralist and postmodernist theory. Importantly, I have argued that these theoretical approaches shed light on the changing nature of essentialism, as it were, especially the ways in which essentialism is itself socially constructed.

CONCLUSION: AND WE ARE NOT EXTINCT!

I would like to conclude this paper with an argument about the position of lesbians and gay men in terms of resistance against the new reproductive technologies and the new genetic essentialism of which they are a part. Precisely because these new technologies are currently facilitating a redeployment of many forms of essentialism which are oppressive to lesbians and gay men, I believe the politics around this issue will become increasingly important. There is a distinct political significance to the simple fact that we do not reproduce ourselves biologically. We reproduce ourselves socially, entirely by means of the social, political and cultural struggles that keep gay and lesbian sub-cultures alive. According to every theory of evolution, biological determinism or genetic essentialism we should be extinct. But we are not extinct. Nor are we threatened by extinction, or dependent upon biological reproduction to make more of ourselves. We may congratulate ourselves for this fact, but we must also assert its significant political importance in the face of all forms of bio-genetic essentialism. Lesbians and gay men should be wary of arguments that we can use the new reproductive technologies to our advantage now, at a time when biological and genetic essentialism are, more than ever, inextricable from the social relations which reproduce and maintain heterosexual privilege.

NOTES

1. For a more detailed description of the development and applications of these techniques see Elkington, 1985.

2. Some feminists, for example, believe that women can use the new reproductive technologies to increase our control over our own reproductive capacities. Likewise, many socialists retain a generally uncritical stance towards "the benefits of scientific progress" in increasing the control of workers over the environment. Both these positions reflect the belief that science and technology are themselves neutral.

3. Recent publications which address these questions include Arditti et al., 1984; Corea, 1985; Corea et al., 1985; Steinberg and Spallone, eds., 1987; Spallone, 1988; Stanworth, ed., 1987.

4. For a further discussion, see Schneider [1968] 1980, 1984.

5. Throughout the passage of the Human Fertilization and Embryology Bill, the British Government did not take a position on the regulation of new reproductive technologies. It has been suggested this is because any position would have inevitably caused controversy and opposition which would be detrimental to election prospects. As a result, public discussion and legislative proposals were facilitated largely by members of the scientific and medical professions, or individual members of Parliament.

6. For further discussion, see Rifkin, 1984.

7. It is important to point out that these "treatments for infertility" do nothing to remedy the condition of infertility. They enable some infertile women to become pregnant, and some infertile men to biologically father children, but they do nothing to remedy the condition of infertility itself.

8. For example, Haraway, 1985.

REFERENCES

Arditti, R., Duelli Klein, R. & Minden, S. (Eds.). (1984). *Test-Tube Women: What Future For Motherhood?*. London: Pandora Press.

Corea, G. (1985). *The Mother Machine: Reproductive Technologies From Artificial Insemination to Artificial Wombs.* New York: Harper & Row, Pub., Inc..

Corea, G. et al. (eds.)(1985). *Man-Made Women: How New Reproductive Technologies Affect Women.* London: Hutchinson.

Creed, B. (1987). From here to modernity: Feminism and post-modernism. *Screen, 2.* 47-67.

Haraway, D. (1985). A manifesto for cyborgs: Science, technology and socialist feminism in the 1980s. *Socialist Review, 80,* 65-108.

Lyotard, J. (1984). *The Post-Modern Condition: A Report on Knowledge.* Minneapolis, MN: University of Minnesota Press.

Rifkin, J. (1984). *Algeny: A New Word, A New World.* Harmondsworth, England: Penguin Books.

Schneider, D. ([1968] 1980). *American Kinship: A Cultural Account.* Englewood Cliffs, NJ: Prentice-Hall Inc.

(1984). *Critique of the Study of Kinship.* Ann Arbor, MI: The University of Michigan Press.

Spallone, P. (1988). *Beyond Conception: The New Politics of Reproduction.* London: Macmillan Pub. Co..

Steinberg, D. & Spallone P. (Eds.). (1987). *Made To Order: The Myth of Reproductive and Genetic Progress.* Oxford: Pergamon Press Inc..

Warnock, M. (1985). *A Question of Life: The Warnock Report on Human Fertilization and Embryology.* Oxford: Basil Blackwell.

Childhood Cross-Gender Behavior and Adult Homosexuality: The Resurgence of Biological Models of Sexuality

Jay P. Paul, PhD

University of California

SUMMARY. Research on the causes of homosexuality frequently treat it as a matter of disturbed gender identity and/or gender role. Recently, attempts have been made to link cross-gender behavior among boys with adult homosexuality. Often this research presumes a common biological determinant to both the childhood behavior patterns and homosexuality in adulthood. Authors have described such childhood cross-gender behavior in boys as part of a "prehomosexual" configuration. This paper argues that the research to date suffers from (1) a failure to differentiate such concepts as gender identity, gender role and sexual orientation, (2) a reliance upon potentially inappropriate dichotomies in describing such concepts, (3) problematic interpretations of research that makes few distinctions between human sexual behavior and sexual behavior among rodents, and (4) the contradictions implicit in seeking simple biological determinants of constructs (such as cross-gender behavior) that are culturally determined. The author argues that any potential biological factors contributing to sexual orientation must be mediated by a complex sequence of experiences and psychosocial factors. Therefore, the essentialists' search for a simple congruence between physiological or biological traits and homosexuality may be expected to fail.

Dr. Jay P. Paul is Associate Specialist at The University of California, San Francisco, Center for AIDS Prevention Studies, 74 New Montgomery Street, Suite 600, San Francisco, CA 94105. He also works as a psychotherapist in private practice in San Francisco.
A draft of this paper was presented at the *Homosexuality, Which Homosexuality?* Conference, Free University, Amsterdam, The Netherlands, December 1987.

41

Sexology as a formal discipline is relatively new. Our research on human sexuality has provided far more questions than answers in many areas. Yet sexuality remains a topic about which few ambiguities are tolerated, and a subject on which practically everyone has a decided opinion–typically presented as indisputable fact. This tendency to confuse beliefs with evidence is especially unfortunate when it appears within a supposedly rigorous scientific discipline. A case in point is the focus and interpretation of research findings on cross-gender behavior in childhood as a sign of a broader "prehomosexual" configuration. This paper will review some of the published work in this area, contending that scientists have uncritically incorporated our culture's longstanding folk belief in homosexuality as a form of flawed maleness or femaleness. This attempt to provide a common causal explanation for *childhood* cross-gender characteristics and adult homosexuality follows the failure of research to distinguish adults identified as homosexual on the basis of cross-gender aspects of personality, constitution, or circulating hormonal levels.

The linking of childhood cross-gender behavior and adult homosexuality has spurred research that utilizes retrospective self-report data and prospective research that has followed small samples of extremely "feminine" boys. Other critiques have addressed the methodological problems in utilizing retrospective data (Ross, 1980; Sagarin, 1973). However, it appears that the weaknesses in the conceptual underpinnings guiding this line of research need further elucidation.

"SEXUAL IDENTITY": A FAILURE TO AGREE ON CONSTRUCTS

A fundamental problem in much of the existing research in this area is the lack of semantic or conceptual consensus in describing the component constructs clustered under the general term "sexual identity." Some authors fail to define their understandings of specific constructs, which can confuse the reader. Further, such inconsistencies between different authors are only a part of the problem–a single author may fail to utilize terms in a uniform manner within his or her own work.

Despite the lack of any scientific basis for such a view, many authors have either treated sexual orientation as a facet of gender, or have confounded gender role behavior and sexual orientation. Childhood gender role behavior is viewed not simply as *predictive,* but as an age-dependent *expression* of sexual orientation (Bakwin, 1968; Harry, 1982; Money & Ehrhardt, 1972; Zuger, 1978). A brief review of the work of John

Money provides a glimpse of the conceptual problems typical to others in this area.

The Case of John Money

Money has used a sweeping unitary construct, "gender identity/role," which includes everything from a sense of maleness or femaleness to sex-typed characteristics to patterns of sexual arousal and response (Money & Ehrhardt, 1972). Money has spent years of studying individuals whose genetic, hormonal, and physical make-up highlight the existing variations within just the category of biological sex. He has also spent much time on research on the impact of surgical and hormonal interventions, as well as the impact of socialization factors. Given this, some of his conceptualizations are curiously impoverished and unidimensional. He seems to equivocate with regard to the respective contributions of "nature" and "nurture" throughout his publications. He doesn't offer any clear theoretical synthesis, since he alternates between prenatal hormonal influences and naming socialization factors when explaining sexual or gender variations. Overall, he demonstrates a fondness for explanations rooted in biological determinants. In this respect, he is quite selective in his consideration of the evidence. If a case fails to follow the presumed hormonal imperatives he has outlined, he looks for another way to demonstrate the urgent call of biology. In describing a genetic male hermaphrodite reared as a girl (Money & Ehrhardt, 1972), he is forced to confess that the eroticization of gender apparently developed independent of biological influences. He then affirms the imperatives of biology by proposing that "a prenatal androgenic effect . . . may have programmed the brain to be sexually responsive to visual images in a way more typical for a boy than a girl" (p. 151).

Then he obfuscates things further by describing homosexuality as "not, in fact, a sexual phenomenon at all, but a love phenomenon–an inability to fall in love with a person of the other sex, and an ability to fall in love with a person of the same sex as one's own" (Money & Russo, 1979). This would seem to remove homosexuality entirely from the domain of biology, unless Money can convincingly argue a biological basis to such a psychological concept as "love." By this definition, he not only reinforces a dichotomizing of sexual orientation, but he also leaves open a number of curious conceptual questions. This definition might lead to categorizing exclusively heterosexual persons with difficulties in forming intimate attachments to members of the other sex as "latent homosexuals."

Some Conceptual Definitions

Before proceeding further, it is important to clarify the author's understandings of certain concepts necessary to this discussion. The set of constructs used here includes biological sex, gender identity, gender role, and sexual orientation; they are given meanings similar to those used by Shively & De Cecco (1977). These constructs are multi-faceted and complex, oversimplified by the dichotomies commonly associated with them: male/female, masculine/feminine, heterosexual/ homosexual.

Biological sex is–except in highly unusual cases–a readily discernable anatomic feature for any observer of the neonate. But it is beyond biological science to define sex in strict, clear-cut terms. There are always ambiguous cases; then, the determination that an infant is "male" or "female" is a judgment call involving the consideration of the external morphology, internal reproductive organs, chromosomal patterns, and hormonal levels, as well as the impact of attributed sex in socialization.

Gender identity is a psychological rather than an anatomic reality, but it too is a categorical variable. It refers to the individual's personal sense of their gender, an assignment usually congruent with biological sex. Gender identity refers to the individual's inner conviction of their maleness or femaleness. At the same time, however, it is clear that a set of categories from which an individual chooses is defined and shaped by the individual's culture. What appears to be a basic dichotomy of male/female in our culture is not always the case in other cultures. Imperato-McGinley and her colleagues (cited in Hoult, 1983-1984) studied villages in an area of the Dominican Republic where due to a 5-α-reductase deficiency syndrome, it was not uncommon for males to be born with ambiguous external genitalia and appear to be females until the onset of puberty. The villagers here developed a special gender category for children who apparently began as females and ended up as males. There are also societies where the constructed categories of gender meld aspects of what our culture considers male and female. A well-known example of this is the "berdache" status among Native Americans tribes (Roscoe, 1987); others include the hirjas of India, the mahu of Tahiti, and the xanith of Oman (Nanda, 1990).

Gender role is a variable concerned with the quantitative rather than categorical distinctions: the degrees of masculinity and femininity connoted by an individual's behavior, personality attributes, and appearance. Masculinity and femininity refer to the complex of physical, behavioral, and psychological features culturally associated with males and females. As they are dependant upon social norms, the composition of these constructs is comparatively unstable and may vary with culture, social class, and age. The last two decades have seen a reconceptualization of masculinity and femininity as independently varying dimensions rather than as polar opposites on a single continuum.

Sexual orientation refers to the degree to which the erotic and romantic color one's same-sex and other-sex relationships. As it is not necessarily intrinsic to a conceptualization of sexual orientation, this definition does not make the common assumption that sexual orientation is a categorical variable. The labels of bisexual, heterosexual, and homosexual suggest an isomorphism to a person's sexual behavior, sexual fantasies, erotic arousal, and affectional relationships that is not consistent with research evidence (Blumstein & Schwartz, 1977; Masters & Johnson, 1979). In addition, such categories emphasize discontinuities rather than consistencies along the full range of variations in erotic and affectional preferences. This is not to say that the commonly used categories of homosexual, heterosexual, and bisexual are without meaning. Such labels may have great utility in studies that treat them as loosely descriptive social constructs rather than as intrinsic traits that are predictive of the sum of an individual's erotic and affectional desires.

Those who maintain that such categories are innate, such as Harry (1982), ultimately depend upon an essentialistic paradigm for defining an individual's basic "heterosexuality" or "homosexuality," (as opposed to "situational homosexuality" or "situational heterosexuality"). Variations are collapsed by arguing that a single dimension (such as physiological responsiveness to erotic stimuli, sexual fantasy, or sexual behavior) is determinative of one's "true" sexual orientation. More complex erotic and affectional patterns, such as bisexuality, are treated as subterfuges created by socialized behavioral overlays of the "core" trait. This brings to mind the obsession of some of the last century's sexologists for categorizing what was "congenital" versus "acquired" sexual behavior. Harry ends up weakening his own argument for a simple biological determinant of sexual orientation. Due to gender differences in socialization patterns, he proposes that the nature of sexual orientation is different for men and for women. He suggests that women emphasize the affectionate (as opposed to the erotic) aspects of relationships more than men do and thus "may be able to establish sexual relationships with less attention to the physical body from whom they receive affection" (Harry, 1984, pp. 117-118).

ETIOLOGICAL MODELS–THE DOMINATION
OF BIOLOGY

Two basic etiological schemes are given for the development of gender identity, gender role, and sexual orientation. The first is biological, the second, psychosocial. Of course, these are not mutually independent, but the relative contributions of biology and experience are given different weights by different authors. No one could totally dismiss the biological bases of aspects of human sexual behavior; nor could one deny that learning and experience can influence aspects of brain physiology and chemistry. The controversy here is more a matter of how directly and immutably early biological factors can be related to sexual behavior and sexual orientation.

Research on the determinants of sexual orientation has focused on possible causal antecedents of homosexual behavior, as if heterosexual behavior was somehow a biological "given." Thus, even alleged psychosocial theories of sexual orientation and gender behavior may rest upon assumptions of a biological substratum (e.g., Bell, Weinberg, & Hammersmith, 1981). In addition, the dominant psychoanalytic paradigm of psychosexual development infused sexual object-choice with meanings for gender identification, since sexual orientation and gender identification were long considered facets of the same developmental process of resolution of the Oedipal conflict.

There is a further confusion about the implications of labeling something as biologically determined versus a product of experience and culture. Somehow biologically-determined characteristics are seen as less pliable than are environmentally-shaped traits. Critiques of behavioral plasticity tend to obscure the differences between plasticity as a characteristic of the human species versus as a trait of an individual, and to mistakenly equate immutability with nature, and plasticity with nurture (Bakwin, 1968; Whitam, 1983).

The search for a biological basis for homosexuality (even when seen as a necessary but not sufficient condition) tends to depend upon simplistic models that involve a conflation of biological, psychological, and social categories of sex, gender, and sexual behavior. The attractions of the notion of a biologically determined homosexuality is one that has made curious allies of such scientists as Doerner, who views homosexuality as a potentially preventable neuroendocrine disorder, and sociologists such as Whitam and Harry, who see an essentialist formulation as a strong political argument for "gay rights." This belief is not new. A century ago, Karl Heinrich Ulrichs used it in an attempt to change Prussian laws against sodomy. Both cultural biases and political considerations have long been a part of scientific formulations of homosexuality. Whether well-intended or not, such intrusions can only hamper our understandings of the complexities of human sexuality.

The Prenatal Hormonal Paradigm

The argument for a biological substratum to gender and/or sexual "deviance" has recently focused on the hypothetical effect of prenatal hormones on fetal sexual differentiation of the brain. Such hormonal research has been rightfully criticized (Futuyma & Risch, 1983/1984; Gartrell, 1982; Hoult, 1983/1984; Meyer-Bahlburg, 1977;1979; Ricketts, 1984; Ross, Rogers, & McCulloch, 1978; Sigusch, Schorsch, Dannecker, & Schmidt, 1982) on the basis of both flawed methodology and conceptualizations.

Conceptualizing homosexual behavior as gender deviant, and resulting from biological factors both oversimplifies human sexual behavior and relies on gross extrapolations from animal models of sexual behavior. Defining rodent homosexuality raises difficult conceptual questions. Can certain sexual behaviors or roles per se be defined as "homosexual" independent of partner gender? It is problematic to view the mounting and thrusting behavior of hormonally "masculinized" female rats (or the presenting behaviors in hormonally "feminized" male rats) as an adequate or appropriate model of human homosexual behavior (Ricketts, 1984). Alternatively, should we base our definition of homosexuality upon the choice of a same-sex partner? This leads to questions as to the "sexual orientation" of the other rodent with whom the hormonally-treated rat attempts coitus. If we are to judge homosexuality as a supposed inversion of coital roles, then this presents a problem for applying such a rigidly biological model to humans, where sex is more than a procreative act, roles are more varied, and there are far more sexual conjunctions than the insertion of penis into vagina. Furthermore, "inversion of coital roles" describes specific behaviors, not necessarily an exclusive trait, which is how homosexuality is typically conceptualized among those advocating biological explanations. Hormonal research has yet to find meaningful correlations between testosterone levels and preferred role in coitus (insertive, receptive or both) (Doerr et al., 1973), or between hormonal levels and general cross-gender role behavior (Pillard et al., 1974).

Various authors have pointed out that sexual behavior is less mediated by hormonal levels in the fetal environment as one moves up the evolutionary ladder from rats and guinea pigs to even non-human primates, such as rhesus monkeys. The plasticity of sexual behavior needs to be emphasized in the context of the greater overall behavioral plasticity in humans (Goy & Goldfoot, 1975; Seaborg, 1984). It is recognized that:

> infrahuman species might be arranged in a hierarchy from lower to higher, with an increasingly variegated range of behaviors available at the higher levels. This might be true in particular of the capacity for varied forms of sexual behavior. When one reaches the human species, however, another factor enters–social constraints on variations in sexual behavior. Thus the paradox would emerge that the species inherently capable of the most varied sexual behavior might in fact exhibit the fewest variations. (Goy & Goldfoot, 1975, p. 419)

GENDER DEVIANCE AND SEXUAL ORIENTATION

The presumption of sexual deviance as necessarily rooted in gender deviance flies in the face of contrary anthropological evidence which emphasizes the differing cultural associations between gender and sexuality. In some cultures, it is not the "sexual object" but the sexual role (active versus passive) that is infused with gender meanings (Parker, 1985). Furthermore, whereas male homosexuality has feminizing connotations within some cultures, it is viewed as a necessary masculinizing process by such cultures as the Sambia of New Guinea (Adams, 1985; Herdt, 1981). The culture-bound nature of definitions of what is masculine and what is feminine evade the attempts of essentialists to describe particular clusters of behaviors as being innately male or innately female. Mead (1963) pointed out the diversity of what is construed as masculine and as feminine in various cultures. Furthermore, the effects of rearing have been demonstrated to be more reliably linked to displays of gender-typed behaviors and characteristics than have any biological factors (Maccoby & Jacklin, 1974).

To those that believe in a hormonally-induced gender dimorphic organization of the brain which influences subsequent sexual orientation, there remains a question of why such research on childhood cross-gender traits and adult homosexuality has concentrated almost exclusively on males. Any such underlying causal mechanism should be valid for females as well. Furthermore, what is defined as masculine and feminine varies over the life cycle. Researchers such as Green (1987) acknowledge that this cross-gender syndrome is not maintained as a consistent pattern into adulthood. The conceptualizations used in this research often ignore the vast contemporary psychological and sociological literature on gender roles. Although some would treat the stereotyped masculine or feminine play of early childhood as springing from basic biological differences between the sexes (Bakwin, 1968; Green, 1987; Whitam, 1981), it can be readily linked to a cognitive-structural model of the acquisition of gender roles. Thus, "the heightened stereotyping observed in young boys is a direct result of the child's effort to conform to criteria of masculinity that are still inaccessible to him" (Ullian, 1981, p. 497).

A key issue here is our cultural appraisal of masculinity versus femininity. Why is there no equivalent concept for effeminacy when talking about girls? Webster's Seventh New Collegiate Dictionary defines "effeminate" as "(1): having unsuitable feminine qualities: UNMANLY (2): marked by weakness and love of ease." Clearly, we are talking about a value-laden and derogative concept, one that may be a very subjective attribution. Schatzberg and his colleagues (Schatzberg, Westfall, Blumetti, & Birk, 1975; Westfall, Schatzberg, Blumetti, & Birk, 1975) decried the failure to provide a precise "clinical definition" of effeminacy in the literature. To fill that gap, they devised an "Effeminacy Scale" of 67 binary scale items. Unfortunately, the mean scale score reported for homosexuals was only 7.0 (as compared with 3.7 for heterosexual subjects), suggesting that what they termed "effeminacy" varied considerably in its manifestations from individual to individual, possibly with little overlap. An attempt to be more precise highlighted just how imprecise and global the term effeminacy is. This may be related to more recent conceptualizations of masculinity and femininity as "fuzzy sets"–concepts that have an agreed-upon general meaning (as in a prototype), but which cannot be defined in a comprehensive manner to include all possible instances of the concept (Deaux, 1987).

Sociocultural factors explain the high salience of male cross-gender behavior as compared with the "tomboy" characteristics of girls. The male gender role is more strongly tied into heterosexual behavior in our culture (Gross, 1978). Bell, Weinberg, and Hammersmith (1981) found recollected childhood gender nonconformity to be more salient for males than for females in attempts to "predict" adult homosexuality. Stereotypes of male homosexuals appear more negative than stereotypes of female homosexuals. There is evidence (Page & Yee, 1985) that males are judged more harshly for deviations from "appropriate" gender role behavior. Cross-gender behavior by males not only impugns their sexual maleness, but involves them in less valued role behavior. Cross-gender behavior by females may cast aspersions on their sexual femininity, but allows them proficiency in more highly regarded sex-typed behaviors.

Researchers need to focus more on the ascribed meanings given to certain behavioral patterns and traits. Too many authors confuse social constructions of gender with biology, and gender nonconformity as a "problem" existing independent of any cultural context. Sexual scripts may be influenced by the meanings imputed to an individual's manner, early social behavior patterns and appearance by his culture. Cass (1979) described the first stage in homosexual identity formation being one of "identity confusion," where the individuals ask themselves if they might be homosexual, since their behavior may be called homosexual. Given the symbol systems attached to cross-gender behavior in our culture, someone who is not stereotypically gender-typed may find their behavior ascribed a special sexual meaning before they have any clear erotic attractions.

Harry (1982) points out that by late childhood, boys characterize those who are feminine in behavior or manner as "faggots" rather than "sissies." Before the actual sexual meaning of the label has significance for them, a child's peers may apply it to him. Once defined as a "faggot," how does this influence the development of sexuality? Additionally, reports of parents' concerns in studies of "effeminate" or "gender-disordered" boys show them to worry about their son growing up to be homosexual, rather than fearing his being transsexual or transvestite. Thus, these boys may be less able to unquestioningly assume their heterosexuality. In addition, those who assume a homosexual identity may tend to qualify their masculinity on the basis of entrenched cultural ascriptions to homosexuality.

Studies of child cross-gender behavior tend to dichotomize sexual orientation and treat it as immutable. Green (1987) found that his "sissy boy" sample (broken down into categories on the basis of composite Kinsey scores) could be described as 27% heterosexual, 32% bisexual, and 41% homosexual. Yet he failed to treat the bisexual population as distinct in any way from the homosexual population. Other authors rarely, if ever, acknowledge a continuum of sexual behavior and fantasy, thus reifying both the homosexual/heterosexual and the gender-deviant/gender-appropriate dichotomies. When authors such as Cass (1983/1984) emphasize the fluidity of sexual labels, and the fact that it is our construction of sexual orientation that "dictates the rigid and permanent quality" of any such identity, they are challenged by others such as Harry (1984), who prefer to deal in absolutes. However, neither masculinity/femininity nor sexual orientation can be said to be consistent over the life cycle, and it scarcely benefits scientific thought to presume that early manifestations of either are somehow any more rooted in the biological make-up of the individual than later displays.

It appears that any attempt to develop a simple, linear biological cause-and-effect model of the development of adult homosexuality must be doomed to failure. Bell, Weinberg, and Hammersmith's (1981) attempts to "explain" the development of homosexuality (in a work somewhat deceptively titled *Sexual Preferences*) led them to suggest numerous paths to adult homosexuality or bisexuality. They then propose that there are numerous types of homosexuals, based upon their developmental origins–some for whom recollected childhood gender nonconformity is a relevant experience. It is not surprising that they tread speculatively into the hypothetical realm of biological precursors of homosexuality, as their focus suggests a presumption of homosexuality as a series of diverse deviations from a heterosexual norm. However, they do a service in acknowledging how much more complex any such causal links would necessarily be than stereotypical etiologies in the popular imagination.

If we are to come to any understanding about what we term "sexual orientation," we need to remember that human sexual behavior is more than procreation, that sexual conjugations have different meanings in different cultures and different contexts, and that the individual plays an active role in selecting from, weighing, and interpreting various experiences to create a self-identity. The hypothetical links between biology and gender role behavior have weak support (at best) once we move beyond rats and procreative roles, and discount more complex research findings in the area of human gender role differences. The reductionism implied in the dominance of notions of a single biological substratum to both cross-gender behavior and adult homosexuality cannot be supported either on conceptual grounds or on the basis of the existing research evidence. Those who continue to do research along these lines would do well to scrutinize the assumptions behind their work. Their supposedly objective scientific inquiries may be fueled by underlying agendas that bias their conclusions.

REFERENCES

Adam, B. (1985). Age, structure, and sexuality: Reflections on the anthropological evidence on homosexual relations. *Journal of Homosexuality, 11*(3/4),19-33.

Bakwin, H. (1968). Deviant gender-role behavior in children: Relation to homosexuality. *Pediatrics 41*(3), 620-629.

Bell, A., Weinberg, M., & Hammersmith, S. (1981). *Sexual Preference: Its Development in Men and Women*. Bloomington: Indiana University Press.

Blackwood, E. (1985). Breaking the mirror: The construction of lesbianism and the anthropological discourse on homosexuality. *Journal of Homosexuality, 11*(3/4), 1-17.

Blumstein, P., & Schwartz, P. (1977). Bisexuality: Some social psychological issues. *Journal of Social Issues, 33*(2), 30-45.

Cass, V. (1979). Homosexual identity formation: A theoretical model. *Journal of Homosexuality, 4*(3), 219-235.

Cass, V. (1983/1984). Homosexual identity: A concept in need of definition. *Journal of Homosexuality, 9*(2/3),105-126.

Deaux, K. (1987). Psychological constructions of masculinity and femininity. In: J. Reinisch, L. Rosenblum and S. Sanders (Eds.) *Masculinity/Femininity: Basic Perspectives.* New York: Oxford Press (pp. 289-303).

Doerr, P., Pirke, K., Kockett, G., and Dittmar, F. (1976). Further studies on sex hormones in male homosexuals. *Archives of General Psychiatry, 33,* 611-614.

Futuyma, D., & Risch, S. (1983/1984). Sexual orientation, sociobiology, and evolution. *Journal of Homosexuality, 2*(2/3), 157-168.

Gartrell, N. (1982). Hormones and homosexuality. In W. Paul, J.D. Weinrich, J.C. Gonsiorek, & M.E. Hotvedt (Eds.), *Homosexuality: Social, Psychological and Biological Issues* (pp. 169-182). Beverly Hills, CA: Sage Publications Inc.

Goy, R., & Goldfoot, D. (1975). Neuroendocrinology: Animal models and problems of human sexuality. *Archives of Sexual Behavior, 4*(4), 405-420.

Green, R. (1985a). Gender identity in childhood and later sexual orientation: Follow-up of 78 males. *American Journal of Psychiatry 142*(3), 339-341.

Green, R. (1985b). Potholes on the research road to sexual identity development. *Journal of Sex Research, 21*(1), 96-101.

Green, R. (1987). *The "Sissy Boy Syndrome" and the Development of Homosexuality.* New Haven: Yale University Press.

Gross, A. (1978). The male role and heterosexual behavior. *Journal of Social Issues, 34*(1), 87-107.

Harry, J. (1982). *Gay Children Grow Up: Gender Culture and Gender Deviance.* New York: Praeger Publishers.

Harry, J. (1984). Sexual orientation as destiny. *Journal of Homosexuality, 10*(3/4),111-124.

Herdt, G. (1981). *Guardians of the Flutes: Idioms of Masculinity.* New York: McGraw-Hill Inc.

Hoult, T. (1983/1984). Human sexuality in biological perspective: Theoretical and methodological considerations. *Journal of Homosexuality, 9*(2/3), 137-155.

Lebovitz, P. (1972). Feminine behavior in boys: Aspects of its outcome. *American Journal of Psychiatry, 128*(10), 1283-1289.

Maccoby, E., & Jacklin, C. (1974). *The Psychology of Sex Differences.* Stanford: Stanford University Press.

Masters, W., & Johnson, V. (1979). *Homosexuality in Perspective.* Boston: Little, Brown & Company.

Mead, M. (1963). *Sex and Temperament in Three Primitive Societies.* New York: Dell. [Originally published 1935].

Meyer-Bahlburg, H. (1977). Sex hormones and male homosexuality in comparative perspective. *Archives of Sexual Behavior 6*(4), 297-325.

Meyer-Bahlburg, H. (1979). Sex hormones and female homosexuality: A critical examination. *Archives of Sexual Behavior, 8*(2), 101-119.

Money, J., & Ehrhardt, A. (1972). *Man and Woman, Boy and Girl: The Differentiation and Dimorphism of Gender Identity From Conception to Maturity.* Baltimore, MD: John Hopkins University Press.

Money, J., & Russo, A. (1979). Homosexual outcome of discordant gender identity/role in childhood: Longitudinal follow-up. *Journal of Pediatric Psychology, 4*(1), 29-41.

Nanda, S. (1990). *Neither Man nor Woman: The Hijras of India.* Belmont, CA: Wadsworth Publishing Co.

Page, S., & Yee, M. (1985). Conception of male and female homosexual stereotypes among university undergraduates. *Journal of Homosexuality, 12*(1), 109-118.

Parker, R. (1985). Masculinity, femininity, and homosexuality: On the anthropological interpretation of sexual meanings in Brazil. *Journal of Homosexuality, 11*(3/4), 155-163.

Pillard, R., Rose, R., & Sherwood, M. (1974). Plasma testosterone levels in homosexual men. *Archives of Sexual Behavior, 3,* 453-458.

Ricketts, W. (1984). Biological research on homosexuality: Ansell's cow or Occam's razor? *Journal of Homosexuality, 9*(4), 65-93.

Roscoe, W. (1987). Bibliography of berdache and alternative gender roles among North American Indians. *Journal of Homosexuality, 14*(3/4), 81-171.

Ross, M. (1980). Retrospective distortion in homosexual research. *Archives of Sexual Behavior, 9*(6), 523-531.

Ross, M., Rogers, L., & McCulloch, H. (1978). Stigma, sex and society: A new look at gender differentiation and sexual variation. *Journal of Homosexuality, 3*(4), 315-330.

Sagarin, E. (1973). The good guys, the bad guys and the gay guys. *Contemporary Sociology, 2*(1), 3-13.

Schatzberg, A., Westfall, M., Blumetti, A., & Birk, C. (1975). Effeminacy. I. A quantitative rating scale. *Archives of Sexual Behavior, 4*(1), 31-41.

Seaborg, D. (1984). Sexual orientation, behavioral plasticity, and evolution. *Journal of Homosexuality, 10*(3/4),153-158.

Shively, M., & De Cecco, J. (1977). Components of sexual identity. *Journal of Homosexuality, 3*(1), 41-48.

Sigusch, V., Schorsch, E., Dannecker, M., & Schmidt, G. (1982). Official statement by the German Society for Sex Research (Deutsche Gesellschaft fuer Sexualforschung e. V.) on the research of Prof. Dr. Guenter Doerner on the subject of homosexuality. *Archives of Sexual Behavior 11*(5), 445-449.

Ullian, D. (1981). Why boys will be boys: A structural perspective. *American Journal of Orthopsychiatry, 5*(3), 493-501.

Westfall, M., Schatzberg, A., Blumetti, A., & Birk, C. (1975). Effeminacy. II. Variations with social context. *Archives of Sexual Behavior, 4*(1), 43-51.

Whitam, F. (1981). A reply to Goode on "The homosexual role." *Journal of Sex Research, 17,* 66-72.

Whitam, F. (1983). Culturally invariable properties of male homosexuality: Tentative conclusions from cross-cultural research. *Archives of Sexual Behavior, 12*(3), 207-226.

Zuger, B. (1978). Effeminate behavior present in boys from childhood: Ten additional years of follow-up. *Comprehensive Psychiatry, 19*(4), 363-369.

Reproductive Strategies and Gender Construction: An Evolutionary View of Homosexualities

Mildred Dickemann, PhD

Sonoma State University

SUMMARY. In this chapter the author addresses the following question: Can the historical occurrence of various forms of homosexuality and bisexuality be explained as part of the management of reproduction in response to environmental conditions? She believes that explanations for the occurrence and forms of homosexuality appealing to genetics are biologically indefensible and historically inadequate. However, Darwinian behavioral theory, and specifically that subset termed life history theory, provides an explanatory framework. An individual's life course consists of behaviors coerced by parents and chosen by the individual in response to environmental conditions, forming a coherent reproductive strategy. In the process, alternate male and female genders, such as cadet sons, spinsters, and religious celibates are explained and the normative male bisexuality of Classical Athens and modern Mediterranean/Latin societies is elucidated. The rise of modern homosexuality in industrial nations results from the demographic transition to low mortality and low fertility, relaxing the reproductive management of children by parents and permitting a greater role for temperament in individual sexual and gender choices.

Mildred Dickemann is Professor Emeritus of Anthropology at Sonoma State University.

Presented at the H.W.H. Conference, Free University, Amsterdam, December, 1987

55

Several attempts have been made to explain "homosexuality" using concepts from Darwinian theory, all (Hamilton 1959; Kirsch & Rodman 1982; Trivers 1974; Wilson 1975; Weinrich 1977, 1982) resting on the assumption that homosexual behavior is genetically determined. Most propose an inclusive fitness advantage to possessors or their families, that is, greater perpetuation of the homosexual's genes through investment in reproducing relatives sharing those genes (but see Trivers 1985), thus assuming that all homosexuals are non-reproductive. Most treat "homosexuality" as a single entity, perpetuating the Western view of the homosexual as a deviant "intersex." Without resort to untenable assumptions about varying gene frequencies within and between populations, these hypotheses cannot explain the historical and ethnographic variations in frequencies of overt homosexual behavior, by society, class, and special circumstance. Weak in their grasp of Darwinian theory, these theories are genetically indefensible and historically inadequate.

Yet evolutionary theory does, I believe, have relevance to our subject, specifically the area of behavioral ecology, derived from comparative study of plants and animals, which makes predictions about the forms of sexuality and reproduction that occur in specific environmental contexts, including the social environments of conspecifics. The cluster of propositions known as life history theory (Anderson & King 1970; Cody 1966; Cole 1954; Demetrius 1975; Gadgil & Bossert 1970; Horn 1978; Lack 1954; MacArthur & Wilson 1967; Stearns 1976; Tinkle 1969) includes reproductive strategies, sex allocation, parental manipulation and investment, and in social organisms, inclusive fitness or kin selection theory. This approach views individual life courses as sequences of adaptive behaviors, evolved through natural selection to produce maximal reproductive gain. In long-lived organisms with parent-offspring proximity, the benefit of a behavior or behavioral sequence may be to the parent, not the offspring, the latter being coerced or programmed to behave at the expense of its own interests. Social behaviors are generally compromises between the individual's interests and those of its parents (Trivers 1974). This is all the more true in humans given the existence of elaborate structures of social coercion.

This level of evolutionary analysis makes probabilistic statements about recurring patterns of behavior, and does not presume to explain rare variations (though such explanations, at lower analytical levels, can be accommodated when available). It requires *no* presumption of genetic bases for individual variants nor for recurring patterns, *no* genes either for heterosexuality or for homosexuality, beyond the basic morpho-physiological differences of males and females, expressed in their differing reproductive capacities. Rather, behavioral ecology proposes that humans, like most other organisms, possess behavioral plasticity, whose function is to produce adaptive behavioral responses to changing environmental circumstances. Application of life history theory to humans provides a new way of conceptualizing *genders,* as life courses whose social construction concerns the *reproductively relevant* aspects of role and identity, whether or not that gender includes reproduction. Thus, this analysis of homosexual and bisexual behavior is part of a larger attempt to demonstrate the existence of *multiple genders* in human societies and their predictability from the perspective of neo-Darwinian theory. It avoids both "essentialist" emphasis on morphogenetic or physiological factors in explaining heterosexual and homosexual gender differences and also extreme "social constructionist" denial of the significance of reproductive roles. In addition, it may provide a general theory of the occurrence of specific heterosexual and homosexual genders in specific historical and ethnographic contexts, one integrating biological theory with historical and ethnographic data (cf. Adam 1985; Blackwood 1985).

I first review relevant aspects of this theory set, then discuss multiple genders in humans, and finally turn to homosexuality and bisexuality. Life history theory views life courses as series of sequential steps or stages, involving (metaphorical) "decisions" about major life parameters that affect survival and reproduction, including sex, rate of growth, age at maturity, length of reproductive life, level of fertility, degree of investment of energy and resources in offspring, and longevity. Some aspects of life courses may be tightly programmed, others highly responsive to change in environment: responsive, or plastic, attributes may be morphological, physiological, or behavioral. Plasticity may involve switching from one behavior mode to another, or grading of behavior in response to degree of environmental difference or change. Humans differ from other organisms only in the degree to which behavioral fine-tuning is employed. Thus, all mammals prevent wasted reproductive effort through anovulation of females under caloric deprivation or high metabolic demand, and through abandonment of sick or injured offspring. Humans, in addition, manage reproductive effort through social tabus controlling sexuality, age of marriage, frequency of intercourse, abortion, infanticide, length of nursing, age of social adulthood of offspring, and other means. The very long period of heavy investment in offspring in our species predicts that we should rely heavily on such graded behavioral responses.

For all parents, sex of offspring is a critical choice, as it affects chance of mating and reproducing. Many plants vary the sex of offspring depending on the microenvironment. More elaborate is sex reversal, the ability of some plants, invertebrates, and fish to change sex during the life span, in response to the numbers of individuals of both sexes in the group, and the numbers of dominants, a way of taking advantage of changing reproductive opportunities throughout the lifespan. In some cases, three different life histories may be present in the same population: permanent males, permanent females, and those who have switched sex (Charnov 1982; Robertson 1972; Warner *et al.* 1975).

Alternate reproductive strategies within the same morphogenetic sex may be determined developmentally, the most dramatic examples being social insects such as the honeybee, whose hives are composed of thousands of worker females, additional thousands of reproductive but non-laboring males, and only a few queens during the year, the last produced by differential nutrition during the larval stage. Workers spend their lives as non-reproductive helpers, investing their energies in the reproductive success of their mother and sister queens. It is not generally known that even the chastity of the worker bee is plastic, or facultative, as in the absence of a queen, workers' atrophied ovaries enlarge and produce eggs. Though many factors are at work, the evolution of these distinct genders in social insects seems to be in part a response to such variables as scarcity of nest sites and high predation in contexts of high density and intense competition (Seeley 1985; Traniello 1978; West-Eberhard 1975, 1978, 1979, 1981, 1982). In birds, alternate reproductive strategies are generally temporary. The helper at the nest is a male or female who delays reproduction due to the difficulty of establishing a territory or finding a mate, instead assisting in the rearing of its siblings. But in some cases, individuals may spend their lives in such non-reproductive helper roles (Emlen 1978, 1981, 1984; Ligon 1981; Stacey & Bock 1978; Woolfenden 1981; Woolfenden & Fitzpatrick 1984).

In mammals, dominance hierarchies, and the reproductive advantage of dominant males, frequently produce satellite male strategies. Where dominants hold territories or otherwise control access to females, satellite males engage in sneak copulations on the margin of the territory or harem. Thus, in Rocky Mountain bighorn sheep, a higher rank male typically tends individual ewes in a traditional rutting area, achieving high levels of copulation. Subordinates attempt to breach his defenses by attack and rapid mounting; copulation rates using this strategy are less than half as high. In addition, they may attain copulations by separating a ewe from the group for several days (Hogg 1984). Generally satellite male strategies are employed by junior males, before full dominance and maturity are attained, as in our own species. They have been reported in many insects, birds, fish, frogs, and mammals, including elephant seals and nonhuman primates (Alcock 1979; Cade 1979; Dunbar 1984; Emlen 1976; LeBoeuf 1974; LeBoeuf & Peterson 1969; Otte & Stayman 1979; Thornhill & Alcock 1983). But alternative strategies may become permanent life courses or genders. For example, in the gelada baboon, a dominant male controls a harem of females. There are two options available to a maturing male: he may attempt to take over the harem, ousting the owner, or may live as a follower dependent upon sneak copulations. There is a slight reproductive advantage to the harem strategy, but only if it is initiated early in adulthood (Dunbar 1984).

The reproductive morphology and physiology of birds and mammals are too complex to permit sex reversal. Therefore, their adjustments to varying reproductive opportunities must be achieved behaviorally. Paradoxically, those organisms most *rigidly* constrained by morphogenetic sex characters are those most *flexible* in behavioral aspects of sex and reproduction. This applies *a fortiori* to humans. The developmentally or behaviorally achieved alternate life courses of social insects, birds, and mammals parallel human genders, lacking only the socially constructed ideologies and self-conscious identities of our own. Such alternate genders, within a single morphogenetic sex, probably rarely coincide exactly with those of the opposite sex. Thus, most of them may more accurately be categorized as sub-genders within a general male or female gender set. This is probably the usual case with humans, as well (cf. Callender & Kochems 1985; Whitehead 1981).

Alternate male genders, or sub-genders, are familiar from European history. They result from the control of resources, means of production, and human labor by high status families. Patrilineal inheritance at these ranks produces more reproductive success than investment in females, due to greater male than female capacity to produce offspring. Investment of resources in males attracts females, as brides or concubines or for casual liaisons. Since the division of lands reduces political power and lineage survival, but high fertility is necessary to offset high mortalities, primogeniture, with the dispersal of second and later sons, is the usual inheritance strategy.

First sons inherit major titles, offices, and lands, enjoy higher rates of marriage into wealthier families, earlier marriage, higher fertility, and higher survivorship and reproduction of offspring. Cadet sons, destined for the lower nobility and military or clerical roles, have markedly different life courses. As in other organisms, they may accede to the senior role if it is vacated by death, or through a political takeover, but more often will experience delayed marriage or lifelong celibacy, sometimes involving chastity, but more usually promiscuity and liaisons, often across caste or ethnic boundaries. Rates of mortality are generally higher; reproductive success is lower. These cadet sons may pose a problem for their families and society at large. Georges Duby (1977, 1978, 1980) has proposed that the primary function of the Crusades was to draw off the large numbers of wandering knights (cadets) from Europe, directing them into a politically promising (though failed) adventure.

In later centuries, cadet sons from the nobility and peasantry formed the legions carrying out Spanish-Portuguese exploration, conquest and colonization of Africa, Asia, and the New World (Boone 1983, 1986). The differential allocation of senior and cadet roles is replicated on a more modest scale by the peasantries of such patrilineal agrarian societies. Demographic analysis of this phenomenon has only begun; however, qualitative comparisons make clear that this pattern is widespread in agrarian, pre-industrial societies characterized by environmental, economic, and political instabilities (Dickemann 1979a, 1979b, 1981). For his parents, the senior son is a high-investment, lower-risk tactic, the cadet a lower-investment, higher-risk tactic, providing insurance in case of failure of the senior line, and possible familial gain through dispersal and colonization. The celibate religious role remains unstudied. However, Duby notes that celibate uncles in the medieval period regularly bequeathed their wealth back to the senior male line, thus employing the inclusive fitness strategy.

Both of these cadet roles, at some times and places, were characterized by bisexuality or even preferential homosexuality, as in the religious elite at the court of Charlemagne (Boswell 1980), or probably the Knights Templars. It is important to note that these roles were *allocated parentally* by birth order. Contrasting life courses, with differing sexualities, reproductive and non-reproductive, heterosexual, bisexual, homosexual, were imposed and supported by the social order. The birth order allocation of contrasting genders is one of the strongest evidences we have against genetic-endocrine theories of sexual orientation. *If sexuality can be allocated by birth order, what need is there to propose a gene for homosexuality?*

Can the occurrence and forms of homosexuality and bisexuality be predicted by a theory of parental and social gender allocation, as part of the management of reproduction? I believe so. The familiar Athenian case makes sense in these terms (Boswell 1980; Dover 1978; Licht 1969). The elite Athenian citizen male ideal prescribed a life course containing two sequential stages, adolescent and adult. Adolescent attachment to an older man, who provided emotional support, protection, education, and political favors, was idealized. Simultaneously, adolescents had access to women of lower status, young men of their own age, and female and male prostitutes, but not to elite women, who were controlled by a Mediterranean code of virginity and marital fidelity, enforced through seclusion, chaperonage and strong social sanctions. Male prostitutes, non-citizens and slaves, and adolescent boys, might perform the anal "passive" sex role, but not adult male citizens, as this violated the gender definition of adult masculine assertiveness. After adolescence, the adult male enters a second life stage, marrying, siring a family, inheriting land, perhaps assuming office. Complementary sexual and affectional relations with young boys would be accompanied by sex with male and female prostitutes. Intercrural and anal "active" or "insertor" acts were deemed gender-appropriate, but not the "insertee" or "passive" role. This resulted not only from the categorization of sex acts as symbolic of male dominance and female passivity, in this sex-hierarchical society, but more deeply, from the equation of masculinity with procreation, and hence with the inseminator role in sex contacts.[1] Exclusively homosexual men were rare, but not condemned unless engaging in "passive" receptor intercourse. Thus elite Athenian males had access to a variety of partners, but were expected to perform a reproductive role, and constrained from violating the sanctity of elite women and from practicing gender-dissonant "feminine" forms of intercourse, once adult.

To explain this pattern, we must examine its context. Greek city states were patrilineal, though less stratified, more democratic, than larger agrarian monarchies. Investment of land and title in males produced competition between families to place their daughters with high status grooms, guaranteeing better survival and reproduction. That competition, expressed in part through the offer of dowry to increase the bride's value, also included the family's guarantee that the bride was virgin at marriage, would be faithful in marriage and raise daughters similarly sexually controlled. This concern for female fidelity is a result of the need, in contexts of heavy *male* investment in offspring, to assure the paternity of such offspring. Paternity confidence concerns have generated a variety of solutions in animal species wherever males invest heavily. In humans, the greater the intensity of competition for high status grooms, the greater the intensity of control over women, seclusion, veiling, and elaboration of a code of female modesty and purity (Dickemann 1981). In this regard, Athens was moderate, like many recent Mediterranean societies. In consequence, high status women associated only with men of their own kin group, and husbands. Extremely contrasting personalities, values, and social sex roles separated elite men and women in temperament and interests, as well as spatially. Male authority and female subservience eliminated the potential for emotional and intellectual sharing. But the stratification of society produced a large lower class desperate for survival, from whose ranks male and female prostitutes emerged, as a consequence of elite sex segregation.[2]

What of the man/boy love aspect of the Athenian ideal? It is significant that fathers of boys evaluated and approved the choice of adult lovers, on the basis of advantages offered to the son. Athenian society was politically decentralized. Sociopolitical networks played an important role in the citizen's achievement, so early acquisition of social skills and contacts was crucial. Yet, formal education was minimal. In fact, similar forms of man/boy love occur in other societies with decentralized, open political competition between males, whether literate urban or non-literate horticultural (Weinrich 1976; Gray 1985; Herdt 1984). Thus Athenian male sexuality is predictable from a few variables: social stratification with a controlling patrilineal elite and a large poverty class, seclusion of women, decentralized political system involving individual political networks, absence of elaborate formal education, and perhaps, the high libido of young men. (There are no data on the sexuality of secluded women.)

A similar, though not identical, system of male sexuality characterized the elites of despotic agrarian feudal and monarchical societies in China, Japan, North India, and the Middle East (Adam's 1986 "ancient" model of homosexuality). Here too, patrilineal inheritance resulted in intense paternity concern, with the seclusion and devaluation of women as household workers and childbearers, dangerous to men, concomitantly more extreme. Prostitution, concubinage, and the Greek *hetaira* role were all replicated. But these centralized societies imposed greater polygyny on elite males, monarchs holding harems of as many as 3,000 women. This greater reproductive demand on elite males arose from their greater instability of tenure and the higher mortalities, infant and adult, in these societies. The evolution of male homosexual love resulted from alienation between the sexes. But more elaborate religious institutions than in Greece produced celibate male roles as well. Thus, at both court and "chapel," man/boy love became the ideal, and a mystical/ erotic literature emerged. I have no data on the allocation of elite religious roles, but it is clear that lower status roles were entered by men too poor to obtain wives. Thus the bisexuality of elite males is similar to that of Athenians, but is accompanied by more exclusive homosexuality in segregated male institutions, and lacks the emphasis on the educative function of man/boy love between individuals of the same socioeconomic rank.

For most patrilineal societies, data on female sexuality are meager.

However, in some cases, the emergence of alternate female genders provides us with some understanding of environmental context. In the period from 1790 to about 1860, the U.S. underwent rapid transformation to a modern industrial society, with an urban labor force, male and female, and intense class stratification, resulting in extreme distance between rich and poor. As the upper class crystallized, elite female gender definition changed. As we would predict, emphasis on the domestic, modest, subservient wifely role of the marrying woman increased, as did distance between men and women. But soon, another female gender, that of the spinster, appeared. More than maiden aunts serving as household servants, public spinsters acquired new roles, and a supporting ideology of the pure spinsterly calling emerged, a secular Victorian ideology surprisingly similar to that surrounding the European nun. Elite families, competing for grooms, have often found it impossible or impossibly costly to marry all their daughters with dowries. In some cases, as in post-Buddhist India, the solution to this dilemma was infanticide at birth of most or all daughters; in others, some of these children were allocated to celibacy. The European nunnery demanded a dowry, but always less than the marital dowry. American Victorian spinsters required expensive educations to enter newly developing female professions, especially teaching; new female colleges were created serving in part as secular equivalents to the nunnery. In the late 19th and early 20th centuries, as many as 50% of all graduates of elite eastern women's colleges never married (Dickemann[1987]; Solomon 1985).

What of the sexuality of these women? The sparse European record suggests continuing attempts by authorities to repress same-sex relations (Brown 1986; Crompton 1981). In 19th century U.S., "passionate" or "romantic" friendships were common and accepted among women, as close friendships were idealized between men. For marrying women and men, friendship offered emotional support not possible in increasingly role-segregated marriages. For celibate women, such friendships often became long-term cohabitations, so-called "Boston marriages," frequent among female academics. The sexual content of these relationships is mostly unknown, for good reason. Sex was *not a specified attribute* of this gender role, since elite female sexuality, in all these societies, concerned reproduction alone. The proper woman was not only sexually undemanding, submissive, but sexually unresponsive, anorgasmic. In these societies, only whores had orgasms. The separate celibate female sub-gender shared in this notion of sexual purity, because to produce sexually assertive women would have destroyed the family's credibility in its more critical enterprise, the production of marriageable daughters.

Only when *marrying* daughters acquired the right to sexual assertion, many decades later, could spinsters, and lesbians, also enjoy gender identities that included public recognition of their sexuality. The imposition of asexuality upon women, whether marrying or celibate, as opposed to men, the reduction of female sexuality to reproduction, characterizes elites in all stratified patrilineal societies. Whether or not it also reflects a fundamental physiological difference between women and men in degree of libido, or degree of plasticity of libido, I leave as a question for others.

We need much more work on the allocation, sexuality, and familial functions of celibate genders, female and male. There is evidence in Europe that higher birth order daughters were assigned to nunneries, paralleling the pattern of male allocation. This assignment of low birth order men and women to reproduction is one component of the high fertility strategy of pre-demographic transition families, which includes early betrothal and marriage. In 19th century U.S., birth order loses significance as individual achievement and education play greater roles in industrial society, and late marriage reflects upper-class stability. Thus, temperament could play a greater role in gender allocation; but more data are needed on this score.

I turn last to speculation regarding ourselves, the modern phenomenon of overt homosexuality, gay identity, and gay community, of which at least some aspects are predictable from the Darwinian perspective. Around the turn of the century, Western Europe, the U.S., Canada, and other nations completed the "demographic transition," which had begun in European urban elites as early as the 1600s. As a result of declining mortalities and greater socioeconomic and political stability, birthrates declined to replacement levels. In the last 50 years, much of Northwestern Europe has passed through a so-called "second demographic transition," resulting in fertility below replacement and high levels of divorce, delayed marriage, and lifelong celibacy. These societies have reduced infant mortality to near zero; advanced social support systems provide medical care, maternity leaves, child care, and public education, while a large female wage labor market employs almost all women. To reproduce oneself, only 1+ offspring are necessary, and there is little investment gain from marriage. These most advanced industrial societies represent the extreme of heavy investment in a few offspring, a strategy characterizing all organisms in stable predictable environments with controllable resources, though here investment is more through contributions to state subventions than directly to offspring. The decline of patrilineal inheritance and the unimportance of marriage as a means of reproductive success result in reduced familial and social imposition of marital and sexual controls on offspring. Coercion into heterosexual, reproductive genders declines, so personal choice of sexual and affectional partners for both men and women becomes more possible.

To test this proposition, I would hypothesize that where the demographic transition is less advanced, patrilineal emphasis will still obtain, more men will be allocated to reproductive, inheriting roles, and more familial control over marriage, sex role segregation, and female modesty-submissiveness will occur. Rather than open homosexuality, high frequencies of middle and upper class male married bisexuality should occur; with female sexuality repressed, lesbianism will be closeted and socially denied or ignored. Journalistic reports (Cummings 1986; Turner 1986) suggest that such a gradient does obtain in Europe, from the greater open gay life of Northwest Europe to the greater married male bisexuality of Southern and Eastern Europe, while various authors (cf. Fry 1985; Kutsche [1986]; Parker 1985; Taylor 1985) have reported on Latin American variants of the same pattern.

A longitudinal test would hypothesize increasing numbers of individuals reproducing at low levels and living open gay lives either post-reproductively or simultaneously. Unfortunately, few studies give data on reproduction.[3] The proportion of U.S. lesbian mothers appears to be increasing rapidly, both through the entry of previously heterosexual mothers and through lesbian conceptions. Apparently an increasingly common life course, at least for lesbians, involves early heterosexuality and reproduction with a subsequent switch to gay lifestyle in midlife. While such a life course is made possible by high survivorship, reduced familial controls, and lower necessity for marital support, I believe this midlife switch represents merely a point in the continuing adaptation of reproductive strategies to economic evolution. If the trend toward socialism continues, heterosexual liaisons will become truly optional and reproduction will be fully severed from marriage. I have dealt almost exclusively with pre-modern elites and modern middle and upper classes. Time prevents the application of this theoretical framework to working class, poverty class, and ethnic minority populations. Nor have I discussed so called "situational" homosexuality in sex-segregated institutions, because such separate categorization is misconceived. All sexuality is in part situational–the product of the interaction of familial and social pressures, social opportunities, and individual temperament and experience. Whether among prison inmates, bisexual married men, football teams, or Victorian spinsters, homosexual contacts are a *component*, either mandatory or optional, of that gender or life course definition. Gender rules always dictate the circumstances in which homosexual contact is appropriate, whether it is mandatory or not, age of the actor, choice of partner, form of the sex act, and its meaning in relation to total gender identity for the actor and for her or his milieu. Which individuals, in any specific social gender category, prefer more or less homosocial or homosexual contact, is of course a matter of temperament. Temperamental differences may indeed rest in part on innate factors, but that is a far cry from a gene for homosexuality. Variations in form and frequency of approved homosexual and bisexual behaviors cannot be explained genetically or physiologically, but accord at least tentatively with predictions from behavioral biology regarding environmental contexts and reproductive strategies.

If individual human life courses are generally produced by parental and societal socialization whose primary goal is reproductive success, the persecution of overt homosexuality as a perceived threat to reproductive interests becomes comprehensible. Discrimination is regularly justified in terms of defense of "the family" (i.e., the reproductive unit), children, and codes of sexual (i.e., reproductive) propriety and purity. The political implications of this analysis are clear. Wherever, in whatever class or society, social support systems are weakened, economic instabilities increase and employment opportunities, especially for women and single parents, decline, infant mortalities will rise, and with them, greater familial emphasis on fertility, on marriage, and on gender separation and female subordination.[4] While married male bisexuality will increase, persecution of overt homosexuality will intensify. This is the message of Darwinian biology. The ultimate guarantee of safety for an openly gay lifestyle is only superficially paradoxical: a stable industrial social system providing the most adequate, most egalitarian support (social, economic, medical, and educational) for *independently reproducing* adults, will provide us, as well, the environment of greatest personal freedom in all relations of sex and love.

NOTES

1. Note that in original usage *"macho"* refers to a man who achieves status not merely by sexual but by *procreative* success, and that intensely patrilineal societies regard the womb as a mere vessel or soil in which the male-donated conceptus matures.

2. Note that Humphreys (1970) found a frequent pattern of conjugal role and activity separation in marriages of bisexual men.

3. In the 1970s, 10-20% of male homosexuals in Western Europe and North America appear to have been previously married (Weinberg & Williams 1974: 17%; Bell & Weinberg 1978: 20%, of which 1/2 had children); while about 25%

of lesbians were previously married (ranging in various studies from 14 to 35%, summarized in Peplau & Amaro 1982).

4. Note the positive correlations between tolerance for homosexuality and for sexual permissiveness and reduced sex role separation reported by MacDonald & Games 1974; see also Levitt & Klassen 1974, and for married bisexual men, themselves, Ross 1983: 115-116.

BIBLIOGRAPHY

Adam, B.D. 1985. Age, structure, and sexuality: Reflections on the anthropological evidence on homosexual relations. *J. Homosexual. 11.* Reprinted in *Anthropology and Homosexual Behavior*, Blackwood, E. (ed.), pp. 19-33. New York: The Haworth Press, Inc. 1986.

Alcock, J. 1979. The evolution of intraspecific diversity in male reproductive strategies in some bees and wasps. In Blum, M.S. & Blum, N.A. (eds.), *Sexual Selection and Reproductive Competition in Insects,* pp. 381-492. New York: Academic.

Anderson, W.W. & King, C.E. 1970. Age-specific selection. *Proceedings,* National Academy of Sciences 66 (July 1970): 780-86.

Blackwood, E. 1985. Breaking the mirror: the construction of lesbianism and the anthropological discourse on homosexuality. *J. Homosexual. 11.* Reprinted in Blackwood, E. (ed.), *Anthropology and Homosexual Behavior*, pp. 1-17. New York: The Haworth Press, Inc.

Boone, J.L. III 1983. Noble family structure and expansionist warfare in the late Middle Ages. In Dyson-Hudson, R. & Little, M.A. (eds.), *Rethinking Human Adaptation: Biological and Cultural Models,* pp. 79-96. Denver, CO: Westview.

———,1986. Parental investment and elite family structure inpreindustrial states: A case study of late medieval-early modern Portuguese genealogies. *Amer. Anthropol.* 88 (Dec 1986): 859-878.

Boswell, J. 1980. *Christianity Social Tolerance, and Homosexuality: Gay People in Western Europe from the Beginning of the Christian Era to the Fourteenth Century.* Chicago: University of Chicago.

Brown, J.C. 1986. *Immodest Acts*: *The Life of a Lesbian Nun in Renaissance Italy.* New York: Oxford University.

Cade, W. 1979. The evolution of alternative male reproductive strategies in field crickets. In Blum, M.S. & Blum, N.A. (eds.), *Sexual Selection and Reproductive Competition in Insects,* pp. 343-379. New York: Academic.

Callender, Ch. & Kochems, L.M. 1985. Men and non-men: male gender-mixing statuses and homosexuality. *J. Homosexual.* 11. Reprinted in Blackwood, E. (ed.), *Anthropology and Homosexual Behavior*, pp. 165-178. New York: The Haworth Press, Inc.

Charnov, E.L. 1982. The Theory of Sex Allocation. Princeton, NJ: Princeton Univ.

Cody, M. 1966. A general theory of clutch size. *Evolution* 20: 174-184.

Cole, L.C. 1954. The population consequences of life history phenomena. *Quart. Rev. Biol.* 29 (June 1954): 103-37.

Crompton, L. 1981. The myth of lesbian impunity: Capital laws from 1270-1791. *J. Homosexual.* 6: 11-25.

Cummings, P. 1986. Gay life in Eastern Europe: A special report. . . . *The Advocate* (4 Nov. 1986): 28-33.

Demetrius, L. 1975. Reproductive strategies and natural selection. *Amer. Natural.* 109 (May-June 1975): 243-249.

Dickemann, M. 1979a. Female infanticide, reproductive strategies, and social stratification: A preliminary model. In Chagnon, N.A. and Irons, Wm. (eds.), *Evolutionary Biology* and *Human Social Organization* pp. 321-357 North Scituate, MA: Duxbury.

_____,1979b. The ecology of mating systems in hypergynous dowry societies. *Soc. Sci. Information* 18 (1979): 163-195.

_____,1981. Paternal confidence and dowry competition: A biocultural analysis of purdah. In Alexander, R.D. & Tinkle, D.W. (eds.), *Natural Selection and Social Behavior: Recent Research and New Theory*, pp. 417-438. New York: Chiron.

_____,[1987]. Multiple genders and reproductive strategies in humans: Steps toward a radical sociobiology. Paper presented to Anthropology Colloquium on the Evolution of Human Behavior Program, Warner-Lambert Lecture Series, Women in Science Program, Ann Arbor, Michigan, 7 Oct. 1986; revised Aug. 1987.

Dover, K.J. 1978. *Greek Homosexuality*. New York: Random House; Cambridge, MA: Harvard Univ.

Duby, G. 1977. *The Chivalrous Society*. Trans. Cynthia Postan. Berkeley: Univ. of California.

_____,1978. *Medieval Marriage: Two Models from Twelfth-Century France*. Trans. Elborg Forester. Baltimore, MD: John Hopkins Univ.

_____,1980. *The Three Orders: Feudal Society Imagined*. Trans. Arthur Goldhammer. Chicago: Univ. of Chicago.

Dunbar, R.IM. 1984. *Reproductive Decisions: An Economic Analysis of Gelada Baboon Social Strategies*. Princeton, N.J.: Princeton Univ.

Emlen, S.T. 1976. Lek organization and mating strategies in the bullfrog. *Behav. Ecol. Sociobiol* 1: 382-313.

_____,1978. The evolution of cooperative breeding in birds. In Krebs, J.R. & Davies, N.B. (eds.), *Behavioral Ecology: An Evolutionary Approach*, pp. 245-281. Oxford: Blackwell; Sunderland, MA: Sinauer.

_____,1981. Altruism, kinship, and reciprocity in the white-fronted bee-eater. In Alexander, R.D. & Tinkle, D.W. (eds.), *Natural Selection and Social Behavior: Recent Research and New Theory*, pp. 217-230. New York: Chiron.

_____,1984. Cooperative breeding in birds and mammals. In Krebs, J.R. & Davies, N.B. (eds.), *Behavioral Ecology: An Evolutionary Approach* (2nd ed.), pp. 305-339. Oxford: Blackwell.

Fry, P. 1985. Male homosexuality and spirit possession in Brazil. *J. Homosexual.* 11. Reprinted in Blackwood, E. (ed.), *Anthropology and Homosexual Behavior*, pp. 137-153. New York: The Haworth Press, Inc.

Gadgil, M. & Bossert, W.H. 1970. Life historical consequences of natural selection. *Amer. Natural.* 104 (Jan.-Feb., 1970): 1-24.

Gray, J. P. 1985. Growing yams and men: An interpretation of Kimam male ritualized homosexual behavior. *J. Homosexual.* 11. Reprinted in Blackwood, E. (ed.), *Anthropology and Homosexual Behavior*, pp. 55-68. New York: The Haworth Press, Inc.

Hamilton, W.D. 1959. Altruism and related phenomena, mainly in social insects. *Ann. Rev. Ecol. System.* v: 193-232.

Herdt, G. (ed.) 1984. *Ritualized Homosexuality in Melanesia.* Berkeley: Univ. of California.

Hogg, J.T. 1984. Mating in bighorn sheep: multiple creative male strategies. *Science* 225 (3 Aug. 1984): 526-529.

Horn, H.S. 1978. Optimal tactics of reproduction and life-history. In Krebs, J.R. & Davies, N.B. (eds.), *Behavioral Ecology: An Evolutionary Approach*, pp. 411-429. Oxford: Blackwell; Sunderland, MA: Sinauer.

Humphreys, R.L. 1970. *Tearoom trade: Impersonal sex in public places.* Chicago: Aldine

Kirsch, J.A.W. & Rodman, J.E. 1982. Selection and sexuality: The Darwinian view of homosexuality. In Paul et al. (eds.), *Homosexuality: Social, Psychological, and Biological Issues*, pp. 183-195. Beverly Hills, CA: Sage Publications Inc..

Kutsche, P. [1986]. Gay male identity in Costa Rica. Paper presented to the Ann. Mtgs., Amer. Anthropol. Assn., Philadelphia, December 1986.

Lack, D. 1954. *The Natural Regulation of Animal Numbers.* Oxford: Clarendon Press of Oxford Univ.

LeBoeuf, B.J. 1974. Male-male competition and reproductive success in elephant seals. *Amer. Zool.* 14: 163-176.

LeBoeuf, B.J. & Peterson, R.S. 1969. Social status and mating activity in elephant seals. *Science* 163: 91-93.

Levitt, E.E. & Klassen A.D. Jr. 1974. Public attitudes toward homosexuality: Part of the 1970 National Survey by the Institute for Sex Research. *J. Homosexual.* 1 (1974): 29-43.

Licht, H. 1969. *Sexual Life in Ancient Greece.* Trans. J.H. Freese. London: Panther.

Ligon, J.D. 1981. Demographic patterns and communal breeding in the green woodhoopoe, *Pheoniculus purpureus*. In Alexander, R.D. & Tinkle, D.W. (eds.), *Natural Selection and Social Behavior: Recent research and New Theory*, pp. 231-243. New York: Chiron.

MacArthur, R.H. & Wilson, E.O. 1967. *The Theory of Island Biogeography.* Monographs in Population Biology 1. Princeton, NJ: Princeton Univ.

MacDonald, A.P. Jr. & Games, R.G. 1974. Some characteristics of those who hold positive and negative attitudes toward homosexuals. *J. Homosexual.* 1: 9-29.

Otte, D. & Stayman K. 1979. Beetle horns: Some patterns in functional morphology. In Blum, M.S. & Blum, N.A. (eds.), *Sexual Selection and Reproductive Competition in Insects*, pp. 259-292. New York: Academic.

Parker, R. 1985. Masculinity, femininity, and homosexuality: On the anthropological interpretation of sexual meanings in Brazil. *J.Homosexual.* 11. Reprinted in Blackwood, E. (ed.), *Anthropology and Homosexual Behavior*, pp. 155-163. New York: The Haworth Press, Inc.

Pitharas, L. 1986. Letter from Greece: On the park bench: Contradictions define gay life in Greece. *The Advocate* (14 Oct. 1986): 28-31.

Robertson, D.R. 1972. Social control of sex reversal in a coral-reef fish. *Science* 177: 1007-1009.

Ross, M.W. 1983. *The Married Homosexual Man: A Psychological Study*. London: Routledge and Kegan Paul.

Solomon, B.M. 1985. *In the Company of Educated Women: A History of Women and Education in America*. New Haven, CT: Yale University.

Stacey, P.B. & Bock, C.E. 1978. Social Plasticity in the acorn woodpecker. *Science* 202 (2 Dec. 1978): 1298-1300.

Stearns, S.T. 1977. The evolution of life history traits: A critique of the theory and a review of the data. *Ann. Rev. Ecol. System.* 8 (1977): 145-171.

Taylor, C.L. 1985. Mexican male homosexual interaction in public contexts. *J.Homosexual.* 11. Reprinted in Blackwood, E. (ed.), *Anthropology and Homosexual Behavior*, pp. 117-136. New York: The Haworth Press, Inc.

Thornhill, R. & Alcock, J. 1983. *The Evolution of Insect Mating Systems*. Cambridge, MA: Harvard University.

Tinkle, D.W. 1969. The concept of reproductive effort and its relation to the evolution of life histories of lizards. *Amer. Natural.* 103 (Sept.-Oct. 1969): 501-516.

Traniello, J.F.A. 1978. Caste in a primitive ant: Absence of age polyethism in *Amblyopone Science* 202 (17 Nov 1978): 770-772.

Trivers, R.L. 1974. Parent-offspring conflict. *Amer. Zool.* 14: 249-264.

———,1985. *Social Evolution*. Menlo Park, CA: Benjamin/Cummings.

Turner, J. 1986. Gay in Eastern Europe (Letters to the Editor). *The Advocate* (9 Dec. 1986): 6.

Warner, R.R., Robertson, D.R. & Leigh Jr., R. 1975. Sex change and sexual selection. *Science* 109 (14 Nov. 1975): 633-638.

Weinrich, J.D. [1977]. Human Reproductive Strategy. II. Homosexuality and NonReproduction: Some Evolutionary Models. Ph.D. Diss., Harvard Univ., Ann Arbor, MI: University Microfilms.

———,1982. Is homosexuality biologically natural? In Paul, Wm. *et al.* (eds.) *Homosexuality: Social, Psychological, and Biological Issues*, pp. 197-208. Beverly Hills, CA: Sage.

West-Eberhard, M.J. 1975. The evolution of social behavior by kin selection. *Quart. Rev. Biol.* 50: 1-33.

———,1978. Temporary queens in *Metapolybia* wasps: Nonreproductive helpers without altruism? *Science* 200 (28 Apr. 1978): 441-443.

_____,1979. Sexual selection, social competition, and evolution. *Proceedings, Amer. Philos. Soc.* 123 (August 1979): 222-234.

_____,1981. Intragroup selection and the evolution of insect societies. In Alexander, R.D. & Tinkle, D.W. (eds.), *Natural Selection and Social Behavior: Recent Research and New Theory*, pp. 3-17. New York: Chiron.

_____,1982. La communication chez les sociétés d' insectes. Communication in social wasps: predicted and observed patterns, with a note on the significance of behavioral and ontogenetic flexibility for theories of worker "altruism." Colloque International U.I.E.I.S. Section Française (16-18 Sept. 1982). Barcelona: Bellaterra.

Whitehead, H. 1981. The bow and the burden strap: A new look at institutionalized homosexuality in native North America. In Ortner, S.B. & Whitehead, H. (eds.), *Sexual Meanings: The Cultural Constriction of Gender and Sexuality*, pp. 80-115.

Wilson, E.O. 1975. *Sociobiology: The New Synthesis*. Cambridge, MA: Belknap Press of Harvard University.

_____1978. On *Human Nature*. Cambridge, MA: Harvard University.

Woolfenden, G.A. 1981. Selfish behavior by Florida scrub jay helpers. In Alexander, R.D. & Tinkle, D.W. (eds.), *Natural Selection and Social Behavior: Recent Research and New Theory*, pp. 257-260. New York: Chiron.

Woolfenden, G.. & Fitzpatrick, J.W. 1984. *The Florida scrub jay: Demography of a cooperative-breeding bird*. Monographs in Population Biology No. 20. Princeton, NJ: Princeton University.

The Social Construction of Homosexuals in the Nineteenth Century: The Shift from the Sin to the Influence of Medicine on Criminalizing Sodomy in Germany

Jörg Hutter, Dr. rer. pol.

University of Bremen

SUMMARY. Psychiatry and forensic medicine developed a medical model of deviance locating the source of homosexual behavior within the individual and postulating a physiological condition that is assumed to cause the deviant behavior. The shift in deviance designation from sexually sinful behavior to sexually unhealthy individuals affected social control and sexual criminal law in Germany during the second half of the 19th century. This research project analyzes the process of legislation and the application of sexual law in the German Reich during the period between 1860 and 1920.

The sexological discovery of homosexuals in the 19th century is indubitably of marked significance. Sexual science created a name, a theory of the origins, and probably the seed of a new identity. However, this discovery was not concerned with fathoming a true body of knowledge but with the production of normative definitions. This is shown especially in the contradictory nature of research results of that period. Scientific findings which should have underlined the demand for the non-punishabil-

Jörg Hutter is a graduated Sociologist at the University of Bremen Fachbereich 8 P.O. Box 33 04 40, D-2800 Bremen 33.

ity of homosexual practices, were instead used by jurists to legitimize the norms of criminal law. The patterns of interpretation from that period are sociologically and historically significant, as they are still being found today in the collective identity of homosexuals.

THE SOCIAL CONSTRUCTION OF KNOWLEDGE

Collective patterns of interpretation concerning human sexuality are in particular produced and enforced by medical science. The communicative foundation of this science determines how the patterns of interpretation grow in strength, weaken and change. The most important structural characteristic of such a scientific definition of reality is selection, which decisively determines which product of scientific research will be retained. In a cooperative process of elimination, the originally diverse research results are reduced to the 'true' results, which are then given the status of facts.[1] Through this, the individual scientist is put in the position of categorizing a type of behavior, which at first sight appears very diverse and unstructured, into one or another types of social fact. Early selections of fact influence further research, as new problems are viewed through the lens of existing knowledge, which pre-determines new solutions.[2] What is already known influences the manner of acquiring new knowledge. A historical view particularly shows that a change in collective thought-patterns happens slowly and that for members of scientific communities it happens unnoticed.

In his monograph, first published in 1935, Ludwik Felck considered the development of scientific patterns of interpretation or, in Fleck's nomenclature, "styles of thought" on syphilis.[3] His considerations are more plausible than the ones connected with the term 'paradigm' as used by Thomas Kuhn. Kuhn said that the emergence of a scientific crisis would lead to a change of paradigm, which would mean a completely new orientation of scientific directions.[4] But the slow and unnoticed change of the sum of objectivized human knowledge in the fields of sexual experience and practice results in a reality being created while hiding the fact that scientists are involved in the production of this reality. In this way 'normal' sexuality can be objectivized as a divine law or as an universal law of nature.[5]

Within a scientific framework, the scientific production of patterns of interpretations can be variable. However alternative versions are threatening in that they show that one's own definition of reality is not necessarily the only true one. Thus, definitive versions are created through conflicts between competing groups of scientists by those who have the most power. The enforcement of certain patterns of interpretation is then not a question of scientific cognition, but one of power. This is shown especially clearly in collaboration of the sciences of medicine and law, which form a juridical-medical power-structure.[6] The generation of this power structure is referred to as medicalization.[7]

THE SEXUAL THEORIES

The first characteristic of the sexual theories of the 19th and 20th centuries is a split between sexuality and society. Sexuality was considered to be an individual matter, so research interests seeking the nature of human sexuality, sought and found it inside the single individual. Therefore, the absence of sociology in the sexual field is understandable as sociologists are mainly interested in the structure of society. Thus, the study of sexual experience remains to this day mainly a subject for the sciences dealing with individuals, e.g., criminology, psychiatry or psychology.

The individualization of sexual experiences which took place in the last century proved to be extremely efficient for the regulation and limitation of erotic behavior. It allowed for classification and allocation systems which were used by jurists as a source of normative definitions. The important work of the sexologist Richard von Krafft-Ebing, *Psychopathia Sexualis*, can be considered a masterpiece of classification of sexual deviations from the standpoint that the purpose of natural instinct is procreation.

The second feature of the 19th century sexual theories is that they define males and females as possessing divergent characteristics. To illustrate this we can take Magnus Hirschfeld's definition, which forms the foundation of his Intermediate Theory. "Females are, the germ cell, the ovum, the womb, the ovaries, the vagina and the vulva, as well as the female pelvis, menstruation and the growth of the mammary glands. In addition to this, the physical constitution of the female is built for conception, characterizing the entire sexual and emotional life of women as receiving. Males are, the semen, the testes, the spermatic cord, the penis and the growth of the larynx. The sexual and mental life in men is of a more aggressive, giving nature."[8]

The third feature is that homosexual behavior is regarded as a stable behavior orientation which defines the social character of the person concerned. Whereas in the past the sodomitic act was seen as a temporary abberation, homosexuals are now described as beings in their own right.

Generally speaking, the aim of 19th century sexual scientific research was to search for the structure of the sexual instincts of human beings probing into the realms of knowledge of the body. Research results were used partly as a weapon to strengthen the scientifically-based demand for the impunity of homosexual behavior. This proved however, as I will show, to lead nowhere. The scientific arguments were on the whole very contradictory and were used in ways which they were supposed to have disqualified.

The sexological ideas which influenced the scientific discourse of the 19th century can be traced back to Antiquity. The most important ideas are: the instinctual doctrine, the degenerative theories, and the humoral doctrine (which often characterized the masturbation debate). A more comprehensive explanation has to be omitted here.[9]

THE APPLICATION OF THE PENAL CODE

I would like now to analyze closely the influence of medicalization on the application of the sexual penal code. In my opinion, the question of why such a hold on the subject of the punishability of homosexual behavior existed at all leads to no important findings. After all, why should a behavior which has been threatened for centuries with the heaviest penalties now be excluded from prosecution? Plausible suppositions cannot be drawn from the decisions made in the past, because penal code is often legitimized through a system of internal logic, regardless of the content of the decisions. This is proved by the juridical working-techniques of comparative law and references to the history of its origins. Codified norms are consistently labeled purely external.

Between 1871 and 1920 there were 26 applications, petitions and appeals to Para. 175 of the Penal Code of the German Reich. None of these attempts to change the law were successful. The work of preparing the Prussian Penal Code took 60 years, in which time 11 printed bills were published. However, only the last of these bills played a decisive part in building the foundation for the Prussian Penal Code of 1851. The similarity between the Prussian Penal Code and the German Penal Code of today shows the difficulty in passing formal reforms.

However, as is being investigated in Bremen's research project, norms change through being applied. In spite of the fact that the written word does not change and the law is interpreted in the good old traditional way, the rules of application change, because they are based upon collective patterns of interpretation. Homosexual behavior has always been judged negatively, but at different times new negative meanings were attributed to this behavior. This is how not only the patterns of interpretation but also the rules of application altered. The change in meaning however, was a slow and unnoticed one, because the patterns of interpretation which underlay the application of norms took on the form of timeless facts.

Two types of legislatory procedure will now be examined. Firstly, the forming of a penal code for the North German Union, which was taken word for word in 1871 as a penal code for the whole German Reich. Secondly, the debate concerning the preliminary draft for the German Penal Code of 1909. Unfortunately, as far as I know, up until today neither jurists nor historians have pursued a study into the sources of legal history. Parts of the files in Merseburg and Potsdam were viewed for the first time by our research group.[10]

The case of a petition handed to a ministerial commission of the Prussian Ministry of Justice by a self confessed homosexual man–or "Uranists" as they used to call themselves–is of great significance because for the first time someone personally involved articulated himself. In this document a sexual theory is introduced which unites the three above mentioned aspects for the first time:

- The individualization of sexual experience
- Male and female divergency characteristics and
- The viewing of homosexual behavior as an aspect of human nature.

Even though these ideas were not accepted by medical profession of this time, the theory had marked influence on the classifications of later psychiatrists and forensic experts.

Extracts from the above mentioned petition from junior judicial officer, Karl Heinrich Ulrichs, to the commission of the ministry of justice read:

> Natural science, you know, recognizes the fact that uranist love-life is by no means perverse–as it usually is seen–in nature . . . but is rather due to a *physio-mental hermaphrodism,* expressed by the formulation "Anima muliebris virili corpore inclusa" [= a female soul enclosed in a male body. Author's note].[11] One *cannot and must not demand in any way* from a soul–a soul which is inclined to a love-life of a female disposition–a sexual inclination towards women–to similar poles–, or that the soul should *not* follow its *natural* sexual traits–this towards men, unequal poles. The hermaphrodite, with a female soul in his male body, is also a human being, and has also received the right from nature to a love-life . . .[12]

The appeal was referred to a scientific deputation for medical affairs, who, at the request of the Prussian justice minister, was to give its expert opinion on certain legal questions. Concerning the punishment of homosexual practices, the medical experts came to the conclusion that they "were in no position to supply any reasons why fornication with animals or between persons of the male sex, should be a punishable offence." [13] In a handwritten draft of these experts' opinion, there is a passage which was later omitted in the published version. It reads:

> We do not feel obliged to answer in any greater detail the letter brought to our attention by Herr Ulrichs, as his speculations are totally lacking in any scientific foundation and the issue of whether pederasty is hereditary seems completely irrelevant. [14,15]

Here, the influence which Ulrichs's theory had on the works of von Krafft-Ebing is clearly detectable. Krafft-Ebing started by speaking disdainfully of junior judicial officer Ulrichs, who appeared on the scientific scene in the mid-'60s, but he slightly distorted Ulrichs's ideas, using them for his own clinical classification. He differed only by replacing the term 'soul' with 'brain' and thus speaks of a cerebrally determined neurosis. That it is possible for a person in a normal anatomical and physiological condition to develop contrary sexual feelings proved for him that this must be due to a diseased constitution of the nervous system. Sexual instinct is pathological, or rather perverse, if it is not keeping with the purpose of nature [meaning procreation].

Apart from this pathologicalization and the suggestion of physical causes other parallels with Ulrichs can also be drawn. Krafft-Ebing developed a clinical classification which differentiates between the two poles, male and female. On the first level of his classification, sexual emotions of a predominantly homosexual type appear though heterosexual emotions also exist, so that he speaks of these as a psychosexual hermaphrodism. On the second level of the scale homosexuality, the inclination towards one's own sex, is found. On the third level the whole physical being is correlated to abnormal sexual emotion. This refers to effemination in men and viraginity in women. If the physical form and the abnormal sexual emotion are converging we are confronted with androgynism in men and gynandrism in women. This is the highest level of degeneration. [16]

The idea of feminine feelings towards men is only expanded upon here by differentiating between degrees of importance. In other words: The connection between sexual orientation and sexual divergency is by no means peremptory. Just as logical is the assumption that equal poles attract, which means that these mental associations of a psychosexual her-maphrodite were not necessary.

Contradictory medical arguments within the advisory commission's preliminary draft for the German Penal Code of 1909 can therefore be used for or against the abolition of the article 'unnatural fornication.'

I will examine the protocol of the penal code commission concerning the first reading of the preliminary draft. One member of the commission puts forward a motion for the abolition of the article and justifies his application by saying that punishing cases of hereditary homosexuality cannot be consistent with the principles of justice. This argumentation is similar to that of Ulrichs, mentioned above. At that time it was easily dismissed by pointing out that it was only speculative and void of any scientific foundation. Now, however, this could be countered with appro-priate medical argumentation. This means, and I quote:

> In the few cases in which offenders have acted upon a certain natu-ral compulsion, the regulations concerning diminished responsibility would serve to guarantee justice being done. [17]

With a vote of 14 against 2 the application for the abolition of the paragraph under discussion was rejected. It is therefore understandable that Hirschfeld, by using the argument that homosexual emotions and practices are always hereditary and therefore an irreversible characteris-tic, wanted to achieve the abolition of para. 175 of the penal code of the German Reich.[18] But the mere fact that the deliberations of the penal code commission were so obscure prevented any intervention, as the passage from a sincere plea by Hirschfeld to the Minister of Justice shows. The minister was requested kindly to give a word for word account of the amendment made by the penal code commission.[19]

Hirschfeld, like Krafft-Ebing and Ulrichs before him, connected the assumed natural differences between man and woman with a sexual orien-tation. His theory of an intermediate sex classified reproductive organs, other physical characteristics, and the sexual instinct on a scale between the two poles, female and male.

EXPANSION OF THE FACTS CHARACTERIZING THE CRIMINAL ACT BY MEDICALIZATION

As mentioned above, the influence that medical research had upon the application of the law was of great importance, as the application of the law determined the understanding of the term 'unnatural fornication'. For male offenders this meant that more and more behavioral variations were considered punishable within the meaning of 'unnatural fornication'.

The model for the German Reich's Penal Code was the Prussian Penal Code, which in turn was evolved from the Prussian Allgemeinen Landrecht (ALR) of 1794. The ALR took the place of the Constitutio Carolina Criminalis (CCC) of 1532 which was in force for the whole old German Reich. Article 116 of CCC was as follows: "If a human being and an animal, man with man, woman with woman practice defiled acts, they should be, as it is the general custom, sentenced to death by fire." In Para. 1069, Part II of the ALR of 01.06.1794 this behavior was named 'sodomia sui generis et sexus' and was punishable by imprisonment and exile. This expression referred to sexual practices between humans and animals, and homosexual practices among people of both sexes. Neither other regional laws nor the Code Penal Napoleon are of any interest, as the amended laws of the ALR were the outlines of the Prussian Penal Code, from which Para. 143 was transferred into the Reich's Penal Code of 1871, as Para. 175. These paragraphs (143, 175), concerned 'unnatural fornication', meaning bestiality–sexual practices between humans and animals–and pederasty–practices similar to sexual intercourse among men. Herewith punishment of sexual practices between women in the jurisdiction of the German Reich was no longer pursued.

In 1906, with a view towards the German jurisdiction, the German jurist Wolfgang Mittermaier presented an extensive comparison between the German and foreign Penal Codes in which he declared that the constituent facts concerning unnatural fornication were expanding in meaning.[20] Within the jurisdiction the meaning of the word fornication was debated intensely. In its substantiations the ALR still used the word fornication, without having an exact definition of the term. Later a differentiation between the terms intercourse and indecent practices occurred, which Mittermaier concluded was a noteworthy step towards a greater strictness of the law.[21] However it is obvious that such a differentiation did not solve the dilemma of a clear definition of the word fornication. The problem now was defining the differences between intercourse–or in case of homosexual practices similar to intercourse–and indecent practices. Following the Jurisdiction of the Prussian High Court and the German Reich's equivalent concerning this legal problem is, as Mittermaier also stated, extremely interesting.[22]

Next it should be noted that the semantic content of the terms which label homosexual behavior was constantly changing. Expressions such as sodomy, pederasty, unnatural fornication, perverts, uranists, contrary sexuals or homosexuals, all mean something specific. In addition, the underlying patterns of interpretation were changing with the times. Therefore it is not easy to detect the exact meaning of the content, as the reasons given by the jurists and the legislators only simulated a background of reasoning for their decisions.

Primarily, the constant appeals to the old legal scholars only legitimized their own decisions. Even though it was often claimed that they were still following the good old traditional ways, the motives and the verdicts were constantly changing.

In a judgment published in 1857 by the highest Prussian court, it was decreed that the practice of mutual masturbation had taken place if the penis had been placed between the legs.[23] With complete reliance on the history of the origins of Para. 143 of the Prussian penal code, a practice was only seen as punishable if it was like sexual intercourse, which is not so in the case of mutual masturbation. Also, the reasons for the verdict of 13.04.1863 were given as being that an unnatural immissio seminis in corpus [ejaculation inside the body] must have taken place for it to be a punishable offence, but that emission was not sufficient grounds for sentencing.[24]

However the verdict of the 15.03.1876, contradictory to the earlier verdicts, laid down the principle that penetration of the penis into the body of the other person was not necessary, but that practice similar to intercourse on the body of another person was sufficient to punish the offender![25] Thus the constituent facts of the offense were expanded to the disadvantage of the men affected by this law. This tendency was carried further by the Highest Court of the German Reich. Relying on the history of Para. 175 of the Penal Code of the German Reich, the court argued that an ejaculation inside the body was not necessary.[26] It was sufficient for the penis to be stimulated on the body of another person. This view was confirmed in further judgments.[27] In 1880 performing the act while clothed was strictly excluded from punishable offenses.[28] In 1898, however, this was considered criminal.[29] Still other judgments confirmed this definition and demanded only the uncovering of the penis of the "active party."[30]

Mittermaier concluded from this that something new was simply decreed here which the courts thought appropriate at the time without considering history. Nothing but an outward appearance remained of the definition of "practices similar to sexual intercourse."[31] However, with these conclusions, Mittermaier could not explain why these developments had occurred, he could only describe them.

The slow change in the meaning content can only be understood if we compare it to the collective patterns of interpretation of human sexuality of that time. The flood of forensic and psychiatric publications, rich with medical reports and the presentation of particular sexual practices not only provided information of what is possible within sexual behavior, but also drew interest towards the entire personality of the sexual offender. Homosexuality constituted an entity which was not only an object for medical but also for juridical eyes. Behind the term 'contrary sexual emotion' we find not only the act itself, which is what the judges allegedly formed their judgments upon, but also the idea that the offender's entire inner being is alienated from its own sex.[32]

THE ESTABLISHMENT OF COMMITTED FORNICATION AS FACILITATED BY MEDICALIZATION

Homosexual behavior was not seen as pathological until 1850. In all forensic textbooks up until that time, diagnosing the act of pederasty was the main point of interest, and not the personality characteristics of the offender.[33] The thoughts of the father of forensic medicine, Paolo Zacchia, appeared at regular intervals. In his "Questiones medico legales" [the collected forensic medical examinations], he explains the diagnostical features by which he was able to detect anal fornication in misused boys. Hermann Friedrich Teichmeyer's introduction on the subject is the same as that of Zacchia: Fornication is not only committable with girls, virgins and widows but also with men, by wanton naturally perverted people."[34] His list of diagnostical features was: Lacerations of sphincter muscle, rectal fistula, inflammation of the anus, emaciation, consumption and dropsy. A quotation by Johann Daniel Metzger in 1793 concerning pederasty is typical: "Immorality and a lack of culture in human understanding has brought about two types of intercourse. Namely, pederasty, or the violation of juveniles, and sodomy, associations with animals. Only in rare cases are they grounds for a forensic examination."[35] In this quotation two features are clearly shown. First, that pederasty is an immorality and not a mental disorder. Second, that cases of this kind were rarely tried, which of course does not mean that homosexual behavior occurred less frequently. This shows, rather, a change in the juridical reaction.[36]

After 1860 sexuality was researched in a 'Natural-Scientific-Empirical' manner. In a study of rape and pederasty Johann Ludwig Casper criticized most of the German medico-forensic authors for their lack of empirical experience.[37] Whether because of a lack of experience of their own and a hidden moral, or because the doctors concerned felt it was beneath their dignity to study such matters, they merely copied what Zacchia had said on the features of passive pederasty. Casper had, however, examined eleven people and found that the most important diagnostical feature was an "infundibular" depression of the buttocks. In other respects Casper's comments had a marked influence on further work. He described, among other things, the psychological aspects of this "disagreeable error" by maintaining that this aberration was hereditary in most cases. This statement found an animated echo among doctors and led the way to pathologicalization through psychiatry.

Casper's French colleague, August Ambroise Tardieu, however, viewed the diagnostical features of sexual offense more generously. In the translated version of his monograph, Tardieu listed in contrast to Casper's ideas physical features, as well as the numerous signs of damaged health through passive and active pederasty.[38] Particular mention is made of deceptions during examinations, as pederasts had the habit of hiding the traces of their 'shameful deeds'. It was recommended when confronted with the situation to get the person in question into the more difficult position of laying his knee on the edge of a chair, or to carry out the examination longer, until the muscles relaxed.

The frank letter of 1869 from Karl Maria Benkert, the pseudonym of Kertbeny, to Dr. Leonhard, the Prussian Minister of Justice, in which Kertbeny advocated the abolition of Para. 143 of the Prussian Penal Code, confirmed the growing trend of the accused being convicted on medico-forensic, circumstantial evidence. Kertbeny claimed that hardly any traces of pederasty were to be found on the bodies of the persons concerned. If the offenders were not caught In Flagrante Delicto it was impossible for the forensic doctor to prove that the act had happened. Even Casper warned in vain of the deceptive nature of such symptomatology, and also said that unnatural fornication has no more health damaging effects than any other form of fornication.[39]

Benjamin Tarnowsky still referred in 1886 to the "esteemed monograph" by Tardieu, in which he had discussed every single aspect of sodomy.[40] It is assumed that Tardieu's specifications were followed more closely than those of Casper. Hence, those suspected of homosexual practices were to a great extent examined by coercive measures. In Tarnowskys' opinion less experienced researchers, for example Casper, who denied the significance of infundibular widening of the anus, would argue against undoubted symptoms.

The occupations of the forensic doctors were legitimized by an amendment to the criminal procedure. Before this amendment, according to the Prussian Criminal Procedure of 1805, an inquisition was the procedure for determining who the offender was and if a crime had been committed. As a precondition for sentencing all that was required was a confession, or two eye-witness accounts. Serious circumstantial evidence was sufficient to adjudge guilt and for an extraordinary sentence to be passed, a so-called sentence on the grounds of suspicion. The criminal procedure was supplemented by the decree of 03.01.1849, which concerned the introduction of spoken and public proceedings with a jury in investigatory cases. In trials, accusations took the place of inquisitions.

The change in the criminal procedure made, among other things, the use of circumstantial evidence in trials possible and herewith made the sanctioning of deviant sexual behavior more efficient. Forensics made it much easier for the science of criminal law to assess normative values by being able to refer to expert opinion. Thus the establishment of the facts of the case and the possibility of conviction were assured.

SELECTIVE PROOF OF GUILT ACCORDING TO FORENSIC PSYCHIATRY

The selective proof of guilt shows most clearly the psychiatricalization of the penal code. Forensic psychiatry supplied a concept of mental disease, which showed that mental illness fundamentally threatens social order, and that it is therefore necessary to have a qualified professional body of scientific knowledge, so that a constructive contribution to the stability of social order can be made. Jurists were often requested to consult genuine experts. For example: The psychiatrist Paul Möbius in a forward to the translated version of *Psychiatrische Vorlesungen* by Frenchman Valentin Magnan, says that judges must have knowledge of the doctrine of mental disorder in the degenerated, as it is their duty to treat and judge correctly, and so to protect society from any damage the offenders may cause.[41] Further, in relation to ascertaining culpability, the psychiatrist Krafft-Ebing, in talking about homosexual behavior, says: "The contrary sexual emotion is a psychic anomaly of such a complicated nature, that only an expert can tell the difference between fact and fiction."[42]

A nosology of deviant behavior, *Psychopathia sexualis* contained several diagnosis possibilities as well as offering a catalogue of possible treatments.[43] For the purpose of identification of delinquents, stigmata were searched for which betrayed the offender, e.g., men behaving homosexually, a womanlike appearance, neurasthenia etc. While the classical penal code emphasized the punishment of crimes already committed, later the therapeutic treatment of offenders who were regarded to be more ill than bad was considered to be of more importance. As early as 1880 the psychiatrist Emil Kraepelin argued for a standardized categorization of all individuals under the criterion 'danger to the public.' An individualized treatment of the offenders, whose discharge was not to be stipulated would be necessary.[44]

In German speaking countries Krafft-Ebing was the main representative of the natural-scientific instrumental patterns of interpretation. In his *Psychopathia sexualis* he strictly differentiated between acquired and hereditary cases of 'contrary sexual emotion,' for which a complicated classification scheme was developed in which single practices were not held to play an important role. Much more decisive was the proof of a perverse emotion, so that 'Perversion' of the sexual instinct and 'Perversity' of the sexual practice could be distinguished between. To distinguish between perversion as a disease and perversity as a vice, analyses of the whole personality of the offender are called for. Krafft-Ebing calls sexual acts without perversion avoidable, inbred cases of contrary sexual emotion which happen very frequently. Only the proof that an offender has been fighting against his instincts with all strength of will could lead to the conclusion that a compulsive act has occurred. This then annuls the capacity for penal responsibility. This also has to be proven even in the case of hereditary contrary emotion. Though most contrary sexuals suffer from elementary disorders, this does not annul their capacity for penal responsibility.[45]

In 1870 the psychiatrist Carl Westphal pointed out the relevance of the capacity of penal responsibility in court. He protested against the view that all individuals who practice 'unnatural fornication' be defined as pathological cases.[46] Even though there are some cases of pathological theft, this does not mean that the majority of all cases of murder, theft or unnatural fornication have to be pathological.

This shows that sexual science was involved in a power struggle but still managed to win the recognition of the courts. The hereditary disposition of homosexual emotion was not fought for unconditionally. So as not to fall out of favor with the jurisprudence, the concept of the hereditary disposition of homosexual emotions now included the existence of an acquired homosexual emotion, which was regarded punishable with the full weight of the law. The competency of justice and medicine was shared in that the offenders responsible for their crimes were sent to prison, and the sick offenders were committed to asylums.

THE ATTEMPT BY JUDICIARY COMMISSIONS USING MEDICAL ARGUMENTS TO CRIMINALIZE FEMALE HOMOSEXUAL BEHAVIOR IN THE PRELIMINARY DRAFT TO THE PENAL CODE IN 1909

It is still not known why the punishability of homosexual contacts among women was dropped in the jurisdiction of the German Reich. The assumption often held that it was because of an error in translation is not convincing, as jurists as a rule had a sound knowledge of Latin. The penal code, in Para. 175, threatens punishment exclusively for the male variation. This differentiation made by the legislature is even today substantiated by the High Court Jurisdiction of Federal Republic: "The natural difference between the sexes and a thoroughly justified difference in the criminal-political judgment of both types of homosexual fornication."[47] The principle of the equality (Art. 3 III Law Of The Federal Republic Constitution) of woman and man is declared not applicable. Psycho-physiological differences therefore vindicate different handling of the sexes concerning homosexuality.[48]

Long before the general findings of unnatural fornication were formally restricted to male homosexuality, a far-reaching liberalization of the application of the law concerning female homosexuality took place. In the 18th century, as far as we know, no women were sentenced for homosexual practices, even though the law of the time would have enabled a punishment to be passed.

In the Constitutio Criminals Carolina (CCC) of 1532 homosexual practices among men and women were threatened with death penalty by fire. Article 116 CCC lists first practices similar to intercourse between human beings (sodomia propria sexus), second intercourse between human beings and animals (sodomia propria generis), and third every other form of satisfying sexual instincts, especially masturbation (sodomia impropria). Ejaculation was not seen as sufficient for the completion of illicit sexual practices, but the penetration of the penis into an orifice of the body had to occur. In the 18th century, a general commutation of punishment for all forms of illicit sexual practices appeared, at least imprisonment then took place of the death penalty. Until the 19th century the intensity of criminal prosecution was low.

In Para. 1069 of the Prussian ALR of 1794 the penalty for 'sodomy and any other similar sins, which are so bad that they cannot be named here' was imprisonment and subsequent exile. This meant sanctions against sexual practices between human beings and animals as well as the homosexual practices of women and men. However, practically speaking, unnatural fornication among men was still of the most importance. The forensic-doctor Ludwig Julius Caspar Mende documents this in his manual of forensic medicine. Debauchery among women is "only a sort of masturbation." Which, according to the then current legal views, "is not a matter for an intimate examination," and therefore no matter for forensic medicine. The practice only takes on the character of a crime when a woman using an artificial penis tries to imitate the sexual practice by "playing the part usually taken by the man."[49]

According to the then current legal standpoint, the practice had to be similar to sexual intercourse to fulfill the terms of 'sodomia propria sexus'. A practice similar to sexual intercourse occurred when the penis was introduced into the body, and an ejaculation took place inside the body. This restrictive picture of sexual intercourse made the reasons for non-punishability in legal commentaries and amendment debates superfluous.

In the proposals for the amendment to the ALR in the first half of the 19th century, the general findings concerning sodomy were read closely. The definition of the term sodomy in the amendment to the draft for the Prussian Penal Code of 1843 was limited. It was understood to mean abuse of juveniles and sodomy with animals. In the draft for a penal code of 1847 it was proposed for the first time that punishability of homosexual behavior be limited to men, without announcing any grounds for this change. With the passing of the Prussian Penal Code of 1851 this proposal was accepted. Herewith according to Para. 143 Prussian Penal Code, illicit sexual practices were now defined as only being sexual practices between human beings and animals and practices similar to sexual intercourse among men.

In contrast, it is astonishing that Austria kept to the principles of the 'Old Reich' and threatened all homosexual practices with punishment. The clause in question of the Austria Penal Code of 1803 was transferred to the Austria Penal Code of 1852 as Para. 129. The offense is described here as 'fornication against nature'.

After 1900 psychiatric-medical reasoning led primarily to jurists being able to require the punishment of homosexual practices among women. With a temporal delay which seems to be typical of research into the female mode of life, the research results eventually found their way into the legal discussion. Krafft-Ebing wrote in the later editions of the *Psychopathia Sexualis* concerning the 'contrary sexual emotions' of women, that the non-punishability existed because of two errors:

1. It was assumed that only performance of practices similar to sexual intercourse was pederasty–even though, as today's experience

shows, at least among contrary sexuals, this type of sexual satisfaction rarely took place.

2. It was believed that women among themselves were not able to commit this crime.

In a psychological point of view the only factor which matters for women as well as men, is that during any sexual act orgasm–sexual satisfaction–has been attained. In women an ejaculation occurs analogous to that of men, therefore the act which leads to this sort of ejaculation has to be regarded as a coitus equivalent. Stimulation is attained by oral-genital contact or by intimate rubbing of the genitals, both of which could be considered practices similar to sexual intercourse within the meaning of the German Criminal Law.[50] It appears therefore, as Krafft-Ebing says, that the Austria Penal Code was more thorough in that it made provisions for this delict.

NOTES

1. Smith, D.E., K ist geisteskrank - Die Anatomie eines Tatsachenberichtes, in: Weingarten, E., F. Sack, J. Schenkein (ed.), Ethnomethodologie -Beiträge zu einer Soziologie des Alltagshandelns, Frankfurt (Weingarten, E. et al.) 1976, p. 372.

2. Knorr, K., Die Fabrikation von Wissen, in: Kölner Zeitschrift für Soziologie, Sonderheft 22 Wissenssoziologie, 1980, p. 331ff.

3. Fleck, L., Entstehung und Entwicklung einer wissenschaftlichen Tatsache, Frankfurt (Fleck, L.) 1980, p. 129, following pages.

4. Kuhn, T., Die Struktur wissenschaftlicher Revolutionen, Frankfurt (Kuhn, T.) 1961, p. 110. Though as Kuhn says on p. 8 ". . . I should like to draw attention to Ludwik Fleck's almost unknown monograph, Origins and Developement of a Scientific Fact (Basel 1935), a work, which anticipates many of my own thoughts." Another flaw in the Kuhn idea is the stress he applies to the natural science methodology, which is dependent upon the patterns of interpretation of that time. More interesting for me are the contents of this knowledge and not the assumed relations between this and the methods.

5. Berger, Peter L. and T. Luckmann, Die gesellschaftliche Konstruktion der Wirklichkeit, Frankfurt (Berger, P.L. and T. Luckmann) 1969, p. 95. In the following I use, as Berger and Luckmann do, the term "objectivisation" which is closely interwoven with Marx's term "estrangement." A clear terminological explanation of this term is not possible so this is why Berger and Luckmann did not use it. More precise: Berger, P.L. and T. Luckmann, loc. cit., p. 58.

6. Foucault, M., Mikrophysik der Macht, Berlin (Foucault, M.) 1976, p. 73

7. Conrad, P. and J.W. Schneider, Deviance and Medicalisation–From Bad-ness to Sickness, St. Louis/Toronto/London (Conrad, P. and J.W. Schneider) 1980, p. 28f.

8. Hirschfeld, M., Die Homosexualität des Mannes und des Weibes, 2. ed., Berlin (Hirschfeld, M.) 1914, p. 350.

9. Of all the representatives of the humoral doctrine I consider S.A. Tissot as being the head of the field. In the humoral doctrine the term 'masturbation' is presented. Tissot's monograph "Onanisme un dissertation physique sur les mala-dies produites par la masturbation," Paris 1760 is exceptional. In German speak-ing countries, J. Häussler's essay "Über die Beziehungen des Sexualsystems zur Psyche Überhaupt und zum Kretinismus im Besonderen," Würzburg 1826, and H. Kaan with his "Psychopathia sexualis," Leipzig 1844. As representatives of the instinctual doctrine I include F.J. Gall "Lehre über die Verrichtungen des Gehirns"; A. Comte, "Die positive Philosophie" im Auszug von Jules Rig, 2. Vol., Heidelberg 1883, p. 455-472; and J.C. Santlus with his "Über die Zunah-me der Geisteskrankheiten und ihren Zusammenhang mit den Geschlechtsfunk-tionen und Geschlechtskrankheiten," Erlangen 1858. The degenerative theories are well represented by B.A. Morel in his monograph "Traité des maladies men-tales," Paris 1860 and by V. Magnan's "Psychiatrische Vorlesungen," Leipzig 1892. In the historical developement of ideas well represented by Fischer-Hom-berger, Esther, "Medizin vor Gericht," Gerichtsmedizin von der Renaissance bis zur Aufklärung, Bern/Stuttgart/Wien 1983, and Leibbrand, W. and A. Wettley, "Der Wahnsinn," Geschichte der abendländischen Psychopathologie, Freiburg/ München 1961, Leibbrand, W., "Formen des Eros," Kultur–und Geistesge-schichte der Liebe Freiburg 1972.

10. An exception is found here in the edition of the printed preliminary drafts of the Penal Code which had already been read by Schubert and Regge from Kiel. cp: Schubert, W. and J. Regge (ed.), Quellen zur preußischen Gesetzge-bung des 19. Jahrhunderts, Vaduz (Schubert, W. and J. Regge) 1981.

11. Emphasis shown by underlining in the original letter.

12. ZSTA, Potsdam, Rep. 14.01. des Reichskanzleramtes, Akte Nr. 625, Bl. 40-43.

13. ZSTA, Potsdam, Rep. 14.01. des Reichskanzleramtes, Akte Nr. 625, Bl. 66-67.

14. The term pederasty here means homosexual behavior as a punishable offense. This included anal and also oral sex, but for a long time did not include mutual masturbation.

15. ZSTA, Potsdam, Rep. 14.01. des Reichskanzleramtes, Akte Nr. 625, Bl. 67.

16. Krafft-Ebing, R.v., Psychopathia sexualis, 14. ed., Berlin (Krafft-Ebing, R.v.) 1912, p. 267ff.

17. ZSTA, Potsdam, Rep. 30.01. des Reichsjustizamtes, Akte Nr. 5939, Bl. 88ff.

18. Hirschfeld, M., Die Homosexualität des Mannes und des Weibes, 3. ed., Berlin (Hirschfeld, M.) 1920, p. 325.

19. ZSTA, Potsdam, Rep. 30.01. des Reichsjustizamtes, Akte Nr. 5691, Bl. 256.

20. Mittermaier, W., Verbrechen und Vergehen wider die Sittlichkeit, in: Birkmeyer, K. u.a. (ed.), Vergleichende Darstellung des deutschen und ausländischen Strafrechts, 14. vol., Berlin (Birkmeyer, K.) 1906, p. 154f.

21. the same, p. 79.

22. the same, p. 154.

23. Archiv für preußisches Strafrecht, Berlin (Goltdammer) 1857, p. 268ff.

24. Archiv für Preußisches Strafrecht, Berlin (Goltdammer) 1863, p. 425ff.

25. Oppenhoff, F.C., (ed.), Rechtsprechung des Königlichen Obertribunals in Strafsachen, Berlin (Oppenhoff, F.C.) 1876, p. 200.

26. Rechtsprechung des Deutschen Reichsgerichts in Strafsachen, 1. vol., Berlin 1880, p. 395.

27. Entscheidungen des Reichsgerichts in Strafsachen, 2. vol., Berlin 1880, p. 237; 3. vol., Berlin 1881, p. 200.

28. Entscheidungen des Reichsgerichts in Strafsachen, 2. vol., Berlin 1880, p. 239.

29. Archiv für Strafrecht, Berlin (Goltdammer) 1998/99, p. 112ff.

30. Entscheidungen des Reichsgerichts in Strafsachen, 36. vol., Berlin 1903, p. 33.

31. Mittermaier, W., Verbrechen und Vergehen wider die Sittlichkeit, in: Birkmeyer, K. u.a. (ed.), Vergleichende Darstellung des deutschen und ausländischen Strafrechts, 4. vol., Berlin (Birkmeyer, K.) 1906, p. 155.

32. This quotation comes from the psychiatrist Carl Westphal who created the term 'contrary sexual emotion', which was suggested by a colleague whom he admired greatly for his work in the fields of philology and archaeology. With this term he wanted to express that it is not the sexual instinct but the emotions of the entire inner being which alienate one from one's own sex. Westphal, C., "Die conträre Sexualempfindung. Symptom eines neuropathischen (psychopathischen) Zustandes," in Archiv für Psychiatrie und Nervenkrankheiten, Berlin 1869. Notes: see p. 107.

33. Henke, A., Lehrbuch der gerichtlichen Medicin, Stuttgart (Henke, A.) 1832, p. 105f.; Mende, L.J.C., Ausführliches Handbuch der gerichtlichen Medizin, Leipzig (Mende, L.J.C.) 1819, p 507; Nicolai, G.H., Handbuch der gerichtlichen Medicin, Berlin (Nicolai, G.H.) 1841, p. 168; Schürmeyer, J.H., Theoretisch-practisches Lehrbuch der gerichtlichen Medicin, Erlangen (Schürmeyer, J.H.) 1850, p. 351f.

34. Teichmeyer, H.F., Institutiones medicinae legalis vel forensis, Jena (Teichmeyer, H.F.) 1751, p. 31 and Zacchia, P., Questiones medico-legales, liber III, titulus II, questiones V, edition Frankfurt (Zacchia, P.) 1688, p. 382.

35. Metzger, J.D., Kurzgefasstes System der gerichtlichen Arznywissenschaft, Königsberg/Leipzig (Metzger, J.D.) 1793, p. 309f.

36. Engelhardt, D. v., Sittlichkeitsdelinquenz in Wissenschaft und Literatur der 2. Hälfte des 19. Jahrhunderts, in: Sexualität und soziale Kontrolle. Beiträge zur Sexualkriminologie, Heidelberg (Engelhardt, D. v.) 1978, p. 146f.

37. Casper, J.L., Über Nothzucht und Päderastie und deren Ermittelung seitens des Gerichtsarztes, in: Vierteljahrsschrift für gerichtliche und öffentliche Medicin, Berlin (Casper, J.L.) 1852, p. 21-78.

38. Die Vergehen gegen die Sittlichkeit, in: Blätter für gerichtliche Anthropologie, Friedreich, J.B. (ed.), Erlangen (Friedreich, J.B.) 1860, p. 323-362. On page 323 the monograph is being reviewed, entitled: Die Vergehen gegen die Sittlichkeit in staatsärztlicher Beziehung, betrachtet von A. Tardieu (German: by F.W. Theile), Weimar (Tardieu, A.) 1860. Explanations concerning pederasty can be found on p. 353-363.

39. Kertbeny, M., Para. 143 des Preußischen Strafgesetzbuches vom 14. April 1851 und seine Aufrechterhaltung als Para. 152 im Entwurf eines Strafgesetzbuches für den Norddeutschen Bund, Leipzig (Kertbeny, M.) 1869, p. 83.

40. Tarnowsky, B., Die krankhaften Erscheinungen des Geschlechtssinnes, Berlin (Tarnowsky, B.) 1886. Concerning the diagnosis of pederasty p. 109-113. Tarnowsky published the monograph "Der Sexualtrieb und seine krankhaften Äußerungen vom doppelten, dem juristischen und psychiatrischen Standpunkt" in 1893 in Petersburg. (French: Paris 1898; Engl.: London 1904).

41. Magnan, V., Psychiatrische Vorlesungen, 2. vol., Leipzig (Magnan, V.) 1892, p. V.

42. Krafft-Ebing, R.v., Psychopathia sexualis, 14. ed., Stuttgart (Krafft-Ebing, R.v.) 1912, p. 328.

43. The most important monographs about deviant sexual behavior were so entitled. For the first time Kaan, H., Psychopathia sexualis, Leipzig (Kaan, H.) 1844, who almost exclusively dealt with masturbation or Krafft-Ebing, R.v., whose standard work with this title was published in 17 editions between 1886 and 1924, the last edition, the 18th in München 1984!

44. Kräpelin, E., Die Abschaffung des Strafmaßes. Ein Vorschlag zur Reform der heutigen Strafrechtspflege, Stuttgart (Kraepelin, E.) 1880, p. 39.

45. Krafft-Ebing, R.v., Psychopathia sexualis, 14. ed., Stuttgart (Krafft-Ebing, R.v.) 1912, p. 12.

46. Westphal, C., Die conträre Sexualempfindung. Symptom eines neuropathischen (psychopathischen) Zustandes, in: Archiv für Psychiatrie und Nervenkrankheiten, Berlin (Westphal, C.) 1869, nb. p. 108.

47. Entscheidungen des Bundesgerichtshofes, in: Neue Juristische Wochenschrift, 1951, p. 810.

48. cp. Entscheidungen des Bundesverfassungsgerichtes, 1951, p. 389.

49. Mende, L.J.C., Ausführliches Handbuch der gerichtlichen Medizin, Leipzig (Mende, L.J.C.) 1819, p. 510f.

50. Krafft-Ebing, R.v., Psychopathia sexualis, 14. ed., Stuttgart (Krafft-Ebing, R.v.) 1912, p. 298.

BIBLIOGRAPHY

Archiv für Preußisches Strafrecht, Berlin (Goltdammer) 1.1853-18.1870.

Archiv für Psychiatrie und Nervenkrankheiten, Berlin 1.1868-62.1920.

Archiv für Strafrecht, Berlin (Goltdammer) 9. 1880-46. 1898/1900.

Berger, P.L. and T. Luckmann (1969), Die gesellschaftliche Konstruktion der Wirklichkeit, Frankfurt (Berger, P.L. and T. Luckmann).

Casper, J.L., (1852), Über Nothzucht und Päderastie und deren Ermittelung seitens des Gerichtsarztes, in: Vierteljahrsschrift für gerichtliche und öffentliche Medicin, Berlin (Casper, J.L.).

Comte, A. (1883), Die positive Philosophie, im Auszug von Jules Rig, translated by J.H. Kirchmann, Vol. 1, Heidelberg (Comte, A.).

Conrad, P. and J.W. Schneider (1980), Deviance and Medicalisation–From Badness to Sickness, St. Louis/Toronto/London (Conrad, P. and J.W. Schneider).

Engelhardt, D.v., (1978), Sittlichkeitsdelinquenz in Wissenschaft und Literatur der 2. Hälfte des 19. Jahrhunderts, in: Sexualität und soziale Kontrolle. Beiträge zur Sexualkriminologie, Heidelberg (Engelhardt, D.v.).

Entscheidungen des Bundesverfassungsgerichtes, Karlsruhe 6. 1951.

Entscheidungen des Reichsgerichts in Strafsachen, Leipzig 1.1879-77.1943/44.

Fischer-Homberger, Esther (1983), Medizin vor Gericht. Gerichtsmedizin von der Renaissance bis zur Aufklärung, Bern/Stuttgart/Wien (Fischer-Homberger, E.).

Fleck, L. (1980), Entstehung und Entwicklung einer wissenschaftlichen Tatsache, Frankfurt (Fleck, L.) (1.ed. Basel 1935).

Foucault, M. (1976), Mikrophysik der Macht - Über Strafjustiz, Psychiatrie und Medizin, Berlin (Foucault, M.).

Gall, F.J., (1805), Lehre von den Verrichtungen des Gehirns, Dresden (Arnoldische Buchhandlung).

Häussler, J. (1826), Über die Beziehungen des Sexualsystems zur Psyche überhaupt und zum Kretinismus im Besonderen, Würzburg (Häussler, J.).

Henke, A. (1832), Lehrbuch der gerichtlichen Medicin, Stuttgart (Henke, A.).

Hirschfeld, M. (1914), Die Homosexualität des Mannes und des Weibes, Berlin (Hirschfeld, M.).

Kaan, H. (1844), Psychopathia sexualis, Leipzig (Kaan, H.).

Knorr, K. (1980), Die Fabrikation des Wissens, in: Kölner Zeitschrift für Soziologie und Sozialpsychologie, Sonderheft 22 zur Wissenssoziologie.

Krafft-Ebing, R.v. (1886), Psychopathia sexualis, Stuttgart (Krafft-Ebing, R.v.); the same (1912), Psychopathia sexualis, 14. ed., Stuttgart (Krafft-Ebing, R.v.).

Kraepelin, E. (1880), Die Abschaffung des Strafmaßes. Ein Vorschlag zur Reform der heutigen Strafrechtspflege, Stuttgart (Kraepelin, E.).

Kuhn, T.S. (1961), Die Struktur wissenschaftlicher Revolutionen, Frankfurt (Kuhn, T.S.).

Leibbrand, W, and A. Wettley (1961), Der Wahnsinn. Geschichte der abendländischen Psychopathologie, Freiburg/München (Leibbrand, W. and A. Wettley).

Leibbrand, W. and A. Wettley (1972), Formen des Eros. Kultur–und Geistesge-
schichte der Liebe, Freiburg/München (Leibbrand, W. and A. Wettley).

Magnan, V. (1892), Psychiatrische Vorlesungen, 2. vol., (german by P.J. Möbius), Leipzig (Magnan, V.).

Mende, L.J.C. (1819), Ausführliches Handbuch der gerichtlichen Medizin, Leipzig (Mende, L.J.C.).

Metzger, J.D. (1793), Kurzgefasstes System der gerichtlichen Arznywissenschaft,
Königsberg/Leipzig (Metzger, J.D.).

Mittermaier, W. (1906), Verbrechen und Vergehen wider die Sittlichkeit, in:
Birkmeyer, K. et al. (ed.), Vergleichende Darstellung des deutschen und
ausländischen Strafrechts, 4. vol., Berlin (Birkmeyer, K. et al).

Morel, B.A. (1860), Traité des maladies mentales, Paris (Morel, B.A.).

Nicolai, G.H. (1841), Handbuch der gerichtlichen Medicin, Berlin (Nicolai,
G.H.).

Rechtsprechung des Deutschen Reichsgerichts in Strafsachen, München/Leipzig
1.1879-10.1888.

Rechtsprechung des Königlichen Obertribunals in Strafsachen, Oppenhoff, F.C.
(ed.), Berlin (Oppenhoff, F.C.) 1863-1877.

Santlus, J.C. (1858), Über die Zunahme der Geisteskrankheiten und ihren
Zusammenhang mit den Geschlechtsfunktionen und Geschlechtskrankheiten,
Erlangen (Santlus, J.C.).

Schubert, W. and J. Regge (1981), Quellen zur preußischen Gesetzgebung des
19. Jahrhunderts, Vaduz (Schubert, W. and J. Regge).

Schürmeyer, J.H. (1850), Theoretisch-practisches Lehrbuch der gerichtlichen
Medicin, Erlangen (Schürmeyer, J.H.).

Smith, D.E.. (1976), K ist geisteskrank. Die Anatomie eines Tatsachenberichtes,
in: Weingarten, E., F. Sack, J. Schenkein (ed.), Ethnomethodologie. Beiträge
zu einer Soziologie des Alltagshandelns, Frankfurt (Weingarten, E. et al).

Tarnowsky, B.(1886), Die krankhaften Erscheinungen des Geschlechtssinnes,
Berlin (Tarnowsky, B.).

Tarnowsky, B. (1893), Der Sexualtrieb und seine krankhaften Äußerungen vom
doppelten, dem juristischen und psychiatrischen Standpunkt, Petersburg
(Tarnowsky, B.).

Teichmeyer, H.F. (1751), Institutiones medicinae legalis vel forensis, Jena
(Teichmeyer, H.F.).

Tissot, S.A. (1769), Onanisme ou dissertation physique sur les maladies produites
par la masturbation, Paris (Tissot, S.A.).

Westphal, C. (1869), Die conträre Sexualempfindung. Symptom eines neuropathischen (psychopathischen) Zustandes, in: Archiv für Psychiatrie und Nervenkrankheiten, Berlin (Westphal, C.).

Zacchia, P. (1688), Questiones medico legales, liber IV, edition Frankfurt
(Zacchia, P.).

Zentrales Staatsarchiv (ZSTA) Potsdam, Repositur 14.01.des Reichskanzleramtes.

Zentrales Staatsarchiv (ZSTA) Potsdam, Repositur 30.01.des Reichsjustizamtes.

III. POLITICALLY INCORRECT IDENTITIES

The Construction of Identities as a Means of Survival: Case of Gay and Lesbian Teachers

Peter Dankmeijer

Amsterdam

SUMMARY. The article, at its most general level, questions the requirement for "coming out" in public, which the author sees as the central demand of gay liberation ideology upon its adherents. Using research on teachers, the article shows that the political demand that teachers come out professionally ignores the central professional and political concerns of several teachers and their need for professional survival. In this study, teachers were found to have varying lifestyles. Coming out fitted the lifestyle only of those teachers who took on the role of crusaders for gay liberation. This role was often a secondary concern for women, who were more strongly identified as feminists than lesbians, and for men for whom

Peter Dankmeijer was trained as a teacher and proceeded to study sociology of education at the University of Amsterdam, Netherlands. Currently he is involved in building national coordination of gay/lesbian emancipation in Dutch schools. Correspondence may be addressed: P. Dankmeijer, Aert van Nesstraat 36, 1013 RH Amsterdam, Netherlands.

homosexuality was not a major aspect of their lifestyle. The author suggests that more attention should be given to the homophobic conditions under which such teachers work than to the requirement that they all come out.

INTRODUCTION

Scientific social studies tend to split up in different directions and researchers seem to delight in sham fights that serve to bring these differences to full contrast. Gay studies is no exception. The distinction between the two competing branches often rests on a single question: are there any constant factors determining human social life, or are we at the mercy of circumstances or in other words, can no general rules be formulated to explain human social life? The essentialism/constructionism dilemma is part of this greater scientific discussion.

Researchers often present the essentialist and constructionist approaches as mutually exclusive. I believe that this viewpoint is not fruitful and will only bring us to blows without positive effects on ideas and research. In this paper I propose a possible solution for this dilemma. The solution I propose developed from (unpublished) research I did in 1986 on gay and lesbian teachers in the Netherlands. In this paper I will first consider the theoretical background on which I worked, then I will present some interesting conclusions from the research. Finally, I will propose the reevaluation of some central concepts concerning gay/lesbian identity construction, and will point to a few important consequences that this reevaluation might have on gay/lesbian emancipation strategies.

THEORETICAL NOTES

The research on gay and lesbian teachers began in an attempt to satisfy the need for an inventory of strategies gay and lesbian teachers could employ in their day-to-day practice. From a survey of scientific and non-scientific literature on this subject, I found that very little was known about homosexual teachers. Some research has been done on the opinions of others about homosexual teachers (De Boer 1974, COC Kennemerland 1982, Kösters 1985), some has been written on discrimination, and a lot of newspaper coverage has been given to escalated conflicts. The publications on "discrimination" gave the clearest view on the practice of homosexual teachers, but even they were not clear enough to formulate a general idea of exactly how teachers behave, when they are able to address discrimination, or what they can try to do about it (Dobbeling & Koenders 1984, Bullinga & Van der Veer 1981, Gerretsen 1985).

The problem with these research projects was their limited theoretical background. Every writer or researcher posed a quite open question, such as: what is the situation of homosexual teachers? It is no wonder they only found general and well-known forms of discrimination and their solutions lacked consistency. To make their results appear somewhat more sound, they padded them with analysis about the heterodominant system which represses the homosexual teacher who cannot act freely. This kind of analysis does not contribute to creative thinking about emancipation and it leaves many questions unanswered. For instance: what is *free* for a teacher, what is exactly meant by *heterodominance,* what practical strategies are available to teachers to survive, to motivate, to maintain order and instruction, and to emancipate?

Thus, finding little valuable information in the known literature about homosexual teachers, I turned to research on teachers in general. The sociological field has quite a tradition of research on teachers. For us, the most interesting aspect is the research which presents teachers as culturally bound people who reproduce our culture within the framework of an institution especially designed for that purpose, the school (Bourdieu 1973). The school not only reproduces "heterodictated" values, but it also defines who is powerful and who is powerless, and it teaches how to behave in prescribed societal situations. Putting it another way, the school itself is part of societal control (Foucault 1981), and there is no question of being free to act in such a system. Research that focuses on the existing school system, no longer works with simple repression hypotheses, but concentrates on the conditions under which teachers and pupils have to operate. Special attention is given to the varying interests of groups and persons, how they develop problem-bound perspectives on the situation, and what range of strategies they can choose from. This is often a very restricted range.

Participating researchers found out that teachers have to juggle their interests when coping with problematic situations (Pollard 1980, Woods 1977). The situation in the classroom is described as a very complex interactional scheme, where varying short and long term interests, for teachers and pupils, have to be taken into consideration while determining which strategy should be chosen. The directness of the interaction in the classroom leads teachers to choose the strategies which serve the interests at hand. The survival of the teacher himself or herself is the primary interest. Pollard explains how the contradiction between ideals and practice, the handling of workload, the upkeep of physical and mental health, the need to enjoy work and the tradition of personal autonomy have led to several traits of teacher culture. Typical teacher identity forms can be derived from this. Thus, a teacher's identity depends for a large part on his or her way of surviving.

Of course, survival is not the only interest teachers have. They want to teach pupils, and often wish to have a rearing function that surmounts the teaching job: they have ideals concerning how pupils should be brought up and what kind of people they should become. These long-term objectives have a vague but distinctive influence on teaching. Not all these goals are completely congruent. In fact, many interests of teaching are competing with each other. It is especially on the levels of survival, motivation, order and instruction and long-term objectives, that frictions between competing interests arise. For example, a teacher might want to stop a child from shouting all the time. A strategy to maintain order could be to pay some individual attention to the child. But by paying attention to him or her the teacher could lose oversight of the group as whole, which would threaten order and survival in another way. In addition, paying attention to one pupil could conflict with the general view on teaching that male students, or pupils in general, should not be favored above others. In this way, any strategy the teacher chooses will be the result of a juggling of interests.

In earlier research on teachers that I did (Bijlsma-Frankema & Dankmeijer 1986) with a team from the University of Amsterdam, we developed a research model to map the juggling of interests that occurs in schools and classrooms. This model was also used in the research-project on gay/lesbian teachers. Important questions I asked were:

1. Which interests do gay and lesbian teachers perceive for themselves?
2. How do they accommodate these interests to them?
3. In which ways do they develop identity in the process of accommodation?
4. What kinds of identities are chosen and what is the meaning of these identities for teachers?
5. How does the self-conceived identity of homosexual teachers influence their practical strategies, problem-bound perspectives and general ideologies

Part of the research consisted of interviewing homosexual teachers about their lifestyles, ideologies, and their ways of teaching, and comparing them with a group of heterosexual teachers interviewed in the same way. I chose to analyze ten interviews with gay men, eleven with lesbian women and fourteen with heterosexuals, half of them female. The lesbian and gay teachers were selected to represent as many ages, lifestyles, areas, types of schools (with different types of pupils) and religions as I could find. Because I was primarily interested in positive strategies, I selected only two teachers who were not "open" about their being lesbian or gay.

CONCLUSIONS OF RESEARCH

I concluded that man/woman differences were dominant. Important differences in style were found both in the group of homosexual teachers and in the control group of heterosexual teachers. Men tended to make a performance in front of the group, while women instead focused attention directly on the subject of teaching and on the group-process, which often was considered an integral part of teaching.

Men have more "clear-cut" strategies; for example, they often have a collection of standard jokes and comments which they use in typical situations. They play a kind of "sounding" game (the concept of "sounding" is adapted from Labov, see Walker & Goodson 1977) with a few individual pupils, in which they attract attention to themselves. Pupils are even encouraged to take part in this game, but they are not allowed to undermine the authority of the teacher. The male teacher survives, maintains order and instruction, and motivates mainly through such games, during which tension is heightened, and attention focused on himself and then directed on the subject matter he is teaching. In this performance, the male teacher develops a specific identity. Male teachers often say that they have to be a "personality" to be able to teach, but what they mean is that they construct an identity which pupils can gaze upon and with which they can play the game of negotiating interests. A well defined teacher identity provides a steady handle with which pupil and teacher can calculate interaction.

Women do not like to be such a focus of attention. They say the attention should flow from them to the pupils. While teaching, they are very much occupied with monitoring group interaction. If they make comments, it is often a reaction to pupils initiatives. They sometimes do not think they are humorous because they do not use clear-cut jokes, but often their reactions are quite original and humorous without bearing the character of "gags." Women try to create a relaxed atmosphere in the classroom. Tension raising remarks from pupils are neutralized as soon as possible. With a research model that uses *strategy* as a key concept, it was sometimes difficult to define the practice of female teachers. They often cannot state formal strategies, because their teaching is a flowing process. The creation of a relaxed atmosphere is very important, but the way this atmosphere is created cannot be forced into clear marked formulae.

The man/woman differences were basic to the way gay and lesbian teachers built their identities. Male homosexual teachers often had a well-defined homosexual style. For all of them the hetero/homo difference was the most important aspect of discrimination. For women the man/woman difference was more important. Although the lesbian teachers showed distinctive lifestyles at home, where I interviewed them, they told me they were reluctant to propagate such styles in the classroom. They adapted themselves largely to the groups they taught, which often meant restricting attention to their own identity.

With the male homosexual teachers, I found three well-defined styles: the gay, the camp and the "normal" style. Homosexual teachers who call themselves gay (flikker) think homosexuals are oppressed because of their open choice of another sexual preference. They present themselves as political warriors in the struggle for sexual freedom. Important strategies they use include wearing badges and talking about sex and freedom of choice. They are largely discriminated against because of their openness about sex, sexual preference and promotion of these things in a "political" way.

Teachers who said they sometimes camp up their act a little (een beetje nichterig doen) think they should be accepted as they are. For them, being "themselves" means that they sometimes–or often–violate sex role patterns of behavior. They joke a lot with pupils and collegues and try to get themselves accepted as normal by being social and by shaking the rigid ideas of stereotypical straights. They are largely discriminated against because they do not behave like stereotypically heterosexual men. Finally there were homosexual male teachers who said they "did not feel themselves very homosexual." They said homosexuality was only a label put upon them by others. In their teaching practice there was little that pointed to a specific homosexual identity. They were rarely discriminated against, and often heterosexual colleagues were more angry at discriminating incidents than they were themselves. This does not mean they concealed their homosexuality, only that it was not very visible. They thought it a minor part of their identity, not relevant to their teaching. The homosexual aspect of their identity was characterized by the strategy of behaving "normal," the best way they found to defend their personal and gay/lesbian interests.

It was threatening for the homosexual men to be in contact with homosexual colleagues who used another style. They all developed their own styles to cope with personal interests, and confrontation with homosexuals having other interests and identities seemed to crush the very basis of their own way of being. For example, a "normal" style teacher often feels threatened by a "campy" colleague, because he fears heterosexual colleagues might be supported in their prejudice that all homosexuals are effeminate, which prejudice is rejected by the "normal" style teacher by not acting camp in a heterosexual context. Men who strongly identify with the "normal" style might even reject camp in any circumstance.

This problem did not exist for the lesbians. On the contrary, they often found a mutual interest in the women's liberation. Their being lesbian played a minor role in school. There were differences between the lesbian teachers but these differences largely existed on the level of ideology. There were women with radical lesbian feminist ideals, who made immediate connections between their daily situation and lesbian feminist theories. Unbalanced power-relationships were quickly noticed by them, not only in a man/woman context, but also with black/white, old/young, handicapped/healthy, and teacher/pupil relations. Other women analyzed less, but still saw a direct relationship between their being a woman and being lesbian. Female and lesbian discrimination were perceived as simply discrimination. Other women did not see this. They perceived being female and being lesbian as two different struggles. In daily life the struggle for women's emancipation had priority.

These differences did not pass the ideological level. In schools every lesbian teacher adapted herself to the group. This does not mean they did not try to do something about emancipation. They did. However, women's emancipation always had priority above specific lesbian emancipation. This is logical considering they were all primarily discriminated against for being feminist or female. Thus, the lesbian women I interviewed did not develop lesbian identities in their schools for two reasons: the importance of the women's struggle in their lives and the fact that their way of teaching did not conform with presenting a very explicit identity.

RE-EVALUATION OF CONCEPTS

Certain concepts play a major role in the definitions of identities which are formed around homosexuality. The main concepts are coming-out, openness, identification, subculture and lifestyle. The traditional way of using these concepts is to say homosexuals conceal themselves for fear of being discriminated against. The main strategy against this should be one of coming-out. These open homosexuals could have an identification function for others who have not yet come out. In education especially this would work benevolently for pupils. Because of discrimination, homosexuals have formed subcultures in which they can safely meet and experiment with lifestyles, while not being bothered by heterosexist oppression.

From this research on gay and lesbian teachers, it became evident that coming-out and openness did not mean the same for everyone. For women, openness meant not to conceal, but it did not mean much more due to their views on education (no attention to yourself) and their views on emancipation (the priority for women's liberation). If they came out, it had more to do with the discovery of the women's movement than with identifying as lesbian. For "normal" style men, the concept of openness was not too relevant because it only stimulated labelling. They viewed coming-out as the period in which homosexuals do not know how to handle the consequences of a newly discovered sexual preference and do stupid anti-emancipating things like provoking the public and behaving "effeminately." For the camps, openness is not very relevant either as they do not have to put an effort into being "open." Their style is recognizable from a distance. Coming-out is not a strategy of openness for them, it is about accepting themselves as who they are.

Only for gay men the traditional way of using these concepts held a real meaning. However, it is interesting to note that it is mainly gay men formulating policy, writing articles and organizing homosexual emancipation. In this way they heavily influence general ideology, even of other homosexuals. I believe that is part of the reason why homosexual teachers say that they want to be an identification object, although only "gay" men interpret "identification" as "openness" and "coming-out." Women often say they want to be an example of a strong woman, a camp says he wants to be an example of a sociable homosexual (een gezellige homo).

From the research it seems clear that our "experimental" lifestyles and subcultural traits are not as freely chosen as we would like to think. Identities and even non-identities must be seen as solutions for problems we are confronted with. Men and women are confronted with different kinds of oppression. Varying situations change the survival threat and lead to different perspectives and strategies. Identities are formed as a result of the complex process of accommodation of personal interests to specific situations. On this basis, ideologies are formed and evaluated. I found several examples of how teachers changed their ideologies to accommodate survival threats. Common perspectives and practical strategies change even more easily. Thus, the construction of identities and the choice of not constructing identities based on homosexuality are both means of survival.

The well known concepts of openness, coming-out, identification, life-style and subculture are heavily dominated by male gay ideology, but are not readily applied to others. I suggest therefore a re-evaluation of these concepts in accordance with the model of interactionism.

Lifestyle should be a key concept in this model. Lifestyles should be considered as a means of self-lodging and accommodation (Woods 1983, 1977, Plummer 1975) to general conditions, but with varying starting points and interests. What we need is a map of how varying perspectives lead to different strategies and what the consequences are for identity construction or commitment to certain identity forms.

Close to the concept of lifestyle is that of subculture. Subcultures must not be seen solely as escapes or experimental areas. Within subcultures people gather because they have mutual interests. The stronger the interest, the greater the commitment to a culture. Often these interests lie on several levels. By mapping out which interests are served and which interests are not apt to be fulfilled, research will gather a more accurate picture of what gay and lesbian interests are about.

The concept of openness should allow for differences. Analysis of how teachers were "open" or "visible" suggested that almost everyone was less open in front regions (formal, public or official situations) and more open in back regions (informal, private or individualized situations), while visibility was strongly connected with style and identity. Such conclusions are more valuable than the simplified open/concealed dilemma.

In this way coming-out should not be restricted to the moment that a homosexual becomes "open." The coming-out process involves much more. In fact, it could be compared with a culture-shock incurred while going from a dominant culture into a subculture. Not only should the process of accommodation with this new position be researched, but also the connected process of choosing another ideology, lifestyle and eventually, the way self-lodging occurs and identity takes shape.

The same goes for identification. The gay male oriented slogans surrounding this theme are not based on sound knowledge. To improve this, two things have to be done. First, there has to be research on how identification processes work and when they occur. Second, we have to consider what kind of identification people choose.

CONSEQUENCES FOR HOMOSEXUAL
EMANCIPATION STRATEGIES

One of the most important demands for emancipation is that there be more open homosexuals. From this paper it will be clear that this demand is typical for gay males, but not always relevant to other groups of homosexuals. With women especially, the interest of being open can compete with other, specific female interests. This also goes for the "normal" style homosexual teachers, who I suspect, form a large part of the homosexual teacher population. Instead of focusing on openness, I would suggest that policy-demands concentrate on the amelioration of the conditions under which gay and lesbian teachers function. Of course, this will cost some energy. It is much easier to say that everybody (else) should be open, than to formulate practical proposals to change all the situations in which we find ourselves discriminated against. But it is these practical proposals which allow for addressing the needs of varying lifestyles, and which will lead to more real solutions. Identification is often used as an argument for "openness." By now, it is clear I no longer favor this argument.

Apart from the discussion of the open/concealed theme, conclusions I have reached should be taken seriously when giving information about homosexuality. It is too easy to say that homosexuals are "normal" when some of them are definitely not in the eyes of dominant groups. It is also too easy to say that homosexuals are more free to choose a lifestyle other than heterodictated ones. We have to realize that these kinds of arguments mirror only the ideologies of certain groups of homosexuals. Balanced information about homosexuality is difficult to give, but it can create interest in the variety of lifestyles and ways of survival in heterodominant society. Finally, there is a demand for research. I suggest we leave the complaint era and make a sound analysis of oppression. Social scientists have to show the positive strategies that are possible for subgroups and for us all. Only with a clear view of our mutual interests and goals do we have a basis to cooperate, especially in the gay and lesbian movement.

REFERENCES

Bijlsma-Frankema & Dankmeijer (1986), Een gezelligheidscultuur in het zicht van werkloosheid. In Grob, Husken & Van der Kley (Ed.), *Eigenwijs in onderwijs.* OOMO reeks, Nijmegen

De Boer, Ton Kroode, Manschot & Stolk (1971), *Meningen over homoseksualiteit* deel III. Stichting ter bevordering sociaal onderzoek minderheden, Amsterdam

Bourdieu (1973), Cultural reproduction and social reproduction. In Brown, *Knowledge, education and social change.* Tavistock Publications, London

Bullinga & Van der Veer (1981), series in *SEK* (COC monthly)

COC Kennemerland (1982), *Homoseksualiteit in het onderwijs. Report of a survey and discussion.* Unpublished manuscript.

Dobbeling & Koenders (1984), *Het topje van de IJsberg* (Homostudies, Utrecht)

Foucault (1981), Discipline. In *Te Elfder Ure,* jaargang 25, no.3 SUN, Nijmegen

Gerretsen, Lammers, Parlevliet, Verschuren & Zegerman (1985), *Juf is óók zo.* SUA, Amsterdam

Kösters (1985), *Maar steun die hij/zij ongetwijfeld van leraren zal krijgen zal niet genoeg zijn.* Unpublished report of a survey, University of Amsterdam

Plummer (1975), *Sexual stigma: An interactionist account.* Routledge & Kegan Paul, London and Boston

Pollard (1980), Teacher interests and changing situations of survival threat in primary classrooms. In Woods (Ed.), *Teacher Strategies.* Croom Helm, London, 1980, 1982

Walker & Goodson (1977), Humour in the classroom. In: Woods (Ed.), *School Experience.* St. Martins Press, New York

Woods (1977), Teaching for survival. In Woods (Ed.), *School Experience.* St. Martins Press, New York

Woods (1983), *Sociology and the school, an interactionist viewpoint.* Routledge & Kegan Paul, London

Gay Fathers in Straight Marriages

Gerd Büntzly, MA

Montabaur/Germany

SUMMARY. The author bases his conclusions about gay parenthood on anecdotal evidence gathered from about 100 gay German fathers. First he notes how the religious ethic that surrounds the nuclear family stands in the way of a father's awareness and expression of his homosexual desires. Like van der Geest, he reports that many women are attracted to gay men and proceed to marry them. After coming to realize that husbands' homosexual affairs are transitory and do not constitute a serious challenge to marital and family bonds, a few couples have been able to preserve their marriages. In most cases the marriages collapse under the combined pressures of wife and gay lover both claiming exclusive proprietorship: "the 'love triangle' can rarely be closed." The author laments the existence of all-male gay communities that ignore the existence of females and force gay husbands and fathers to choose against marriage and parenthood.

CLICHÉS AND PREJUDICES

Gay fathers: many of us seem to know what sort of specimen that is. Our cliché is that of sad, half tragic, and half comic figures who are not able to break with a marriage which turned into a lie many years ago. Poor pigs, unable to cut the chains which tie them to the wellbeing of their families, they look for their satisfaction in public closets, and they often have a dog under whose protection they spend five minutes in the local gay club ("Master and Dog" is a short story by Thomas Mann who himself was a secret homosexual).

Gerd Büntzly is translator and piano teacher in Montabaur/Germany. Correspondence may be addressed: Gerd Büntzly, Rheinstr. 29, D-5431 Heiligenroth, Germany.

This description may show that gay fathers, like many other minorities, are like caricatures as long as they have not found a consciousness of their own: like gays themselves, or like transvestites. But in the last years, they have started a certain movement. I know of gay fathers' groups in the U.S.A., in Canada and in Germany where I live; from Austria and Switzerland, I have several testimonies of similar tendencies to consciousness. Gay fathers do not simply break with their family situation leaving their wives and children in order to live as gays in the future (though, this happens, too, of course), but they try to *integrate* their relationships as homosexuals more and more, at least with their children, and with their wives. There are also cases on the other hand, in which self-conscious gays and lesbians ask themselves if they must inevitably renounce fatherhood or motherhood looking for ways to realize these dreams (cf. Schulenburg, J. 1985, p. 84-104; Schwule Väter, 1983).

METHOD OF MY STUDY

My knowledge of these problems is the result of studying about 100 cases I came across during meetings of gay fathers I organized, and with correspondences and interviews. As a gay father myself, I searched early on for fellow peers, and found more of them than I expected. My study is journalistic, not an empirical one, supported very much by example of real situations; generalizations are therefore more or less plausible speculations. I think this method of journalistic study will achieve my aim more effectively: it does not present a so-called "objective reality," but is designed to inspire action, to encourage those who are still in the closet to come out, and to evoke understanding with "normal" gays and heterosexuals.

Only few women were willing to speak about their experiences with gay husbands, and I completely omitted the subject "Lesbian Mothers" (about the situation in the U.S.A. see Schulenburg, J. 1985.). I think that is a subject to be treated by women themselves. On this occasion, I admit that being a man, i.e., a member of an oppressive group, made me cautious and has been a real limit to my knowledge.

SECRET REPRESSION AND SELF DENIAL

Let us look first at the instruments of repression in a society which in most cases make the coming out process of gay fathers a particularly grievous one, if it does not prevent it altogether. Religious education plays an important role in anchoring family conceptions, and guilt feelings, especially to husband/wife and the children, but also to the parents and parents-in-law, to whom marriage and the founding of a family often establishes a new relationship. Religion also leads to self-denial and denial of our own feelings. Then there is the specific role of society, firmly fixed in laws and penal laws for the deviant on the one hand and privileges for those who are 'normal' on the other. Do not forget that many middle aged German homosexuals had to live under the Nazi Law against Homosexuality (the §175), which only was altered in 1969.

This bundle of repression leads to many catastrophes or near-catastrophes in the household of a nuclear family when the husband discovers that he is gay. The feelings of absolute lack of power are due especially to the fact that nobody is to blame: repression is rooted in institutions or in the individual's own mind. This leads to reports of violent happenings in such families with the destruction of household objects and bodily violence. Several gay fathers report that they suffered chronic diseases like headache or heart complaint which vanished when the personal situation had found a better fit.

THE WIVES

We should not forget the situation of the women: wives of gay men are often in the weaker position as they feel betrayed by a husband turning out gay, and this is a process which is completely out of their influence and control (cf. Meyer, K. & Schirnhofer, P., 1984, June). We only can ask if the woman could not have known before which sort of man she chose, even if the man himself did not know of his homosexual orientation. Indeed there are reasons to believe (Nahas, R. & Turley, M. 1979) that some women choose unconsciously men who are gay. There are many reasons for this, e.g., the fact that a gay man, because of not being so much sexually interested in women, often lacks macho attitudes.

In most cases, however, a process of separation and divorce begins which is not very different from the divorce of heterosexuals. Only in towns like Berlin does the situation seem to be a little different: a growing number of people do not marry anymore; economically, there is a balance between the (generally small) income of the man and the woman. Besides, they often live in larger groups with several adults and their children. These communities lack stability, however. Therefore, the stability which is necessary for the children often lies in institutions like

'Kinderläden' (children's houses where the children can stay and get food during the day), organized by the communities, and paid, at least partly, by the municipality.

Responsibility for the children, however, is ultimately the duty of the biological parents. Communities can help a little in the everyday life, but in most cases they are experiments themselves, experiencing many conflicts and stress. Up to now, the most important thing is the relationship between the gay father and his wife. Are they mature enough to overcome personal difficulties after the definite coming out of the husband? Are they able to see their situation constructed mainly by elements of social life and social repression instead of accusing one another? Often the woman has abandoned her profession in order to be present for the family, and therefore feels betrayed because of the loss of the emotional relationship and having a lower economic status. Normally, she does not feel an urge to have lovers outside the family even if she concedes this to her husband, which must lead to an inequality in this mixture of relationships. Some couples report, however, that tension in family life decreased when gay contacts were allowed: afterwards, the husband was more inclined to turn back to his family. The fear that these gay contacts would be a real challenge to the marriage often diminished when it became clear that these sexual adventures did not reach the deepness of the relationship at home which is often bound by its length of many years. I must admit, however, that in most cases this was the situation only for a limited amount of time; besides it is obvious that this way of avoiding conflicts in the marriage separates the so-called "sex adventures" more or less completely from the everyday life. In the extreme case, one gets a "normal" marriage typical of our society where exciting things like sex tend to destroy the normal way of life and are held outside with precaution; however, everyday life may be an image of calmness, harmony, and fidelity, but has tendencies of boredom, hate, and bitterness. I see here a separating force of our society, which no political or sexual revolution has ever changed.

Some couples who stressed their will to stay together were deeply involved in the Catholic or Protestant Church; therefore, it may be that with them the older religious conceptions of fidelity play a part. By the way, I found many gay fathers engaged in a religious gay group, "Homosexuelle und Kirche" ("Homosexuals and the Church"), a group which claims equal rights for homosexuals in the church. This shows that for those friends, the church is still a value even though they feel its repression daily. For many of them, it is a question of their pure material existence since they are engaged in the church by their profession as ministers or lay staff.

RELATIONSHIPS TO THE CHILDREN

Most of the participants of German national wide gay fathers' meetings (nine up to the printing of this essay, with 30-50 attendants each) have contact with their children, some of them even bring them up alone. The problems arise when the children have more contact outside the family and are exposed to the value judgments of the society which may differ considerably from those experienced at home. Gay fathers often fear their children might innocently speak about the friends of their father or about sexual practices seen at home. At school, gays are often the subject of allusions or jokes, and that will hurt those children a great deal who know about the sexual orientation of their fathers. We found out that the best way for gay fathers in this situation is to have built up a social frame which may consist of tolerant and informed heterosexual or homosexual couples or singles, so that the children can see these various forms of stable human relationships in several confident people. Then, the revelation "My father is gay/my mother is a lesbian" will not be a shock but only the conscious confirmation of an everyday event. But even if this social frame does not exist it is important not to wait too long before talking to the child about the situation of the father which is somewhat different to the conceptions of the majority. "Not too long" means at the age of 9-12 years at the latest. There are several reports confirming how well children normally react to this sign of confidence, and that they feel discretion is in their own interest. Often they become ardent defenders of their fathers and help to spread good information about homosexuality.

JURIDICAL QUESTIONS

In Western Germany, the principle of guilt in divorce cases has been abolished, so homosexuality cannot be the subject of the divorce cases nor of the question of custody. The conservative government, however, has changed the regulations of payments to the weaker party in a way which reintroduces every sort of "dirty business." With regard to the children, practically all regulations are at the judge's disposal; so one will find every sort of moral implication with gays, and every sort of fear or lack of fear concerning the bad or immoral influence of a gay father. Conditions for him, if he wants to have his children at home, can be for example, that his lover would not be allowed to live with him, or that his lover would not be allowed to see him while the child or the children are at his house (cf. Gleitz, W. 1987).

Adoption could be a perfect possibility for gay couples to have children–if society would allow it. Even for heterosexuals, the criteria for adoption are very rigid and orientated on traditional clichés of what a "decent household" has to be; at the moment, gay or lesbian couples have no chance.

GAY LOVERS

Many of the possible gay lovers of a gay father do not want to have a relationship which involves children, let alone women. The situation of a gay father often means that he cannot take a lover home at night. In gay pubs and gay clubs, he often meets people who tend to identify gay emancipation with emancipation from the 'normal' family or heterosexuality. In the end, they prefer a type of closed society, in which women no longer exist. In such a climate, they only see a gay father as somebody who is not able to decide what and who he wants to be. On the other hand, we also have reports of gay lovers who integrated very well in a group with the children and who even have good contact with the children's mothers. Of course, feelings of jealousy arise sooner or later. Nahas and Turley (1979) describe the "love triangle" as a sociological structure which lacks stability. In fact, one's partner–if he or she ever overcomes jealousy–will rarely love one's lover as much as you do yourself. All one can hope for is a mutual respect and a mutual confidence that nobody challenges the economic and psychological base of each other.

THE DIFFICULTY OF INTEGRATION

The model of the triangle also shows that one of the angles is normally stressed more than the other two, and therefore has a comparatively strong position. But being loved by two parties also brings stress and effort which is often more than one can bear. In fact, the conception of the "New Couple," invented by Nahas/Turley (1979) (which is, by the way, a completely empty one, like 'post-modernism' or other such concepts) seem to work for only a limited period of time, as the examples of Nahas/Turley themselves show. I propose the concept of the "*Integration*" of homosexuality and heterosexuality; but I must stress that nobody can give any guarantee for the next day. One married couple I interviewed had even lived together for ten years with the wife's full acceptance of her husband's homosexuality; they have a nine year old son. They told me, however, that the husband decided to separate their beds two years ago, and to give up sex with his wife, because having a sexual relationship with her gave him too many emotional problems over the time. His decision caused a crisis, and she considered it a definite separation, since the sexual relationship was very important to her. But they agreed that they would in any case bring their son up together. She did not object to him staying in the common house, and even bringing home lovers sometimes, though she admitted that it was very difficult for her emotionally.

Most of the gay fathers stress that they are really gay, and not bisexual: they feel attracted primarily to men (a testimony of this also in Schroeter-Kleist, 1984). Only few of them do not want to decide or felt uneasy when they tried to. The question of bisexuality has not yet been resolved, and my research does not deal much with questions of definitions.

CONCLUSION

It seems to me that gay parenting challenges the traditional concept of homosexuality: gay fathers or married gays (the name of a group in Duisburg/Germany, in 1987) look to both sides. They also look for their own identity like other gays; and this search seems even more complicated. But they have a chance, and they are able to give a new, freer image of homosexuality to the younger generation. They also have experienced good relationships with the opposite sex. A conception of homosexuality which simply denies the existence of the female sex, will end as sterile and oppressive as is the traditional sex role distribution in a world again dominated by men.

It was always my opinion that a concept like homosexuality is not a fixed one, defined by unchangeable limits, but more or less a "fight concept": with the confession: "I am gay–I am a homosexual" you can "clear the air," and afterwards you will distinguish better your friends and enemies. Of course, in a society in which two men having sex together are no longer seen like monsters or criminals, such fight conceptions will lose their importance. Unfortunately, I cannot see such a society now, and with the impact of AIDS, we risk a roll-back to the darkest times of victorianism.

REFERENCES AND BIBLIOGRAPHY

Anonymous. (1981). *Gay Fathers: Some of Their Stories, Experience, and Advice.* Toronto: Gay Fathers of Toronto.

Anonymous. (1983, April). Schwule Väter. Ein Bericht aus Amerika. Übersetzt von René aus: *The Advocate,* San Mateo, U.S.A. *Hey.*

Büntzly, G. (1988). *Schwule Väter. Erfahrungen, Polemiken, Ratschläge. Ein Reader.* Berlin: Bruno Gmünder.

Clark, D. (1978). *Loving Someone Gay.* New York: New American Library.

Gantz, J. (1983). *Whose Child Cries. Children of Gay Parents talk about their Lives.* Rolling Hills Estates, CA: Jalmar Press.

Jay, Ph. P. (1986). *Growing up with a Gay, Lesbian or Bisexual Parent: An Exploration Study of Experiences and Perceptions.* Unpublished doctoral dissertation, University of California, Berkeley, CA.

Meyer, K. & Schirnhofer, P. (1984, June). Papa liebt Onkel. Homosexuelle Väter. *Wiener,* Juni 1984.

Nahas, R. & Turley, M. (1979). *The New Couple: Women and gay Men.* Cited from the German translation. (1983). München: Wilhelm Heyne.

Schroeter-Kleist, Bettina. (1984, Sept. 8th) Mein Mann liebt seinen Freund. Gespräche mit Frauen von homosexuellen Männern. *Frankfurter Rundschau.*

Schulenburg, J. (1985). *Gay Parenting. A Complete Guide for Gay Men and Lesbians with Children.* Garden City, NY: Anchor Books, Anchor Press/ Doubleday.

Homosexuality and Marriage

Hans van der Geest, ThD

University of Zurich

SUMMARY. Discusses the problems of heterosexual partnership, when one of the partners engages in a homosexual relation. Notes the biblical data on homosexuality and fidelity. Draws attention to the concept of the New Couple as a possible solution.

WHICH HOMOSEXUALITY?

If we could divide people into two definite categories, hetero- and homosexual, the whole problem of this address could be easily solved. The occurrence of homosexuality within a marriage would point to misunderstanding or deception. Such misunderstandings do exist. People who are not capable of entering into a heterosexual partnership often do marry. This can prove to be a tragedy, for both parties concerned. Conventional moral way-of-thinking encourages this misfortune. As long as it is a scandal to express homosexual desires, one will naturally attempt to prove to himself and to others, that one is "normal." Even today marriage is still prescribed by doctors and counselors as the best remedy for homosexuality.

Not all marriages, in which one or both partners wish for a homosexual relationship, are a misunderstanding. There are people who expressly wish for both forms of sexual relationships. This is not always clear to them before their marriages. Social pressure plays a concealing role. They can however become gradually aware, that they can and want to love someone of their own sex. Even then, when there is no pressure or prejudice against known homosexual leanings, marriage can still take place for the simple reason, that this is what both parties want.

Hans van der Geest teaches Pastoral Theology at the University of Zurich. He is a supervisor of Clinical Pastoral Education in Switzerland. Correspondence may be addressed: Langwattstr. 21, CH-8125 Zollikerberg, Switzerland.

The compulsion to place people in definite categories can be harmful to our lives. It is unnecessary and also misleading to try to assess the percentage-rate of a person's hetero- and homo sexuality. The most important thing is for the person herself or himself to know, if he or she can feel love towards both men and women, or only to one.

However, life is even more complex. The desire for sexual love must be important enough, in order to categorize people according to their sexual preferences. This is, however, a false assumption. Sexuality is not equally important to all people. For some it is an irrelevant side of their lives. These people, however, can also marry, become parents and have good or bad partnerships. To try to place these people in a hetero- or homosexual category would be as ridiculous as trying to categorize people according to the color of their hair.

Married people with homosexual contacts are rarely people who exclusively prefer a partner of their own sex, and their partners are equally rarely deceived heterosexuals. Many quite "average" people discover that they have homosexual desires and fantasies. It would be unkind to regard these marriages as failures.

THE CRUCIAL QUESTION

The only relevant point in the discussion on homosexuality and marriage is the degree of importance attached to the genital-sexual relationship between the one partner and his or her friend. It would certainly be crude, if we reduced a friendship to the sexual relation, as if this was all that mattered. But all other aspects are largely indisputed. In general it is completely acceptable, that a marriage partner has a friendship with someone else, that he can experience depths of conversation or kinds of pastime, which cannot be had in his or her marriage. But only then, when this friendship reaches a sensual level, is it a threat to the marriage. Apparently, the notion that one can have a sexual relationship outside one's marriage affects the other partner so deeply, that all feelings of tolerance disappear.

Whether or not this attitude is right, can be disputed at length, without a final solution being reached. Some feel, that the intimate side of a marriage is simultaneously its core, and should therefore take place only within the marriage. Others feel that sexuality is no different from any other side of a friendship, and that more than one sexual relationship can exist parallel to marriage, as long as all other marital responsibilities remain intact. The long and the short of the matter is, that it is not alike for all people: what the one does and thinks, is not tolerated by the other. Theories arise according to their own wishes. Bible verses can be found for the one as for the other. The final decision rests with the person himself.

THE BIBLE AND HOMOSEXUALITY

One of the greatest difficulties concerning Christian ethics in this matter is, that there are several passages to be found in the Bible, which clearly condemn sexual relationships among men (Lev. 18:22; 20:13; Romans 1:26 f.;1 Cor.6:10; 1 Tim. 1:10). On the other hand, there is not one single passage to be found which considers them in a positive light. It has been pointed out, that these prohibitions have to be clearly understood as resistence to pagan practices of worship. The verses are directed towards the so-called cult prostitution, female (Deuteronomy 23:17) as well as male. In the Baal religion, and later in the hellenistic culture, sexual activity was considered as a participation in godly life. Biblical law disputes this. The main point is not the outward shape of the sexual relationship, but the aim of this contact. The Old Testament and Paul both forbid such sexuality because of the religious power attached to it.

An overall prohibition could not, of course, count where a man-woman relationship was concerned. Only the supposed religion- filled behaviour was condemned. In Israel one probably did not bother about this difference, where homosexuals were concerned, so that this kind of relationship could simply be forbidden overall.

However, this difference is important in our time. It cannot be generally stated, that people who today enter into a homosexual relationship are seeking God in a sexual manner. The biblical commandments do not concern them generally. We can do justice to the afore mentioned Bible verses, when we hear the basis demarcation in them, between experiencing human intimacy on the one hand, and finding the way to God on the other. The way to God is to be found through hearing His word, not through human ecstasy. In this way sexuality can break through all taboos and become simply human. Even today, God's commandment is here to warn us when sexual experience attains idolatry value. This applies not only to relationships within the same sex.

God's commandment calls on us to love. According to His will, sexual love should also be real love. It is not a question of whether or not the partners are of the same sex, but rather, whether or not they are trying to live their lives within the relationship in a responsible way.

The Bible is not always a simple or helpful book for homo-sexuals, most certainly not, if they wish to justify their behaviour by it. For heterosexual partners there are numerous examples to be found, the most ardent being in the Song of Solomon. Homosexuals have no such images to draw on, not even David and Jonathan, or Jesus and his best-loved disciple (John 21:10). The homosexual carries a greater responsibility for his way of life, than a heterosexual person does. This difference cannot be argued.

THE BIBLE ON FIDELITY

The combination of homosexuality and marriage touches on the problem of fidelity. Can people have more than one intimate relationship at the same time, and can this be justified biblically?

Once again, the Bible offers no convenient answer. The institution of traditional, Christian, monogamous marriage is not of a general biblical kind. The Bible shows us marriages and marriage-laws of nomadic and agricultural times. Fidelity is always called for, but in different associations. Exclusivity is at times required, in any case for women, but sometimes also for men, for example deacons and elders (1 Tim. 3:2 & 12; Tit. 1:6). Patriarchs and kings have several wives, without being criticized. But they are supposed to be faithful too. Jacob is faithful to Rachel, after he has married her sister Lea. But he does not reject Lea (Ge. 29 f.). Fidelity is not understood here as being exclusive. The idea, that one can only experience a love relationship with one person, cannot be found in the Bible. Monogamy, bigamy (i.e., bigyny) and polygamy (i.e., polygyny) appear in the Old Testament in various forms of marriage, but on a par with each other.

Are simultaneous love-relationships equal in power and value? It seems to me, that one cannot avoid considering the structure of primary and secondary relationships, if one wishes to define inexclusive sexual fidelity. One relation will be the central, most important one of the two (or more). The other contact or contacts are a complement to the first. The primary partner is owed the highest grade of fidelity. However, the secondary relationships must also have their place ethically. But the commitment is less far-reaching here. Usually, one is pledged to the primary partner living together in the same house, or as mother or father of the children. This calls for a much stronger emotional and more temporal commitment, than mere friendship to another person.

In this light fidelity has to be defined in positive, not negative terms. Exclusivity is a negative term, it defines what is not done. Decisive for fidelity is, however, what is done. Fidelity means: long-lasting devotion, participation and concern for the well-being of the partner, continuous frankness and honesty, also in painful situations. Looked at in this way infidelity can be described as: neglect, lack of interest, concealment or even deception, verbally or through silence. It is not unthinkable, that under this definition of fidelity an occasional intimate relationship to another person can be agreed upon. This is indeed even put into practice by many people. Since the partner knows about it, it is not a deceitful escapade. If it poses a complement to the primary relationship, the second relation does not cause a breach of fidelity. No one can fulfill all his partner's needs. The secondary relationship would be a breach of fidelity, if it should threaten or destroy the primary one.

This way of life is often criticized, because one should not expect to be able to fulfill all one's needs. The demand for this can indeed be very egocentric, immature and inconsiderate. Self-denial is necessary in every true relationship. There are however some basic needs, the fulfillment of which can be beneficial not only to the persons concerned, but also to the primary partnership.

ATTEMPTS AT A SOLUTION

Christian ethics do not offer any concrete solutions here either. The commandment of the Lord, "Love your neighbor as yourself" cannot be regarded to point into one particular direction. This has a deep meaning. People must discover together the true meaning of following the path of love. They cannot dictate it to each other. God's commandments do not give us the power to force or to manipulate our partners, they point out the common participation, in which we can take the right steps. It is no loss, that Christian ethics do not give clear orders. It is a poverty which is both humble and creative, and which, through its freedom, makes love possible.

But God's commandment has surely also a clear profile. I understand joy and sexuality as reflections of God's glory. God affirms our need for love in body and soul, and he regulates it. His glory is no inconsiderate glory, it does not harm us, it saves us. It is faithful. God's commandment requires us to be faithful partners in our intensive relationships.

He who identifies faithfulness with exclusivity will naturally condemn the homosexual relationship of a married man or woman. But faithfulness and exclusivity are not the same thing. Faithfulness is recognizable in lasting devotion, in sympathy and care, in understanding and in loving constancy. Faithfulness is positive and active, whereas exclusivity is negative. It renounces activity. Looking at this difference, the homosexual relationship of a married person can be seen as acceptable for Christian ethics. This does not mean, that all such relationships are automatically acceptable, but neither are they on principle out of the question. The decisive question concerns faithfulness. Which form this takes, or should take, can be decided upon only by the partners in question. Christian ethics cannot dictate concrete solutions.

The problem of the combination of marriage and homosexuality can thus be solved in different ways. There are, however, good solutions, better and bad ones.

1. Divorce

A homosexual relationship in marriage can result in the partner seeking divorce. At times this is the only solution, especially when this partner discovers, that he or she cannot tolerate the presence of another intimate relationship on the side of the marriage partner. Legally the suing partner is today "in the right," if the other partner has sexual relationships outside the marriage. There is, however, no longer such a definite difference made in marriage counselling between "guilty" and "not guilty." Even the courts to-day are no longer unanimous in the question of homosexuality being a valid cause of adultery. A far more human and considerate discussion can take place, if one concentrates on one's own wishes, and forgets all the usual moral points-of-view. I think that every person has the right to denounce faithfulness to his/her partner, if the partner behaves in such a way that is insupportable to him/her.

2. Keeping Silent

Is silence also a solution? There are people who do not inform their partner at all about their homosexuality.

Who would presume to either propagate or condemn this solution? Silence can be loving and considerate, it can also be untruthful, misleading and cowardly. Generally speaking silence is inadvisable in such instances, because it excludes the other partner. I know people, who feel that readiness to inform their partner is a touchstone to their actions. What cannot be told, must be left undone. This approach impresses me greatly, although I do not believe, that it is possible to live this through in every case. But it is sure, that these people take their marriage relationship very seriously.

Such frankness does not always imply an immediate notification of the facts. Many people need a certain amount of time, before revealing themselves. An important point is the duration of the silence.

3. Denial

Deceit is an unkind solution. The person who denies the existence of a homosexual relationship pushes his marriage partnership to a large extent into the shadows. There is no promise here. A homosexual relation in itself does not necessarily mean unfaithfulness. Denying it does.

4. The New Couple

Finally, a person with strong leanings towards persons of his own sex can live, or continue to live, a fruitful and worthwhile marriage or similar relationship. There are couples today who are open from the very beginning, others becoming so during marriage, for a homosexual connection. Such couples do not fit in the conventional picture. They form the so-called "new couple." A book has been written about women, who have a love relationship with men who are either totally or at least partially homosexual. The book is called: *The New Couple*, by Rebecca Nahas and Myra Turley. With many examples the book challenges all prejudices against women and homosexual men not being able to experience a fulfilling love relationship together. Narrow-mindedness is not only to be found in heterosexuals. Homosexuals can be just as narrow-minded, when they are biased and feel that a heterosexual relationship cannot possibly bring them the happiness and fulfillment that they long for.

It is not surprising, that homosexual men often appeal to women. There is no feeling here of being regarded purely as a sex-object, as is often the case in the encounter with aggressive heterosexual men. The women questioned in *The New Couple* state consistently, that they have found homosexual men generally more considerate and sensitive. A man, who does not try to conceal his homosexuality, attracts women simply by the unusualness of his path through life. One woman said: "I can talk about everything with him, without any restrictions."

Women and homosexuals have to a certain degree a common tale of woe. They have both been ignored by society, laughed at and made use of. They are thus similarly characterized and have become emotionally united.

The term "New Couple" means the relationship between a heterosexual woman and a homosexual man. Both wish this relationship to be the primary one in their lives. However, this is not always understood as monogamous. Relations with other people are permitted, as long as these do not in any way affect the primary character of their partnership. This prototype reminds one strongly of the open marriage, as described by Nena and George O Neill.

The goal of the New Couple is to find an alternative to the conventional marriage. The New Couple does not want to present a facade of solid tradition. Its main aim is to form as sensible a partnership as possible. Sexual exclusivity, this bone of contention, disappears. It is neither wished for nor practiced by the New Couple.

Rebecca Nahas and Myra Tyler have established, that the women, who are happy living in such a relationship, have several things in common. Generally they are mature people, whose fulfillment in life does not depend solely on their marriage. Nor do they depend on their husbands for contentment in social and business affairs. They are not feminine in the customary sense, they do not play a conventional role. They feel that they are personally and professionally completely equal to men.

The chief problem for a New Couple is, of course, how to cope with jealousy. Only a very self-confident person can really overcome jealousy. These women are capable of this, otherwise a New Couple partnership would be unthinkable. Most of the women maintain, that it bothers them less, if their husbands are with men friends, than if they are with other women.

Women cannot give their husbands that which they receive from other men. This insight reduces the risk of jealousy. The knowledge too, that their husbands are not carrying on a homosexual relationship just to hurt them, helps them to accept this.

The husbands of these women do not regard their homosexuality as a problem or a burden. They just want to be themselves. Equally, they see no difficulty in also being able to bodily and emotionally love a woman. The New Couple gives them the opportunity to live with their different sexual inclinations, without having to give up their singularity or their loved ones. Until recently, men with homosexual tendencies had no other choice but to hide, or to exist exclusively in homosexual circles. The New Couple relationship offers a liberating alternative. Some men discontinue their homosexual relationships, once they have adjusted their New Couple way-of-living. Others continue with the friendship.

A New Couple partnership is rarely looked upon as life-long. Many reason that it will break up in time. However, one tries to continue it. I assume that the quota of divorce among traditional marriages makes the New Couple people look modest. Perhaps the new sort of relationships have more of a lasting chance, when they are not initially regarded as being indissoluble.

Of course the reverse situation, lesbian women and heterosexual men, also exists. This does not have quite the same characteristics, however. Although not much research as yet has been done, the following points are clear: Women generally discover their attraction to the same sex later on in life. They do not tolerate many partnerships, they seek a more subtle relationship. That women are often financially less well-off than men, is an important factor. If a woman just discovers her lesbian tendencies during marriage, this often leads to the marriage being threatened, for the same reasons as when a man starts to take his homosexual tendencies seriously. However, the exact opposite has also been established. Joan K. Dixon maintains on account of her inquiries, that for many women their marriages function better, also from the sexual point-of-view, after entering into a lesbian relationship.

It is still early days for the New Couple, not all problems are evident yet. How parentship survives during such an existence is still unknown, for example.

As long as public opinion condemns homosexuality, people concerned will continue to deceive not only the public, but themselves as well. This leads to catastrophic results for them, as well as for their families. The New Couple is an alternative which deserves the support of the churches, even though we should continue to consider the problems concerned.

REFERENCES

Baltensweiler, H. (1967). *Die Ehe im Neuen Testament. Exegetische Untersuchungen über Ehe, Ehelosigkeit und Ehescheidung.* Zurich.

Dixon, J.K. (1985). Sexuality and Relationship Changes in Married Females Following the Commencement of Bisexual Activity. In F. Klein & T.J. Wolf (Eds.). *Two Lives to Lead. Bisexuality in Men and Women.* New York.

Maddox, B. (1982). *Married and Gay. An Intimate Look at a Different Relationship.* New York.

Nahas, R., & Turley, M. (1979). *The New Couple: Women and Gay Man.* New York: Authors. German translation: (1983) München.

Wiedemann, H.G. (1982). *Homosexuelle Liebe. Für eine Neuorientierung in der christlichen Ethik.* Stuttgart.

IV. FLUIDITY OF SEXUAL IDENTITY

Can Seduction Make Straight Men Gay?

Herman Meijer

Nederland

SUMMARY. The article raises the question of changing sexual preference: Can a man whose past sexual practice has been almost exclusively heterosexual change his practice to homosexual after being seduced by another man? To those who believe that homosexual preference is homosexual *orientation*, an innate biological predisposition, the answer is a resounding "no." Contrary to this response, the author presents three cases in which the men switch from heterosexual to homosexual relationships (exclusively in two cases) by means of a sexual encounter initiated by another man. The author credits part of the change to the gay liberation movement which rescued homosexual desire from the hidden, forbidden, and shameful. The evidence that these men experienced a genuine change in sexual preference, shows that life-long, exclusive homosexuality, as articulated by gay rhetoric, is more a statement about the culture in which it occurs than the "essence" of homosexuality. The author concludes that putting the question of "What do I like?" before the question of "Who am I?" would allow more sexual freedom for those interested in crossing the line that divides sexual preferences.

Men do not become homosexual by seduction. This has been the conclusion of an almost one century old ongoing debate, which contributed to the abolition of Par. 248 bis in the Netherlands and of comparable legal restrictions of homosexual practice in other countries.

When bringing up the need of abolishing Par. 248 bis, which rendered punishable any "lewd acts" between majors (from 21 years on) and minors of the same sex, Mrs. Singer-Dekker said in the Dutch Parliament: "The Catholic psychiatrist Dr. Sengers lately advocated the abolition of this article. At the same time he did away with the idea, underlying this very article, that one could still make young people above the age of 16 homosexual . . . by seduction" (MvT, p. 8). Reading the Explanatory Memorandum which is quoted here makes it quite clear that at that time (1970) this vision was widely accepted. Nevertheless, the radical gay movement of the seventies made seduction a central issue, a strategy even, willing itself to be seductive, alluring, tempting and enticing.[1] It is not only the use of these words that characterizes this movement, but it is also the practice of seducing which can easily be described as successful.

The paradox might be solved by arguing that there are two ideas of seduction at stake and that it has never been the aim of the radical gay movement to make men (above the age of 16) homosexuals. I prefer to doubt both arguments and to let the paradox be. In this paradox the controversy of essentialism and constructivism is beautifully contained.

THE THEORY OF SEDUCTION

When, in 1911, the Catholic Minister of Justice, Regout, proposed to incorporate the new article, Par. 248 bis, in the Penal Law, which discriminated between hetero- and homosexual acts where minors were concerned, he felt urged to do so by the danger of contagion. When asked if a penal process according to the proposed provision would not cause great domestic grief, he answered: "Isn't it a domestic grief when a family father experiences that his eighteen or nineteen-year old son *has become* homosexual? And would this domestic grief not have been avoided if formerly an article as proposed by me now would have been incorporated in the Penal Law? In that case, perhaps many persons *would not be homosexuals* now. Should we permit this vice, which is increasing already anyhow, to expand still more?" (MvT p. 8, underl. HM).

The commission of the National Health Council (the so-called Commission-Speyer), which advised to the Minister nearly sixty years later the abolition of the article, concluded: "It is clear that the danger of seduction and the possibility that homosexual experiences might lead minors of 16 years and older to an enduring commitment to this form of sexual intercourse, has actually been the only motive for incorporating this penal provision in the law" (MvT, p. 8).

On the contrary, the commission, after having given a broad survey of the scientific views on the genesis of homosexuality, concluded unanimously: "Homosexuality occurs regularly in all times and among all peoples in a certain minority of the population. The conditions, innate and/or acquired, which give rise to the homosexual propensity, *generally* start to work in a very early stage of life, as a rule, already a long time before the start of puberty" (p. 14). Paying ample attention to "seduction," the commission stated: "From practice it is evident, . . . that from the sixteenth year on the sexual propensity has already developed so far that a youth who is heterosexual cannot be turned by 'seduction' into permanent homosexuality. They even stated: "When a youth appears to be homosexual after a homosexual approach, *one has to assume* that the youth was already emotionally in for this approach, that he had waited for it, as it were."

SEDUCTION IN GAY PRACTICE

"Only our homosexual struggle, only *gay pleasure*, can make straight men into queens too" (Mieli, 1977, p. 120).

Obviously, the radical gay movement, if it was not just playing, aimed at a change of the sexual constitution of society. It searched to provoke hidden erotic forces, especially sleeping, or latent, homosexual desire. "We homosexuals must liberate ourselves from the feeling of guilt . . . , so that homoeroticism spreads and 'catches on'. We have to make the water gush from the rock, to induce 'absolute' heterosexuals to grasp their own homosexuality" (Mieli, p. 120). This is not just some moral appeal outside of any practice. There is the practice of Fuori! as a context of this statement. And in this practice at least some experience exists as expressed in this passage: "The homosexual can lead the straight man into a relationship that is genuinely gay, and not a clumsy imitation of heterosexual fucking."

When "flaunting their deviant life style" radical gays did not only attract patented homosexuals, but also, curious boys and amused men willing to go one or two steps further. Radical gays learned to reckon and to play with these men and boys. Although it has never been systematically researched or quantified, there has been an impact of the movement on 'heterosexual' men which has changed their lifestyle either temporarily or lastingly.

As a voice 'from outside' testifies: "In gay radicalism I met a large stream of desire that disarmed and seduced me. Commuting between the narrow hetero-bed and the plush faggot couch I discovered how one can become one's own psychiatrist. As a fallen man, I had lost the tie with my own subconscious. As a faggot I was brought into a large subversive stream of desire. Gay radicalism as a unity of desiring and seducing subversity" (Nugteren, 1979).

SENGERS' TRIAD

As indicated by the first quotation in this paper the Catholic psychiatrist (and homosexual) Dr. W. J. Sengers played a large role in clearing of the debate on homosexuality. The argument of his influential dissertation, "Homosexuality as a Complaint," is that the first aim of treatment of homosexual patients should be their self-acceptance as homosexuals. It is in this context that much importance is being laid upon the "propensity" of people: "In the case of each patient seeking a medical consultation on account of any type of homosexual problem, priority must be given to the diagnosis of the propensity: homophilia, heterophilia, biphilia, or, in the absence of these, aphilia. This diagnosis can only be arrived at with the aid of the triad of sexual attraction, sexual fantasies and sexual dreams; at present these three form the only decisive criteria, the dreams having the validity of an absolute indicator. And accordingly a "homophile" he calls " . . . any man or woman if he or she feels attracted towards members of the same sex, fantasizes about members of the same sex when masturbating and dreams about members of the same sex when having a nightly orgasm."

Did Sengers invent the 'essence' of homosexuality, when establishing his propensity-triad, thus (re)constructing the genuine homophile? Did he find the unalienable or even unchangeable core?

Let us consider some limitations. First, the book and the method is built around psychiatric *patients*. Second, the aim of the book is to defend that people should be able to live the life they are led to live by their propensity. Third, regarding sexual *attraction* Sengers is quite conscious of possible and actual changes. Regarding sexual fantasies he states "their character (thinking of one sex) to be *mostly* constant" and regarding sexual dreams he states, "that does not exclude, though, that homosexual dreams can become, in a further development of the personality, hetero-sexual ones and vice versa" (p. 52).

THREE LATE CONVERSIONS

To test my doubts about the unchangeabilty of people's sexual propensity I interviewed three men whom I knew to have changed their sexual habits from hetero (or mainly hetero) sexual into homo (or mainly homo) sexual. I was curious about the conditions under which the change occurred and how far it reached concerning their 'propensity'. Therefore, both the influence of the (radical) gay movement and the character of the triad have been taken into consideration.

Case 1

D. is a 31-year old man (born 1955) with a technical education. He comes from a nuclear family, the second of four children.

During his school period he never engaged in courtship. Girls were divided into "reachable" and "unreachable." The first were the self-conscious and beautiful girls with whom he thought himself to be hopeless in making advances. The second were the "nice" girls, the approach of whom was impeded by the "threat of keeping company." Keeping company meant to him something oppressing, a ritual of unwritten rules and steadiness. He describes himself during that time as being "shy."

His relationship with boys was non-erotic. He does remember some boys' bodies from athletic activities, but he cannot recall these to have had any special attraction to him at that time.

He did not have sexual fantasies, he did not jerk off.

He did have wet *dreams*. In these, the "unreachable" girls played a central part. As far as he remembers, the dreams had their climax when these girls approached within his reach.

This situation continued when he left home for the first two years of his study. Eventually, he joined a progressive students' movement in '76, where he met like-minded women, and a conscious erotic development arose. Feelings of love and erections in the proximity of women followed. In the beginning of '77 his first sexual contact took place, at her initiative, with the woman whom he would live with from '78 till '81.

After discussions on sex in a men's counselling group, he discovered the pleasure of satisfying himself.

Erotic dreams and masturbation fantasies (if present) in this period were about women. But, when one of his friends became involved in the radical gay movement and developed a corresponding practice, he realized that he felt physically attracted to him. He can remember a dream from that time, in which he fucked the friend. Except for an attempt on the behalf of D. when on holiday with this friend, who at that moment did not feel like having sexual intercourse (May '82), nothing happened which would lead to a change in sexual orientation.

When one day, in February '83, he decided to pass the night in the town where he worked, one of the inhabitants, a gay colleague, paid a lot of attention to him, touching him gently and finally inviting him into his bed. He let himself be seduced. They made love and awoke as lovers. Then a relationship began which lasted until now. In the interview (Feb.'87) D. states that from that time on his relations with men have changed. He has become more sensitive to their attractiveness (or the opposite) and to the way he attracts them, actively, if he chooses.

In his fantasies, when masturbating, "vulgar females" still play a part as exciters of lust, which he himself attributes to a "lack of (male) images." It is evident now that exciting pictures of men can have this function too. Furthermore, he has fantasies of a whirl of pricks and hands.

Erotic dreams (no wet dreams anymore) are filled mainly with men he knows pleasantly sharing his bed. Occasionally vulgar females appear.

D. says that his "gay project" has been, and still is, above all things, about the development of his own feelings of lust and about the discovery of the exciting possibilities of the male body.

Case 2

W. is a 33-year old man (born 1954) with an academic education. He comes from a nuclear family, the eldest of seven children.

His earliest erotic memories go back to primary school: the pleasure of sleeping spoonlike with his younger brother, petting with his two younger sisters and the excitement of changing of clothes with friends at the swimming pool.

An important memory dates from his twelfth year: a friend and his twin brother were staying at his home and slept in the living room. When he came downstairs, early in the morning, he nestled down between them. His father, catching him there, took him out angrily.

From his time in secondary school he remembers an equally strong attraction towards boys and girls, though he had noticed (see above) that sex with boys was forbidden. Close dancing was nice and so was look-ing at the beautiful boys whom school girls had brought to the dance. He engaged in taking girls home, french kissing and touching tits. When he was seventeen he had a girl friend who excited him, but she broke off their relationship. From this early period he remembers a wet dream–something about flying and landing. It had been the first and the last time he had such a dream. From the age of twelve on, he used to jerk off, always on the toilet. He did not fantasize when masturbating. During this time he remembers that he was aroused by a picture of a soldier in a shirt, legs naked, but also by passages of books picturing straight sex.

Once away from home (1973) the "real work" was to begin, he thought, with girls. He made love with several women and had some relationships, the longest lasting for more than a year. In December '76 he made love for the first time with a young man, not too intensely, but enough to make him write in his diary: "I am probably bisexual." This incidental contact lasted until March '77. In January '77 he wrote in his diary: "An avowed homophile I am certainly not, fucking with boys doesn't attract me at all."

In June '77 an attractive bisexual young man invited him into his bed and he entered into it. They made love. In his diary he then began to raise doubts about his 'bi'-construction. This experience, however, was opposed by another, when he, shortly after that, fucked with a woman for the first time and then another during the same month.

April '78 he attended Pink Saturday in Roermond, where, as he states himself, his fascination with "bold gayness" begins. Stimulated by the ambiance he was attracted by a beautiful boy who enticed him. They hugged and made love in the big tent. His old images of gay people vanished. In December '79, after having joined a workshop of gay col-leagues, he wrote in his diary that he finally had the urge to cut the knot. While attending a gay and lesbian party in March 1980, he met a guy he fell in love with, whom it was good making love to and who would show him the way in the gay world. He started calling himself "faggot" and was amused by going to work with make-up.

When W. looks back at this development he is astonished at the long drudging period (Dec.'76 - Dec.'79). Because he could never recall his dreams, it is hard to retrace whether the apparently straight period ('73 - end '79) had any indications in another direction. So far as he remembers his sporadic sexual fantasies were about women.

Case 3

V. is a 36-year old man (born 1950). Originally he was an industrial mechanic, since then he has been a full-time political activist for 11 years. He comes from a nuclear family, the first of nine children.

His earliest sexual memory goes back to his second year of secondary school–sex games with a boy friend and a girl together, initiated by himself and the other boy.

Having started with jerking off shortly after primary school, he remembers having had accompanying fantasies about girls until his seventeenth year. Then fantasies arose about a boy he met daily at the factory.

From his seventeenth year ('67) on, he had relationships with girls lasting several months on the average. With one exception, it was he who stopped, because the relationships oppressed him. For twelve years (until '79) he had similar short-lasting relationships with women, alternated with years without relations. During his solosex periods women alternated with men in his fantasies, equally to what he set his eyes upon in the street.

In '79 he fell in love with a woman with whom he developed a relationship which lasted till '83. Also in that period (by fits and starts) he had thoughts of undertaking something with guys, thoughts which he also consciously–suppressed, because of his social environment.

Whether the alternation of attraction towards women and men was also expressed in his dreams, V. cannot tell, because he cannot recall their contents.

In September '82 something decisive happened. At a political training weekend organized by gay activists, on the question "Is heterosexuality natural?" it became clear to him that the question was not being either straight or gay. But, as he says himself: " . . . that I could make love with guys and yet remain a common person." His fear that making love with guys would mean belonging with the queens and not with others disappeared. So he started to look for men more consciously. Some months after this weekend he was easily seduced by a guy and they made love twice. Then the man broke off, this being a disappointment to V. For some time nothing of this kind happened, except when V. made up his mind to undertake something with a man who attracted him. This intention was interrupted by relationships he entered into, almost simultaneously, with three women (around May '83). Though he enjoyed making love, things became too complicated and finally he put it to an end.

In May '85 he developed a relationship with a fellow he had been longing for. This relationship continues now (Feb. '87).

V. believes himself to be where he belongs. If this relationship were to end, he would want to be with a man. He does not need to call himself 'gay', but "men do excite me more." Attraction and fantasies are correspondingly towards and about men.

SOME EVIDENCE IN THE CASES

These three cases refer to adult men who, after coming out of their adolescence, would have been superficially classified as heterosexuals. At the ages of 27, 26 and 35 they live a life that would be classified as "homosexual with one heterosexual relationship" or perhaps as "bisexual" (case 1), or as "homosexual"(cases 2 and 3).

The radical gay movement and/or radical gays in person, contributed to the changes involved in all three cases. They did so by being seductive on the one hand, appealing to bodily lust, sense of freedom, nonconformism (especially cases 1 and 2), and on the other hand liberating from sexual schematics (especially case 3). It may be a hypothetical question, but without the public presence of a gay movement would D., W. and V. have reached any form of gay life by now? It is worth asking. At least one might say that none of the three had strong enough internal impulses to develop a gay practice without external gay stimuli. Or, to reply to the initial question of "can men become homosexual by seduction," one might say, in referring to these men at least "They do not become homosexual *without* seduction." In the lives of W. and V. one can indicate entire periods in time in which a consequent heterosexualisation might have been successful as well. In the case of D. such a hypothesis is more difficult to raise, but in the supposed absence of sexual alternatives one might draw like conclusions.

Far from hypothetical are the changes that were actually made. So, if the only question would be: can men change from one sexual practice to another (e.g., from straight to gay), being seduced to do so, the answer would simply be yes–these cases being accepted as evidence. To be exact, one might discern between a "contextual seduction," produced by the gay movement and a direct one, produced by gay persons.

But, the concept of propensity being given, one should ask: didn't these men have, from childhood on, a propensity which would lead them, conditions given, necessarily towards any type of homosexual activity? In the cases of W. and V. their earliest memories testify to a physical attraction to both sexes. In the case of D. a physical attraction to females alone exists until the time of change. Regarding the sexual fantasies in the case of W., they are either absent or about women until his time of change. In the case of V. they are about men or women. In the case of D. they are either absent or about women until his time of change. Regarding wet or erotic dreams, neither W. nor V. remembers their content, except the first one of W. which had no specific sexual content. D. does remember his dreams and is positive that their content until his time of change was about women.

Looking back from the changes actually made one concludes that:

- the propensity did not unequivocally indicate a future homosexuality (2 and 3) or did indicate the opposite, i.e., a future heterosexuality
- the propensity may develop in adulthood when taken out of an unequivocally heterosexual environment
- the propensity can change in interaction with a gay sexual practice, even from a "heterophile" one into a dominatingly "homophile" one (case 1).

CONCLUSIONS

When dealing with seduction in 1970 and in 1980 there are at least two different environments involved. It is quite obvious that the argument of the Commission followed a practice in which, socially spoken, homosexual behavior was still abnormal. So seducing into homosexuality meant a leading into abnormality. Anyone who still had the possibility to pass for a straight man, would grasp the chance. It is not so difficult then, to find those famous 5 percent whose behavior and propensity were congruent. Therefore, Tolsma's statement of "permanent homosexuality occurs in our culture only among individuals disposed to it" is indeed a statement about 'our culture'.

Our three cases, of course, do not represent a totally different culture, but a different atmosphere concerning homosexual behavior within a certain subculture. In this atmosphere being seduced to homosexual behavior was not seen as being led into abnormality, but out of normality–a normality which was not necessarily regarded as positive. In case 1 and 2 the enticement of homosexuality was part of the attractiveness of a nonconformist movement.

In case 3 it was the disconnection of acting and being, brought to mind by a movement which proposed homosexual behavior as merely a male possibility–and not an ontological category,–which set free a seduction which had already been.

In these three cases it is obvious that the radical gay movement has been a co-creator of sexual identity. Its influence is manifest at three levels:

- in stimulating love making with men,
- in the terms of self-consciousness, be it as a 'non-heterosexual', a 'post-heterosexual' or 'exceptional' (case 1), be it as a 'faggot' (case 2), be it as 'of no importance' (case 3),
- in the further development of the propensity by the contacts, the images and other stimuli it produces.

By connotating homosexuality with openness to sex, promiscuity and gayness the movement seduced especially those who felt oppressed by normal relationships.

When accepting the homophile propensity and even ontologizing it to a permanent disposition, the gay movement of the sixties and early seventies was, of course, also co-creating sexual identities. By that time it was opportune to postulate–even 'prove'–an innate and/or acquired homophile propensity, at least to safeguard those 5% of the population from curing attempts, discriminatory laws and actual persecution. In this respect the movement has been successful and seems to remain so even in these days of AIDS backlash.

Yet the grass is hiding a snake–the identification of homosexual behavior and homosexual people and, therefore, the elimination of border-passing seduction. The effect of the dominance of propensity-thinking on minors tends to put forth the question "What am I?" before the question "What do I like?" Thus at an even earlier stage people are divided into 'pure' kinds. The effect of the victory of propensity-thinking over seduction-thinking might have been that normal men let themselves be seduced easily, because they believe they cannot become homosexual by seduction. Actually they usually do the opposite, using the argument 'they are not gay' in order to not have themselves seduced.

A gay movement which sticks to propensity-thinking for the matter of self-defence may damage another vital interest, sexual mobility through ages, sexes and classes. Ironically enough, the Speyer-commission, on the basis of a firm belief in early fixed propensities, gives an advice that goes beyond what most gay movements today dare to plead:

> A society which would eliminate all situations of seduction as much as possible, does certainly not benefit public mental health. On the contrary, for youngsters of both sexes it is desirable that they meet with such situations. For a normal development a large possibility of getting acquainted, experimenting, contact and initiation is necessary. (MvT, pg. 14)

NOTE

1. "radical gay movement": "flikkerbeweging," which is poorly translated as "faggots' movement," "flikkerij" ("faggotry") being a whole of life style, sex and subversity.

BIBLIOGRAPHY

Mieli, Mario: "Homosexuality and Liberation, elements of a gay critique"; Gay Men's Press, London, 1980.

Memorie van Toelichting (MvT) in Handelingen der Staten Generaal, zitting 1969-1970, nr. 10347 (this is the explanatory memorandum re abolition art. 248 bis).

Nugteren, Hans: in Marge, jrg. 3/1, 1979, "Ketenen verliezen en valstrikken spannen."

Sengers, Dr. W.J.: "Homoseksualiteit als Klacht, een psychiatrische studie," uitg. Paul Brand, Bussum, 1969.

The Freudian Construction of Sexuality: The Gay Foundations of Heterosexuality and Straight Homophobia

Eric de Kuyper, PhD

Netherlands Film Museum

SUMMARY. In developing his theory of male sexual preference, Freud asserted that heterosexual as well as homosexual preferences required explanation, that neither could be assumed to be innate. His theory of the oedipal complex, however, held that the heterosexual outcome was the "normal" resolution, while the homosexual outcome represented arrested sexual development. In the normal resolution the boy identifies as a male with the father, gives up the mother as a love object, and later substitutes another woman of his choice for the mother. The author of the following article, following the theorizing of Laplanche, claims that there is an unavoidable homosexual component or residue in the heterosexual resolution which is implicit in Freudian theory. In the resolution of the complex the boy has the choice of both parents as love objects or as persons with whom to identify. In the heterosexual resolution the boy identifies with the father as a rival for the mother's affection. But love and identification are not entirely discrete processes. The identification with the father involves love for the father. The heterosexual resolution of the oedipal conflict is bought at the price of the homosexual resolution which, however, is not completely surrendered. The homophobia of heterosexual males, the author asserts, is the result of the remnants of homosexuality in the heterosexual resolution of the oedipal conflict.

Eric de Kuyper was Deputy Director of the Netherlands Film Museum. Before that time he taught at the University of Nijmegen and was chairman of the film department (Film en Opvoeringskunsten). He is now a full-time writer. Correspondence may be addressed to his publisher: SUN, Bijleveldsingel 9, 6500 VB Nijmegen, The Netherlands.

We are told that the male population is divided into two unequal parts, a heterosexual majority of 95% and a homosexual minority of 5%. What I would like to bring to your attention is how in classical Freudian theory homosexuality is not only an "accident"–an empirical fact limited to a minority–but also (in contrast to this theory) a fundamental aspect of heterosexuality. More precisely I will look at how homosexual components are not only important, but decisive in the making of the so-called heterosexual position.

In saying this, I also imply that this society, with its values, standards, etc., what we usually call 'culture', is based on homosexuality. This may seem rather scandalous, for we know how much 'normal heterosexuals' have a problem in accepting not only the homosexual minority, but in accepting homosexuality in themselves.

Thus we will see that homosexuality and homosexual feelings are fundamental components of the process of sexual differentiation through creating the homosexual in the child and constructing masculinity. We also see that not only is this not accepted: it is *negated* (Verneint). To set this negation out with more efficiency, it is followed by the creation, the projection of a minority: the homosexual male, the specialized, 'professional' homosexual. The majority is able to say: "Not we or me, but *them!*"

This aspect of the problem–the mechanism of projection with the homosexual as 'official' . *bad object* (in the sense that Melanie Klein has used the word) for the heterosexual society is not the main purpose of my article but is considered a given throughout this work.

What interests me more is to have another look at Freudian theory. It is amazing to see how the idea of homosexuality as a constitutional element in the construction of the 'normal' heterosexual is fundamental to the core of Freudian theory, specifically in the working of the Oedipus-complex. Freud himself never really explored the consequences of his findings in this particular way. However, when we find an insistence on the questions of homosexuality in the work of Freud especially in the implicit passages where homosexuality, one could say, plays a part as 'leitmotif' (passages which are not officially referred to, e.g., in the lexicon under 'homosexual' or 'homosexuality') it may have something to do with the homosexual dimension of the Oedipus-complex as seen from the heterosexual point of view.

I will use the writings of J. Laplanche as a guide in which we can find a recurrent emphasis on this peculiar theme, the paradoxicality in the Oedipus-complex where what is normal is constructed, and can only be constructed on the abnormality of homosexuality.[1] But neither has Laplanche made use of his findings which can hardly be called discoveries, because his approach of Freud's work verges on 'close reading'. What is 'new' in the case of Laplanche is that he has made the paradox more explicit and that he has exposed it as just another of the many contradictions which lie in the sexual differentiation process. The failure of Laplanche to sketch out the consequences connected with the homosexuality of heterosexuality leaves those interested more specifically in the homosexual problems room to analyze the matter further.

I will limit this discussion of the Oedipus-complex to the male side. I'm sure that working out the female side will lead to more or less the same conclusion (that is: the importance of female homosexuality in constituting the female heterosexual position) and that this would not be difficult to do. We must, however, bear in mind that there is no such thing as symmetry between the male and female problem, between the male and the female process of dealing with the Oedipus-complex.[2]

Let us first summarize the Oedipus-complex, as analyzed by Freud[3] and provided with commentary by Laplanche.[4] The description of the Oedipus-complex starts the child just before it comes out into the open, at its dawn, when it is no longer in its pre-history. Here we have a double relationship surrounding the child, putting the child in relation with three poles (not necessary a triangular one, adds Laplanche!):

> At a very early age the little boy develops an object-cathexis for his mother, which originally related to the mother's breast and is the prototype of an object-choice on the anaclitic model; the boy deals with his father by identifying himself with him.[5]

Next, we enter the field of sexual differentiation.

Freud, as we know, differentiated between a positive and a negative side of the Oedipus-complex. The positive side is the classical love-relation with the mother; the negative side is the rivalry-relation with the father. This means that the relation to the father, preceding the identification, has become a matter of rivalry and is marked by ambivalence:

> His identification with his father then takes on a hostile colouring and changes into a wish to get rid of his father in order to take his place with his mother. Henceforward his relation to his father is ambivalent; it seems as if the ambivalence inherent in the identification from the beginning had become manifest.[6]

The destruction of the Oedipus-complex is connected with the castration problem.[7] The love for the mother must be given up. Two solutions, two ways of coming out of this dead end seem possible: an identification with the mother, or a renewed, reinforced identification with the father.[8]

The identification with the mother is not considered normal.[9]

The normal, reinforced identification with a father poses a problem, because it now becomes an identification, not with a love-object, but with a *rival*. The menace of castration creates a conflict that consists of the love for the mother on the one hand and the destruction of the rival, the father, on the other hand. This is resolved by a contract implying a time factor: a promise that later . . . when one is grown up, things will be settled in the best possible way. Let me add that this contract emphasizes the 'historical' aspects of the Oedipus-complex (it is an infantile sexual theory, and thus part of 'life') as well as the generational aspects of it, which are sometimes ignored in the discussion of the Oedipus-complex.[10]

But let me return briefly to the normal way of identification with the father as the rival and observe that for the boy of whom we are speaking this is an identification with the same gender.[11] It is necessarily a love-relation or it would not be possible to have identification at all "love" is, as we know a specific variety of identification): here it is a relation to the *same sex, a homosexual relation.*

Let us pause before going on with the negative Oedipus-complex which Freud presents as a *kind* of solution for the problem occurring by the introduction of the homosexual tendency, and let us stress the importance of this homosexual relation, a relation to the same sex, for what will soon become a heterosexual positioning. The relationship with another man (in this case the father) is not only tolerated, but strongly enforced by the menace of castration, creating a tension between the original love-object–which is now strongly 'forbidden territory'–and the new love-object, 'you have to love your father, your rival, otherwise . . . ' How can one call this identification with a being of the same sex who has to be loved anything but 'homosexual'; even if we do not yet consider it as a positional choice that will occur during the process of sexual differentiation?

This remarkable phase has been modified by Freud so that the edges have been blunted somewhat. He introduces a more complete Oedipus-complex in which the positive aspects are complemented by negative aspects (this includes bringing up the question of bisexuality).[12] This smoothing out has a very ambiguous result however because it does not obliterate, but rather emphasizes the role of homosexuality or at least an homosexual coupling for the heterosexual male throughout the Oedipal system!

This is how Freud introduces the negative Oedipus-complex:

> For one gets an impression that the simple Oedipus complex is by
> no means its commonest form, but rather represents a simplification
> or schematization which, to be sure, is often enough justified for
> practical purposes. Closer study usually discloses the more complete
> Oedipus complex, which is twofold, positive and negative, and is
> due to the bisexuality originally present in children: that is to say,
> a boy has not merely an ambivalent attitude towards his father and
> an affectionate object-choice towards his mother, but at the same
> time he also behaves like a girl and displays an affectionate femi-
> nine attitude to his father and a corresponding jealousy and hostility
> towards his mother.[13]

In this more complete Oedipus-complex there are four vectors for the
boy: a positive and negative tendency towards the father and a positive
and negative tendency towards the mother. With this set the positioning
takes place and results in a sexual choice. Choice means here that a com-
promise is made between different possibilities stressing one position as
more adequate. The 'choice' has been made, so it seems now, between
a male or female love-object.

What should interest us in this 'normal heterosexual' choice is the
identification to the parent of the same gender. This identification is twice
as strong because it has to be there already as a preliminary basis for a
positioning towards the woman as love-object.

There is some contradiction here, which is very remarkable and is
formulated thus by Laplanche:

> The normative identification (in the sense Freud uses the term
> 'normal': according to the biological sex and what is socially con-
> sidered as normal) has the homosexual choice of love-object as a
> driving force. On the contrary the identification leading to homo-
> sexuality has its origins in a very positive [= heterosexual] rela-
> tion.[14]

The question here–restricted to the heterosexual choice–is, what are
the components of the oedipal complex that are left over in adult life? I
shall not answer that difficult question here, but will narrow it down by
saying the Oedipus-complex is not the literal model for ulterior attachments, although there must be some traces left, a distortion (Entstellung)
as it is called in Freudian theory.

What seems to be very strong is the importance of the homosexual identification in the constitution and construction of heterosexual positioning.

What is also very clear is a strong emphasis on the factors of ambiguity in the ego and the superego (and we do not need the theories on bisexuality to make such a statement). In this field everything is marked not as much by ambiguity, as by contradictory forces: to be or not be as the father; to give up the mother, but still love her; to be able to receive the woman not now, but later. This is not a very consistent system, and it is no mere coincidence that, from a different angle, Lévi-Strauss considers Myth in terms of specific ways of 'solving' contradictions and developing conjunctions on the underlying disjunctions, which may be effective in the social field.

Taking all this into consideration, what interests us here is why, with this 'history' behind him, the heterosexual male is fundamentally homophobic in both an explicit and an implicit way. Of course, one should not forget that he is surrounded by the homosexual theme in himself–the core pattern of his heterosexuality!–and in the menace coming from others who have chosen the identification with the mother and a different relation to the father. The 'other' is in himself and around him.

In some way this homophobia has to do with frustration, with a sort of envy present in *both* sexes–the impossibility of being at the same time the other gender as well of being 'total'. The female side of this problem is well known as 'penis envy': the male side focuses on rivalry (aggressiveness and attraction, based on comparison) between subjects of the same gender.

As J.B. Pontalis has remarked, "there is an evident correspondence between the two themes, between the refusal (Ablehnung) of the feminine, on the male side, and the revendication of the masculine on the female side."[15] To this he adds, quoting Freud:

> Something that both sexes have in common is, through the difference of the sexes, molded into another form of expression.[16]

It is what Freud calls "Ablehnung der Weiblichkeit" and proposes that it replace the Adlerian "maennlicher Protest." This "refusal of the feminine" is strangely enough considered by Freud as:

> biological fact, a piece of that great riddle of sexuality.[17]

How strange indeed that Freud in this late text (1937) refers to the biological, mysterious aspects of this "Ablehnung," something he does not need and does not consider for the equivalent ("für beiden Geschlechtern gemeinsam!"") on the female side.

In a footnote Freud adds that there is a fear of passivity, not towards woman, but towards other males; this is what he refers to under "Ablehnung der Weiblichkeit." It is indeed something else to which Freud refers here than to the Adlerian "maennlicher Protest," which is another side of the castration fear.

One should notice also that there is resentment towards the father (the other male[s]) for obliging the male subject to have a homosexual identification.

With these few remarks I have wanted to open up this field of homosexual research: I have done this by looking for the homosexual in the heterosexual and by establishing that in addition to a 'sublimated homosexual' (in Dutch: een gesublimeerde nicht, a 'would be' homosexual) there is also a 'sublimated heterosexual'!

NOTES

1. More specifically: Laplanche, J. (1980). See also: Laplanche, J. et Pontalis, J.B. (1967).

2. Assoun, P.L. (1983).

3. Freud, S. (1923/1961), p. 31.

4. Laplanche, J., op. cit. pp. 337-338.

5. Freud, S., op. cit. p. 31.

6. Freud, S., op. cit. p. 32.

7. Freud, S. (1924), pp. 397.

8. We leave out the first solution as this has much to do with the actual homosexual position as such. We are dealing here, as I have said, with the homosexual components in heterosexuality, not with the question of the homosexual position.

9. Freud, S. (1923/1961), p. 32.

10. The latter aspects are regularly discussed in the works of Laplanche. See also: Green, A. (1983).

11. See note 9.

12. In many ways the theme of bisexuality functions as an "illusion that there is such securing and evident thing as symmetry," Fédida, P. (1973) p. 159. The different articles in this number of the *Nouvelle Revue de Psychanalyse* all stress the 'myth'-aspects of 'bisexuality theories'.

13. Freud, S., op. cit., p. 33.

14. Laplanche J., op.cit., p.345 (my translation).

15. Pontalis, J.B. (1977) (my translation).

16. Freud, S. (1937), p. 97.

17. ibid. p. 99.

18. This theme (the homosexuality of heterosexuality) is of course present in feminist theories, e.g., Irigaray, L. and Gallop, J., but, understandably, from a different point of view, as 'the effects of it on the female side'. The theme is also present in the perspective of Laplanche, e.g.: Safouan, M. (1974) p. 46 and especially of Green, A. (1983): "Desire is maintained only through the identification with the separating pole. The binding with the object of desire is maintained and coexists through the conjunction with the interposed person as rival" (p. 93). For a more 'deviant' feminist view on the subject, stressing the ambiguous role of the mother, see: Oliver, C. (1980).

REFERENCES

Laplanche, J. (1980). *Problematiques I*. Paris: Presses Universitaires de France.

Laplanche, J., Pontalis, J.B. (1967). *Vocabulaire de la Psychanalyse*. Paris: Presses Universitaires de France.

Assoun, P.L. (1983). *Freud et la Femme*. Paris: Calmann-Levy.

Freud, S. (1961). The ego and the id. In J. Strachey (Ed. and Trans.), *The standard edition of the complete psychological works of Sigmund Freud* (Vol. 19, pp. 3-66). London: Hogarth Press. (Original work published 1923).

Freud, S. (1924). Der Untergang des Oedipuskomplexes. *Gesammelte Werke XIII*, pp. 393-402.

Freud, S. (1937). Die endliche und unendliche Analyse. *Gesammelte Werke XVI*, pp. 57-99.

Green, A. (1983). Atome de parente et relations oedipiennes. In C. Levi-Strauss. *L'Identité*. Paris: Presses Universitaires de France.

Pontalis, J.B. (1977). *Entre le Rêve et la Douleur*. Paris: Gallimard.

Safouan, M. (1974). *Etudes sur l'Oedipe*. Paris: Seuil.

Olivier, C. (1980). *Les Enfants de Jocaste*. Paris: Denoel-Gonthier.

V. GAY AND LESBIAN IDENTITIES IN THE THIRD WORLD

Mati-ism and Black Lesbianism: Two Idealtypical Expressions of Female Homosexuality in Black Communities of the Diaspora

Gloria Wekker, PhD

Oberlin College

SUMMARY. There are different ways in which black women in the Diaspora have given expression to their erotic fascination with other women. In this article two idealtypical expressions of black female homosexuality and the outlines of their underlying cosmologics are sketched: *mati-ism* and *black lesbianism*. Mati (or matisma) is the Sranan Tongo word for women who have sexual relations with other women, but who typically also will have had or still have relationships with men, simultaneously. More often than not they will also have children.

While both types can only be understood via a constructionist view of homosexuality, the institution of *mati-ism* will be shown to have retained more Afrocentric, working class elements, while black lesbianism has more middle class, Eurocentric features.

Gloria Wekker, PhD, is (Visiting) Assistant Professor in Women's Studies at Oberlin College, Oberlin, OH. Correspondence may be addressed: Women's Studies Program, 31 Rice Hall, Oberlin College, Oberlin, OH 44074.

INTRODUCTION

In this article I want to focus on the experience of black women and the ways their erotic interest in those of their own gender have taken shape. I shall begin by giving a resume of the historical and social factors which enable us to think of the black female experience in the Diaspora as a unitary, though multifaceted, process. I shall then indicate that ideas about female homosexuality in black communities in the Diaspora are anything but uniform. By presenting a large excerpt from a public discussion with two black women poets, I hope to elucidate the contours of two idealtypical cosmologies as far as female homosexuality is concerned. I am assuming that their views are representative of those held by larger groups of women in black communities in the USA, Suriname and the Netherlands. These cosmologies may be indicated as *mati-ism* and *black lesbianism*.[1] My argument will make clear that both types can only be understood via a constructionist view of homosexuality.

YOU ARE THE OFFSPRING OF SLAVES

Black women of the Diaspora share a terrible history involving the slave trade based on Africa, a history of being transported like cattle across the Atlantic Ocean, of rootlessness in the "New" World, of centuries of living under a system of slavery, of various degrees of retention in their communities of African elements and after Abolition (Suriname 1863; USA 1865) of living in sexist and racist societies, based on class.[2]

Originating from West Africa, an area which stretches from Senegal to Angola and extending far into the interior, the slaves belonged to various tribes with hundreds of different languages and dialects, different systems of family relationships and many habits and customs. For centuries, slaves of both sexes in the Americas were forbidden to learn how to read and write and hardly had opportunities to develop their creative and artistic gifts. The list of prohibitions to which they were subjected was extensive: no marriages were permitted without the consent of their masters nor other relations among themselves, no control over children born to such relationships–the children were the property of the mother's owner, no right to own property or to wear shoes, and no protection against cruel and unreasonable treatment by the master-class.

For both the North American and the Surinamese slaves, one of the things which enabled them to maintain themselves in the new environment was their African culture, which they endeavored to keep intact in the given circumstances and which, in the unspeakable misery of their existence, gave them a sense of having something to which they belonged and which afforded them some foothold. In the days of slavery and later on, the role women played in preserving, communicating and developing elements of African culture was of inestimable importance. Recent scholarship indicates that the principal residue of the African cultural heritage in the Diaspora should be explored in the realm of social values and orientations to reality rather than in more or less concrete sociocultural forms (Mintz and Price 1976).

Important differences between the history of black women in the USA and that of black women in Suriname can be pointed to. Some of these differences had their effect on the degree to which retentions–especially orientations to reality–were able to continue almost unharmed. One of these differences concerns the ratio of blacks to whites that existed during a great part of the 18th and 19th centuries in the (former) British and Dutch colonies. In North America there was always a considerable numerical preponderance of whites over blacks. The ratio in 1780 was, for example, 15 to 1 (Price 1976). On the estates of the Surinamese colony, on the other hand, a handful of whites endeavored to exert control over an immense number of slaves. The ratio there ranged from 1 to 25 in the urban area, to 1 to 65 in the plantation districts further removed from the capitol (van Lier 1949).

It was partly due to this numerical relationship that a different cultural policy towards the slaves took shape in the two colonies. The British colonists succeeded in forbidding their slaves to speak their original African languages. As a result, black English with a grammar, a syntax and a lexicon of its own developed. In Suriname, on the other hand, slaves were left free to develop their own tongue, a creole called Negro English (now Sranan Tongo), for centuries. They were also allowed to elaborate and work out their own cultures. Government policy in the colony until Abolition and after, until 1876, was aimed at creating as wide as possible a geographical, cultural and psychological gap between the colonists and the slaves. The ban on speaking Dutch was only one of an endless series of ordinances designed with this view in end.

Generally speaking, the Surinamese slaves had more freedom than their North American partners in misfortune and for a longer period of time they were able to cultivate their languages and their ways of life and thought, as long as these did not conflict with the interests of the planter class. That the African constituent in the Surinamese orientation to reality must have been considerable for many centuries is emphasized by the fact that the importation of so-called "saltwater negroes" (i.e., slaves newly transported from Africa) was a continuing necessity until the official ban on the slave trade in 1808. In contrast to the situation in North America, where the capacity of female slaves to produce children was encouraged and in certain periods even subjected to coercion, the Surinamese planters preferred to force as much labor from the slaves as possible in the space of a few years. The maltreatment, undernourishment and murder of slaves repeatedly saw to it that within a few years the entire body of slaves could be "written off." Surinamese female slaves hardly reproduced. Whereas at the end of the U.S. Civil War there were 4 million blacks, the Surinamese census only counted 50,000 ex-slaves at the time of Abolition, while roughly the same number of slaves (350,000 to 400,000) had been imported over the course of the past two and a half centuries (Van Lier 1949). The world the slave owners created in Suriname was one which one left as soon as one could, with one's pockets loaded with money.

Despite the differences between North American and Surinamese history, the correspondences are so marked that one can speak of a unitary, though multi-faceted, experience of black women in the Diaspora.

CONSIDERING THE ROOTS, SURINAMESE STYLE

In describing the history of black women in the Diaspora I have made no distinction between the history of black women in general and "lesbian" women in particular. There are various reasons for this. First, black "lesbian" women have for the greater part of the time they have been in the Diaspora been an integral part of their communities; they were subject to the same orders and prohibitions as other women in these communities. Secondly–this is important as regards their position in their own circles–they often had simultaneous relationships with men and had children.

The earliest information about *mati-ism* in Suriname dates from the beginning of this century, 1912, and refers precisely to its being embedded in the culture of the ordinary Creole population. A.J. Schimmelpenninck van den Oye, a high ranking Dutch government official, remarks in a memorandum on the physical condition of the "underprivileged":

> Speaking about the physically weak condition of so many young women, in addition another reason should be mentioned. I am referring to the sexual communion between women themselves ("mati play"), which immorality has, as I gather, augmented much in the

past decades, and, alas!, penetrated deeply into popular customs. (–). It is not only that young girls and unattached women of various classes make themselves guilty of this, the poorest often going and living together in pairs to reduce the cost of house rent and food for each of them, but women who live with men, and even schoolgirls, do the same, following the example of others. (Ambacht 1912: 98-99)

Somewhat later, in the 1930s, mati culture had taken on such proportions that another reporter, Th. Comvalius, expressed his disturbance about:

the unusual relationships among women in Suriname, which were not dependent on social rank, intellectual development, race or country of origin. Love(?) brought women and young girls of very different walks of life together as intimate friends.(–)While this in itself(–)could be called a "sociological misconception," there is another, dark side to it, the discussion of which is no concern of ours. Probably it was blown over here from the French West Indies. (Comvalius n.d.: 11)

With hindsight, it is possible to state that the institution of mati relationships did not just fall down out of the blue sky. Linguistically, two explanations for the word "mati" are offered : one would trace it to old Dutch "maatje," meaning buddy, mate; the other one is more convincing and links it to Hausa "mata" or "mace": woman, wife. It is now known that in a number of West African regions from which slaves were taken, for example, Ashanti and Dahomey, that female homosexuality occurred in times long past and that it was not burdened with negative sanctions prohibiting it. The anthropologists Herskovits reported that in Dahomey a woman could formally marry another woman and that offspring born to the one woman were regarded as the children of the other woman (Herskovits, M. and F. Herskovits 1938/I). The women slaves who were carried off to the "New" World were therefore familiar with the phenomenon. Elsewhere it is stated about the Saramaka Maroons, the descendants of the runaway slaves who formed viable societies in the rainforests of Suriname from the 17th century on, that in Saramaka society:

Mati is a highly charged volitional relationship, usually between two men, that dates back to the Middle Passage–matis were originally "shipmates," those who had survived the journey out from

Africa together; (–)*Sibi* is a relationship of special friendship between two women. As with the mati relationship, the reciprocal term of address derives from the Middle Passage itself: sibi referred to shipmates, those who had experienced the trauma of enslavement and transport together. (Price, R. and S. Price 1991: 396, 407)

The word "sibi" does not occur with this meaning in Sranan Tongo, the coastal creole; here the term "mati" covers all modalities. It may very well be that, encapsulated in Sranan Tongo "mati," there may at one time also have been the notion of shipmates who had survived together, but at present that connotation is not there anymore.

Features of mati culture that are mentioned in older sources, have been preserved to this day. There were, for example, female couples who wore "parweri": the same dress, women who embroidered handkerchiefs with loving texts in silk for each other: "lobi kon" (love has come) and "lobi n'e prati" (love does not go away), women who courted each other by means of special ways of folding and wearing their *anyisa*, headcloths, and finally the widespread institution of "lobi singi" (love songs). In these songs women sing the praises of their mati, in metaphorical language, and enlarge the faults of their rivals (Comvalius n.d.; Herskovits 1936). One such text is sung as follows:

Roos e flauw	The rose is weak
A de fadon	It has fallen down
Roos e flauw	The rose is weak
A de fadon	It has fallen down
Ma stanvaste	But "steadfast" [3]
Dat e tan sidon	That stays upright.

Mati relationships in 1990 are a very visible feature of Afro-Surinamese working class culture. Spokespersons speak of "one big family," where everyone knows each other and older women clearly predominate. But women and men of younger age-groups also are present. Many female couples have a marked role division, where one partner will play a "male" role, and the other a "female" role. It is, furthermore, important to note that a mati career, for most women, is not a unidirectional path: thus it is very possible that a woman takes a man for a lover, after having had several relationships with women. It also is not unusual for a woman to have a female and a male lover at the same time. Nor does mati life necessarily imply restriction to one partner. As one 35 year old informant told me:

I never have just one lover, at the same time. I have my "tru visi-
ti" ("steady girlfriend") and then two or three other lovers. If my
"steady" is a Creole woman, I take care that the others are of
different ethnic origin or just over here on vacation from Holland,
because Creoles aren't likely to take this arrangement easily. I
handpick my lovers, I don't take just anybody. Because it takes a
lot of time to find a "Ms. Right," I can't afford to begin looking,
after me and my steady have broken up. So I keep them in reserve. [4]

AN AFRO-AMERICAN ANGLE

The literature of black North American women writers, which began
to appear in a rich variety of forms from the beginning of the 1970s,
makes it clear that the societies they describe would have been unthinkable failing the strong ties of love and eroticism among women. The
literature also reveals a certain tolerance of homosexuality in the working
classes, as long as it does not bear a name, and this corresponds with the
situation in Suriname. I want to illustrate this by a single fragment from
the bio-mythographical novel *Zami, A New Spelling Of My Name* by
Audre Lorde. In this fragment the North American black communities of
the 1950s are discussed and Lorde describes the attitude of Cora, a factory worker and mother of Zami's first woman lover, Ginger:

> With her typical aplomb, Cora welcomed my increased presence
> around the house with the rough familiarity and browbeating humor
> due another one of her daughters. If she recognized the sounds
> emanating from the sunporch on the nights I slept over, or our
> haggard eyes the next day, she ignored them. But she made it very
> clear that she expected Ginger to get married again. "Friends are
> nice, but marriage is marriage," she said to me one night as she
> helped me make a skirt on her machine. . . . "And when she gets
> home don't be thumping that bed all night, neither, because it's late
> already and you girls have work tomorrow." (Lorde 1982: 142)

LESBIANISM, SAY WHAT?

In addition to the established custom of women having relationships
with other women and the degree of tolerance for this in black communities, there is another reason for my choosing not to make a sharp distinc-

tion between the history of black women in general and "lesbian" women in particular. There are strong indications that the western categories of "homo," "bi," and "hetero" have insufficient justification in some black situations. The concept of "homosexuality" introduces an etic category that is alien to the indigenous, emic system which exists in some sections of black communities.

Sexuality cannot be considered independently from the social order in which it exists. Ross and Rapp state rightly that the biological basis of sexuality is always experienced and interpreted according to cultural values. The simple biological facts of sexuality are not self-explanatory, they require social expression. The image they employ for the universal rootedness of sexuality in larger social units such as family relationships, communities, national and world systems, is that of the union. One may have the illusion that by peeling off one layer after another one comes nearer to the core of sexuality, after which one realizes that all the different layers together form its essence (Ross and Rapp 1983).

How societies precisely give form to sexuality remains relatively obscure. I am not claiming to describe all the different layers of the emic system of sexuality to which mati-ism belongs. I would, however, like to sketch the outlines of two idealtypical socio-historical structures, situating two differing cosmologies, as far as female homosexuality in black communities is concerned.

In the summer of 1986, black women in Amsterdam had the good fortune to be witnesses to and participants in a public discussion between two eminent women poets, true children of the black Diaspora, Audre Lorde and Astrid Roemer.[5] While many subjects were addressed during this discussion, the burning question, which also aroused a passionate interest among the audience, proved to be the matter of namegiving/nomenclature: how important is it that black women who love other women should call themselves "black lesbians"?

TWO IDEALTYPICAL EXPRESSIONS

ASTRID ROEMER: "I do not call myself 'lesbian' and I do not want to be called 'lesbian' either. Life is too complex for us to give names not derived from us, dirty, conditioned words, to the deepest feelings within me. If I were to call myself a lesbian, it would mean that I should be allowing myself–on the most banal, biological level–to be classed as one who chooses persons who also have female genitals. If I love a woman, I love that one woman and one swallow does not make a summer.

People have a masculine and a feminine component in them and these two components constantly seek to come into equilibrium with each other and with the rest of the world. Who is to say whether I shall not love a man in my later life? The result of that search for equilibrium is not a constant. I should be terribly ashamed as a human being were I to know in advance that for the rest of my life I should love only women. It would, moreover, conflict with feminism, for feminism also insists that men can change."

AUDRE LORDE: "First of all, I want to make clear what I understand by a 'lesbian'. It is not having genital intercourse with a woman that is the criterion. There are lesbian women who have never had genital or any other form of sexual contact with another woman, while there are also women who have had sex with other women but who are not lesbian. A lesbian is a woman who identifies fundamentally with women and her first field of strength, of vulnerability, of comfort lies in a network of women. If I call myself a black, feminist lesbian, I am acknowledging by that that the roots of my strength, and of my vulnerability, lie in myself as a woman. What I am trying to achieve in the first place is changes in my awareness and that of other women. My priority does not lie with men.

There are two reasons only why I call myself a black lesbian. It makes me aware of my own strength and shows my vulnerability too. In the sixties we could do anything we wanted to as long as we did not talk about it. If you speak your name, you represent a threat to the powers that be, the patriarchate. That's what I want to be too. The price I pay for that and the vulnerability it makes me aware of are no greater than what I feel if I keep it a secret and let others decide what they want to call me. That also perpetuates the positions of inferiority we occupy in society.

The other reason I consider it important is that there may be a woman in my audience who, through this, may see that it is possible to speak your name and to go on living. If we, who are in a relatively more secure position enabling us to come out for what we are, if we fail to do so that will only perpetuate the vicious circle of inferiority.

ASTRID: "I think your definition of a lesbian is interesting. In that sense, all Surinamese women are lesbian, because they draw their strength to carry on from women. All the same, I do not see why it is necessary to declare oneself a lesbian. In the community from which I come, there is not so much talk about the phenomenon of women having relations with other women. There are, after all, things which aren't to be given names–giving them names kills them. But we do have age-old rituals originating from Africa by which women can make quite clear that special relations exist between them. For instance, birthday rituals can be recognized by anyone and are quite obvious. Also, when two women are at a party and one hands the other a glass or a plate of food, from which she has first tasted herself, it is clear to everybody and their mother what that means. Why then is it necessary to declare oneself a lesbian? It *is* usual there. Surinamese women claim the right to do what they want to do. They can love women, go to bed with men, have children. We distinguish between the various levels of feeling and experiencing which life has to offer and allow ourselves the opportunity to enjoy these things in a creative manner. This is different from the situation in the Netherlands, where you are shoved into a pigeon-hole and find your opportunities restricted. My not wanting to declare myself a lesbian is certainly not prompted by fear. I also want to remain loyal to the ways in which expression has been given from of old in my community to special relationships between women. Simply doing things, without giving them a name, and preserving rituals and secrets between women are important to me. Deeds are more obvious and more durable than all the women who say they are lesbian and contribute nothing to women's energy."

AUDRE: "I respect your position and I recognize the need and the strength that lie behind it. It is not my position. I think it necessary for every woman to decide for herself what she calls herself, and when and where. Of course, there have always been rituals and secrets between women and they must continue. But it is important to make a distinction between the secrets from which we draw strength and the secrecy which comes from anxiety and is meant to protect us. If we want to have power for ourselves this secrecy and this silence must be broken. I want to encourage more and more women to identify themselves, to speak their name, where and when they can, and to survive. I repeat: and to survive.

Finally, I think it important to state my essential position as follows: it is not my behavior that determines whether I am lesbian, but the very core of my being."

TOWER OF BABEL

So much for the burning discussion among the black poets. The positions taken up here are shared by large groups of women in the black communities of the Diaspora and are typical of two idealtypical cosmologies, where female homosexuality is concerned. The position defended by Audre Lorde is a prototype of that held by groups of black lesbians within the USA, Suriname and the Netherlands. In the attitudes adopted by Astrid Roemer, features can be discerned of the mati paradigm, whose protagonists are also to be found everywhere in the Diaspora yet who, almost by definition, attract less attention.

Perhaps it is unnecessary to say that in practice numerous intermediate positions and hybrid forms exist. Without wishing to force people into one camp or the other, or to question the legitimacy or "political correctness" of either position, I seek to throw light on the outlines of these two idealtypes. Exchanges around the theme of namegiving often give rise to heated discussions, that aren't particularly fruitful, because as in a true tower of Babel people speak in mutually unintelligible tongues.

Central to my thinking on the matter is the fact that orientation to reality–which includes the meaning given to and the form taken by homosexuality in black communities in the Diaspora–is more or less colored by the cultural heritage from Africa. In the cosmology of *mati-ism* more African elements have been preserved, while the black lesbian groups have drawn more inspiration from Western influences. *Mati-ism* is characterized by a *centripetal*, a comprehensive and inclusive movement, whereas in the black lesbian world a *centrifugal*, exclusive spirit seems to be present. This is reflected in the attitudes in various circles to relationships with men. While in the lives of many mati-women men play a role, among the black lesbians this must generally be regarded as excluded. Children in the lives of black lesbians are either a residue from a former lifestyle or a conscious choice within a lesbian relationship. Neither circumstance necessarily asks for continued emotional and/or financial commitment from the father to the child or the mother. The part played by men in the life of mati-women, apart from possible economical support for children, is underscored by the fact that motherhood is regarded as a rite of initiation into adulthood and by many as a sign of being a woman.

Besides displaying a differential level of African elements, *mati-ism* and *black lesbianism* are exponents of two different *class cultures*. Mati typically are working class women, whose claims to social status lie in their capability to mobilize and manipulate kin networks. Indeed, according to Janssens and van Wetering, matisma can be seen as entrepreneurs, who through their extensive kin networks with women and men, try to build up social and real capital (Janssens and van Wetering 1985). While in Suriname, middle and higher class black lesbians are largely invisible, obviously not having found appropriate models to style their behavior, in the USA and in the Netherlands, they have increasingly come out of the closet. Through their education, income and often professional status they are insulated against some of the survival hazards of working class black lesbians.

A further difference distinguishing mati relationships from black lesbian connections is the often wide *age gap* between mati partners, while in the latter circles "equality" along many dimensions, including age, seems to be an aspiration. It is not at all unusual, in the mati world, to find a 20 year old ("yong' doifi," young dove) having a relationship with a 60 year old woman. For the young woman, the emotional and financial security of the older woman, who will typically have raised her children and will get financial support from them, is an important consideration. The older woman, for her part, now as almost sixty years ago when it was first recorded (Herskovits, M. and F. Herskovits, 1936), will demand unconditional loyalty and faithfulness from her "young dove," in return for indulging and spoiling her with presents, notably gold and silver jewellery. Ideally, she teaches her young dove "a mati wroko" (the mati work) and she "trains" her the way she wants the young woman to be.

A further differentiation would seem to lie in the *underlying self* that organizes all life's experiences, sifts through them and integrates them into manageable material. Though this issue awaits further elaboration, [6] the self of matisma would seem to be a *sociocentric* phenomenon, while the self of black lesbians could be characterized as an *egocentric, individualistic* entity. Among matisma, sociocentrism is evident not only in the zeal with which human capital is constantly being mobilized, but also in the perceptions of what a person is. Linked with the folk religion "Winti," persons are perceived to be built up out of several components: kra (= jeje), djodjo and several "winti" or Gods, who each have their specific characteristics.[7] "Kra" with its male and female component can be understood as the "I"; "djodjo," also male and female, are like "guardian angels," gotten at birth. The different "winti" or Gods are divided into four pantheons: those of the Sky, the Earth, the Bush and the Water. Male homosexuals are often believed to have a female "Aisa," the (upper-) goddess of the Earth, who is said to be frightfully jealous of real women the man would get involved with. Female homosexuals are perceived to be "carried" by a male Bushgod, Apuku, who cannot bear to see the woman connected, on a longterm basis, with a flesh-and-blood male.

Black lesbians' personhood, on the other hand, seems more aptly characterized by Western notions of individuality, persons as self-contained "islands," with their own motivations and accountabilities.

An additional distinction between matisma and black lesbians is that concentration on women for the latter is a *political issue,* aimed at male dominated society. In their own communities they often wage war on sexism and homophobia. While they experience their sexual choice as a matter of politics, matisma tend to see their behavior as a *personal issue.* A typical response is: "Mi na wan bigi uma f' mi eygi oso. No wan sma e gi mi njan," (I am a big woman in my own house. Nobody gives me food), meaning it's nobody's business but my own with whom I sleep. In a small scale society like Suriname (400,000 inhabitants), this can be seen as a rather defiant survival posture.

Lastly, one could posit that matisma display *lesbian behavior,* while black lesbians have a *lesbian identity.* I assume that matisma unwillingness to declare oneself can, functionally, be explained with reference to this point. In a society where the avenues to status for working class women are limited, it would not seem wise to declare oneself openly and thereby alienate potential personnel, men and women, from one's network.

EPILOGUE

Within black communities there are many different ways of giving expression to erotic relationships between women. The biological basis of sexual desire takes form in various socio-historical structures, underpinned by differing· cosmologies. Mati-ism and black lesbianism are two of these structures. Lesbians have not always existed in black communities. In some sectors, today, they still do not exist. But this statement is not a complaint about the lack of sexuality between those of the same gender in the black communities of the Diaspora. Rather it is a statement which tells us more about the socio-historical structure of the concept "lesbian."

NOTES

1. Mati is the Sranan Tongo word for "friend," used both in a heterosexual and a homosexual context. It is used by and for men and women. The word *mat-isma* (literally "mati people") specifically connotes women who have sexual relations with other women. By *mati-ism* I mean the institution of those who are mati, in this case women. In Dutch I would use the term "matischap."

2. "For Each Of You," Lorde 1982: 42, 43.

3. This text was recorded at a lobi singi in Paramaribo, November 1990. Stanvaste/"steadfast" is the name of another flower.

4. See my dissertation, "'I am Gold Money' (I Pass Through All Hands, But

I Do Not Lose My Value): The Construction of Selves, Gender and Sexualities in a Female, Working Class, Afro-Surinamese Setting," University of California, Los Angeles, July 1992.

5. This public discussion, organized by the black lesbian group Sister Outsider, took place on June 21, 1986, in the black and migrant women's center Flamboyant in Amsterdam. Astrid Roemer (born in Paramaribo in 1947), is an Afro-Surinamese poet/novelist, living in the Netherlands, while Afro-American Audre Lorde (Harlem, NYC, 1934) now resides on St. Croix, U.S. Virgin Islands.

6. See note 4.

7. See Wooding, C., 1988.

REFERENCES

Ambacht. (1912). *Rapport van de commissie benoemd bij Gouvernementsresolutie van 13 januari 1910.* Suriname: Gouvernement.

Comvalius, Th. (n.d.). *Krioro: Een bijdrage tot de kennis van het lied, de dans en de folklore van Suriname.* Deel I. Paramaribo.

Herskovits, M. and F. Herskovits. (1936). *Suriname folklore.* New York: Columbia University Press.

Herskovits, M. (1938). *Dahomey: An ancient West-African kingdom.* New York.

Janssens, M. en W. van Wetering. (1985). Mati en Lesbiennes. Homosexualiteit en Ethnische Identiteit bij Creools- Surinaamse Vrouwen in Nederland. *Sociologische Gids,* 5/6. Meppel: Boom.

van Lier, R. (1949). *Samenleving in een Grensgebied.* Een sociaal-historische Studie van Suriname. Amsterdam: Emmering.

van Lier, R. (1986). *Tropische Tribaden.* Een Verhandeling over Homosexualiteit en Homosexuele Vrouwen in Suriname. Dordrecht/Providence: Foris Publications.

Lorde, A. (1982). *Chosen Poems, Old and New.* New York: W. W. Norton & Co., Inc.

Lorde, A. (1982). *Zami. A New Spelling of my Name.* New York: The Crossing Press.

Mintz, S. and R. Price (1976). *An Anthropological Approach to the Afro-American Past.* Philadelphia: Ishi.

Price, R. (1976). *The Guiana Maroons.* A Historical and Bibliographical Introduction. Baltimore: The Johns Hopkins University Press.

Price, R. and S. Price (1991). *Two Evenings in Saramaka.* Chicago/London: The University of Chicago Press.

Ross, E. and R. Rapp (1983). Sex and Society: A Research Note from Social History and Anthropology. In: Snitow, A. et al. eds. *Desire, The Politics of Sexuality.* London.

Wooding, C. (1988). *Winti.* Een Afro Amerikaanse Godsdienst. Rijswijk: Eigen Beheer.

Homosexuality and Police Terror in Turkey

Arslan Yuzgun, PhD

Istanbul, Turkey

SUMMARY. Being a way of sexual living as old as human history, homosexuality occupies an interesting place in the life of the Turkish people of the Republic of Turkey. This has been so since the days of the glorious Ottoman Empire. In the year 1987, instead of investigating the roots of homosexuality, the pressing need has become to present a particular view of homosexuality in Turkey today. To be more specific, there is a need to explain the problems of Turkish homosexuals and suggest certain vital solutions. Our country is constantly endeavoring to become "westernized" and it is claimed that steps are being taken toward that modernization. Despite this fact, homosexuals are confronted with such great problems that it is not difficult to justify those who say that there is no democracy in Turkey. I will try to explain these problems with documentary evidence and without exaggeration. In doing so, I shall make use of new material in my book, published under the title of *Homosexuality in Turkey: Yesterday, Today.* Beginning in March of 1986, we compiled a list of the attitudes of the police toward gays, involving pressure and cruelty that can be qualified as torture. Despite this situation, instead of being more democratic and humane, in April 1987 the police force employed terror tactics against homosexuals in Istanbul. This was "the straw that broke the camel's back." Soon after this act of oppression, 18 gays, acting on our suggestions, sued the police for the first time. They then submitted a petition to the Attorney-General and later launched a hunger strike in Taksim Square. These represent movements of importance in the political history of Turkey. From now on homosexuals, too, will have the right to speak out in political affairs.

A HISTORICAL APPROACH TO HOMOSEXUALITY

It is difficult to analyze the sexual attitudes and ways of life of the Turks who spread into Europe after leaving Central Asia and the Near

East. However, as our subject requires, we can say something about the existence of homosexuality. Initially, the religion of the Turks was Shamanism, and homosexuality was regarded as a mark of superiority among the highest ranking clergymen, who were Shamans. Homosexuality spread rapidly and at a certain point it became impossible for a non-homosexual to become a clergyman.

In the Holy Book of Islam, the "Kor'an" and in subsequent words of the prophet Mohammed, we can trace important explanations concerning homosexuality. It was defined by the prophet Mohammed as "sodomy." Although homosexuality was considered a major sin, we notice that homosexuality was a reality that the Prophet often mentioned. In other words, however severely homosexuality was prohibited and punished under religious laws, the necessity of preventing homosexuality shows us that it was quite common even in those times.

It cannot be denied that the Turks underwent a cultural transformation after being converted from Shamanism to Islam. But the existence of homosexuality, which was already common among the Arabs, did not change the attitude of the Turks toward it. Certain religious penalties were, however, in question. If we look at the homosexual way of life under the Ottoman Empire until the Turco-Islamic Synthesis, we can discern attitudes of tolerance that we cannot see in the Republic of Turkey today. In the works of Resat Ekrem Koçu, an author who investigates the Ottoman way of life in detail, there is mention of young lads who committed suicide or who murdered others for their male lovers. Many Ottoman poets, too, such as Necati, Nedim, Vasif and Razi, obviously and frequently chose male love as their subject.

In the hope that it will be of interest, I will quote another example from the Ottoman period. Among the homosexuals of today, many transsexuals are often seen and they add a colorful touch to night life. Hundreds of years ago transsexual operations were institutionalized and in the palaces there was a large hospital (in the "Harem" section) where such operations were carried out. These examples show that although gay relations were seen as "adultery" and punished accordingly, such relations were still common. During certain periods homosexual administrators were dominant in the Ottoman palace. Many Ottoman Sultans and Arch-Viziers are known to have been gay. The most worthy of mention are the Conqueror Sultan Mehmet, who conquered Istanbul, and Murat IV who was well known for the cruelty of his reign. We learn from history books that certain gay hamams (Turkish steam baths) used to be guarded by Janissaries (soldiers) in Ottoman times. In light of this we cannot help feeling pain and shock when we see the police forces of modern Turkey closing gay bars or raiding them day after day, picking up all the gays, taking them away, and subjecting them to hideous treatment.

NUMERICAL ANALYSIS

It is impossible to ascertain the definite number of gays, even in those societies where they live freely and are assisted in their problems by government authorities. In a developing country of fifty five million, in a society where gays are oppressed, it becomes even more difficult to ascertain the number of homosexuals. Being the first person to make a broad study of the subject, I can say that there are nearly half a million male homosexuals in Istanbul. So, despite the effort to ignore this fact, despite the attempt to fight homosexuals and try to obliterate them by oppression, and despite the utmost cruelty of the police forces, gays of today have in part broken free of their chains and created an atmosphere of freedom. Now transvestites and transsexuals, along with clandestine homosexuals, are hitting the streets every night and fighting with police as though on a battlefield. So the gays have left the stamp of their existence on the night life of Istanbul.

Eighty-five point seven percent of Turkish homosexuals wear butch or male clothes, 12.1% are transvestites and 2.2% are transsexuals. These last two rates may, however, be exaggerated, since we focused our study on Istanbul and the Beyoglu quarter there. Among those covered by the survey, 223 of the male Turkish homosexuals conceal their identity due to social pressures. Still, despite all this oppression, the percentage of gays whose families are aware of their homosexuality is 39.9%, while those known to their colleagues at work is 63.7% (they have been more successful in concealing their homosexuality at their work). These two rates clearly show that homosexuals have not yet overcome their fears and prefer to remain hidden. The other interesting figure is for those who claimed that homosexuality was a crime according to Turkish law (7.2%). The figure indicates that there is a mass of homosexuals who are not aware how much their way of life contravenes the law. The percentage of those who were not sure or did not know about the subject is 6.7%. Ironically, none of the Turkish laws make it a crime to be a homosexual or to lead a homosexual life.

CHARACTERISTICS OF TURKISH HOMOSEXUALS

It is necessary to explain some characteristics of Turkish homosexuals, which should, no doubt, be treated on a large scale. Most of the homosexuals in Istanbul have chosen the Beyoglu (Pera) District, particularly for enjoyment rather than for residence. The Cihangir quarter of this district is almost a gay suburb. There are apartment buildings in which almost all the flats are occupied by homosexuals. But 55.2% of Turkish homosexuals still live with their families. This might seem a low rate by European standards. The figure for young Turkish people who stay with their families and are not involved in the homosexual way of life, however, is much higher. So, in this situation, homosexuals were obliged to have their own homes in order to be free. In doing this, they tended to act collectively, causing many two or three-person menages to develop.

If we look at their marital status, we find some interesting figures. The most important point here is that people who remain single cannot have children. This is a great problem for homosexuals is Turkey. The element of sin in the Islamic religion is, in a way, side-tracked. However, one can conceive of the mistaken cross-conditioning of gays, especially passive ones, by telling them they cannot get married and have children. Even the ones deeply involved with this way of life who are used to having gay relations, constantly wish to get married in order to provide security for the future. Having children has become important to them, but it is an idle hope. When we look at the marital status of Turkish homosexuals, we see that 83.9% are single and 15.7% are married. Even this figure proves that the argument that homosexuality prevents one from having children is really worthless. These figures are not important for people who think rationally and scientifically. They are, however, important for those who have been preconditioned. The authorities in Turkey always tend to ignore the fact that children should receive sexual education. Therefore, they always try to limit the distribution of scientific works and even the reading of such works, let alone sexual education in schools. The best evidence of this is that my book *Homosexuality in Turkey* has been deemed detrimental to children and may only be sold in a plain black plastic cover. However, among gays, the figure for those who started the gay life before they were ten years old is 13.9% which is quite a high figure. The figure for those who started between the ages of eleven and fifteen is approximately 37.7% which is enough to frighten the conservatives. Fortunately, this is also a fact. Since these facts are clear, we cannot understand the efforts made to prevent children from receiving sexual education.

Because of these educational concerns, I should say something about the educational level of Turkish homosexuals: 20.6% of the total were primary school pupils, 21.1% were secondary school pupils, 30.9% were high school pupils and 23.8% were university graduates. However, the corresponding figures for Turkey as a whole in 1980 were: 71.8% primary school education, 12.2% secondary school, 10.6% high school and 3.3% university graduates. The figure for homosexuals having Masters and Doctors degrees is 3.5%–a figure far above that for Turkey. This indicates that Turkish homosexuals have received a higher education than the rest of the population. Moreover, some even claimed that their colorful and active life makes them more skillful and adroit than others.

If we examine their sexual behavior, we see that 56.1% of gays are both active and passive, 30.9% of them are exclusively passive and 13% are exclusively active. Since it is not important to most gays whether he play the active or passive role, it proved highly difficult to obtain these figures. Here we should state that, the actual figure for both-active-and-passive gays must be higher, since our survey concentrated on homosexuals who stated their own personal preference.

A situation of amazing injustice exists in Turkey. For example, where active homosexuals are appreciated and boast of their ways, passive gays prove to be the most ill-treated and despised group in the population. In Turkey there are hundreds of thousands, perhaps millions of men who boast .they are "kulampara." In Turkish "kulampara" means "loving a boy," and it distinguishes an active homosexual. The same word and sort of life is also to be observed in Iran. More could be said about the characteristics of Turkish male homosexuals. Because time is limited, I have only been able to discuss the more important points. The reactions to the publication of my book *Homosexuality in Turkey,* in which I also studied homosexuals' reading habits and their desire to use make-up in detail, reveal the proper meaning of my research.

TURKISH LAWS

The truth is that no Turkish law regards homosexuality as a crime. The treatment of homosexuals, however does not reflect this. Even today, being a homosexual is the same as being a criminal without having committed any crime. The horrible events of which I would particularly like to tell you fall into this category.

Although Turkish society does not generally approve of homosexuality, it has always granted gays the right to live and even raised them to the highest positions. Gays would have no problems with the Turkish people, were it not for assaults carried out by some ill-intentioned persons, including attempts at robbery and beatings. Gays are Turkish citizens who belong to families. Real family ties make it unnecessary to ostracize them by prying into their private lives. For this reason, there are many parents now who discover that their children are gay and still treat them well and do not shun them. The number of such parents is on the increase.

Parents may disapprove of homosexuality, due to environmental pressure, but later feel obliged to accept it. The figure for parents who initially became furious and then found their children's homosexuality natural is 92.1%. The figure for those who have severed their ties with their families because of their homosexuality is as little as 7.9%. These figures alone show that Turkish homosexuals do not have great problems with their families or members of society in general. Yet, Turkish homosexuals draw our attention as people submerged in problems. Who, then, created these problems? Although the Turkish Criminal Code does not prescribe any punishment for those leading a gay life, they are punished. Who, then, are the people who continuously *persecute* them? Has any change occurred in the behavior of these people?

THE PROBLEMS OF TURKISH HOMOSEXUALS

One's homosexuality is next to impossible to escape from or to treat by seeing it as an illness. Both gays and straight people should be aware of this fact. Despite this, the police forces in Turkey are continuing their fight against homosexuality as if they had been appointed to obliterate it. They pick up many people they assume are homosexual from various places in the city (roads, houses, clubs, baths and cinemas). These people are then stuffed into a place which is part prison and part lunatic asylum–which they call a "hospital." There, even the healthy ones are diagnosed as having syphilis (fortunately not yet AIDS) and are locked up, beaten, and humiliated. Their hair is cut and they are thrown out of the city. Even this is not enough. They notify employers in writing, causing homosexuals to be interrogated and to lose their jobs. They even notify parents. Thus they try to make homosexuals tired of living.

A policeman is appointed to protect people's lives and security. He above all, should know the law. He should also find those who don't obey the laws and hand them over to impartial Turkish courts. Will causing homosexuals to be fired from their jobs by recording them and then notifying their employers under the mask of "preventing prostitution" really prevent prostitution? On the contrary, even the security authorities cannot produce any solution apart from "sex for money." Those who are left jobless in this way still have to survive.

It can be said that the "gutter press" has significantly increased the problems confronting homosexuals. Exaggeration in the press, using headlines like "The scum are picked up," "the faggot's hair has been cut," "homos are driven out of the city" heartens and encourages the police forces. Even newspapers whose actual bosses were gay often published news attacking and insulting gays, assisting the police force in its cruelty. After protesting these realities, the press began to pay the required attention to the subject. Since then the number of newspapers and journals which approach the topic seriously by studying the problems facing homosexuals has increased.

Although the government boasts that the present administration is democratic, it does not blush at the fact that homosexuals are being registered, subjected to torture, banned from singing, etc.. When we consider applying for individual inquiries to both the European Human Rights Commission and the European Community, their conservative rules are exposed. What sort of respect for human rights is this? Although our statements have been published in the press hundreds of times, the police persist in their attitude and commit crimes by raiding gay bars with sticks and beating the occupants, cutting their hair and registering them. Why do the officers resist change? From now on it is necessary that policemen (who are paid their salaries and support their wives and children from taxes that gays also pay) are humane, democratic, rational and tolerant toward homosexuals.

After being attacked and beaten or robbed, homosexuals appealing to the police encounter a further assault. Instead of obtaining their rights, they leave the police station as criminals. Again they are beaten and their pride broken. The robbers, even the murderers of homosexuals cannot be caught and are not caught. Despite this maltreatment, homosexuals still lead their lives and never consider being anything other than their homosexual selves.

ORGANIZING TURKISH HOMOSEXUALS

Because the educational level of homosexuals is higher than the general level in Turkey, one may wonder what they do to combat the injustices they have to face. The answer is: nothing. When a person who attempts to have some brief sexual gratification is beaten and robbed (this is becoming slightly less frequent), or is continuously punished by the police, he always remains silent. It is this cowardice and fatalism that increases the problems. One may say, "What will happen, if we go to the police station? Are they in our favor?" They are no doubt right in asking this. But does not their silence encourage the police and evil people all the more? The answer is certainly yes.

In the world at large, homosexuals are individuals free from conditioning, sensible and progressive, and thus democratic. One can hardly expect them to be conservatives. Nowhere in the world do conservative rulers approach homosexuality with complete tolerance, because they see homosexuality as a vain "waste of sperm," resulting in a decrease in the population. If the population declines, how can the state dominate other states? For this reason, or by appealing to "morality, custom, tradition," conservatives are never able to take a realistic approach to homosexuals and homosexuality. The democrats and social democrats in particular, remain fairly silent. We wish that all our political parties would concern themselves with homosexuals' problems and seek out solutions to them. Since the existing parties remain silent, it has become vitally important to form a party that will tackle the problems confronting our gay community.

REPULSIVE POLICE TERROR

Turkey is undergoing a rapid and head spinning change. The people of the country are trying to achieve a modern state. Even the most conservative governments are compelled to take similar steps. The basic rights of everybody, ranging from gay people to Gypsies, from Jews to Kurdish people, are supported by large masses of the society. The governments have signed human rights charters, parliamentary commissions have been set up to investigate allegations of torture. While at first people like us combating for these rights were few, this figure has increased, and the press has come to a point where it fiercely defends such undeniable human rights.

Unfortunately the police somehow failed to keep up with these changes. Some legislation that was in apparent breach of human rights has been eliminated, however homosexuality, which has not been an illegal act, has not been viewed in a modern light by the police. The State, which in the past denied "identity" to transsexuals following their sex operations, now grants them these rights. One transsexual singer, much loved by the nation, whose tapes sold millions and showrooms attracted masses, has been allowed to perform on the stage again. The Police Organization which once banned this person from the stage, now invites Miss Bülend Ersey to sing in "Cheering Up Days for Police Forces!" This is a dramatic irony, but it may as well be considered a jolly good change.

In May of this year, a Police Commissioner of the Beyoglu Area, where there is a large percentage of gay men, resumed storms of terror. He ordered raids on scores of gay households, leaving doors smashed. He sanctioned gay people being dragged away from streets, homes, and bars. The period of notorious "hair-cropping" resumed, the truncheons were replaced with thick wooden sticks and plastic hoses and gay people were beaten up ruthlessly. Some gay men were sent away from the town, some were stripped naked, truncheons were inserted in their anuses and they were beaten severely. The events leaked to the press and under our guidance, some homosexuals brought legal action. These developments were brought to the attention of Human Rights Commission of the Parliament and the so-called "liberty-monger" President. We are now calling for immediate measures to be taken. The matter has also been brought to the attention of the opposition party (SHP). These defiant, insolent, relentless police chiefs should be brought to court for their actions. Sooner or later they will change and see that their children may be homosexuals too.

OPPRESSION OF AN AUTHOR WHO DEFENDS GAYS

State powers have carried out oppressive actions against an author who has launched a war against "taboos." My book, *Homosexuality in Turkey,* shortly after its publication, was judged to be detrimental to children by a censorship committee called "The Obscenity Committee." It was banned from sale unless covered and sold in a black plastic bag. The same end came to a dramatic film called "The Cliff" which was about a love affair between two gay men. My subsequent book, *Women with Blue Identity Cards,* was charged with a more serious violation–"public indecency." Naturally, following a chain of hearings, it was decided that it should be burned.

Before publishing my books (which were about the problems of gays), I was not afraid of the police who blackmailed me, threatening that they would reveal my gay identity to the press. And so a series of works were written by me which caused great echoes throughout our country.

I started a legal action to stop the execution of the decision that my books would be covered with black plastic bags and the case was been brought up in the Courts. Following lengthy trials, Turkish courts held that my two books were not "harmful for minors" and they were taken out of their black covers.

Thus, I won my first two legal victories. I also solicited the Court of Appeals to reverse the decision to have my other book burned and the court decided in my favor. However, for my last book *The Temple of the Dog,* aside from the accusations of its being harmful to children or obscene, a case was brought up against me, accusing me of "insulting and degrading the police forces." This was done to stop me from revealing the tortures and brutalities of the police. In this case, they wanted me to be sentenced to five years. By being acquitted from this allegation, I have again won another victory. When issued the verdict for my two books to be sold in black plastic bags, they also required me and the editor to pay a fine of approximately TL 10.000.000. When I was acquitted and my books were brought out of their black plastic bags, the censorship crowd was unpleasantly surprised. Now, I am preparing to bring an action against the Turkish President Mr. Turgut Özal, who introduced the Obscenity Act, for damages amounting to TL one billion. This conservative leader, who has presented me to the Turkish public as an author who writes bad things about children and is an obscene author, will have to account for himself.

There are efforts being made not only for my books but also to solve the unfair suffering of other gay people. When police forces are disturbed by this, they make it a point to disturb us. Sometimes they bring us to their stations to interrogate us, at times they are daring enough to break into our homes. These are but a few examples of the oppression to which we are subjected.

CONCLUSION

Being a country on the eastern edge of Europe, Turkey wishes to integrate with the Western World. This is not pretence. It is required by the necessity of living as a true human being. It is a common policy of the Turkish police to drive out homosexuals, to hate them and punish them in various ways; but homosexuals are part of humankind. Despite all our efforts no positive signs of change have been observed among the police. Change has come about in other fields, but not in the attitude of police.

The Turkish press now sees homosexuality as a reality and is giving it serious consideration. There are now often lengthy articles and discussions on the matter. The press respects human rights and continues to publish within that framework. This change in the press's attitude makes a positive impression on people, causing a humane trend in views about homosexuals. Gays themselves are no longer silent, as they were in the past. They are resisting the haphazard harassment by the police. After the publication of my books, they have realized that it is necessary to work for solidarity. Eighteen homosexuals have appealed to the Attorney-General against police pressure. A group of thirty to thirty-five gays has started a hunger strike. These developments will force the authorities to adopt a more respectful and democratic attitude toward gays and human rights.

REFERENCES

Demircan, Ali Riza: *Islama Göre Cinsel Hayat,* Istanbul, 1985.
Ilhan, Atilla: *Yanlis Kandinlar Yanlis Erkekler,* Istanbul, 1985.
Koçu, Resat Ekrem: *Istanbul Ansilopedisi,* Istanbul, 11 cilt.
Mungan, Murathan: *Son Istanbul,* Ankara, 1985.
Yüzgün, Arslan: *Türkiye'de Escinsellik (Dün, Bugün),* Istanbul, 1986.
Yüzgün, Arslan: *Uçurum,* Istanbul, 1986.
Yüzgün, Arslan: *Mavi Hüviyetti Kadinlar,* Istanbul, 1987,
Yüzgün, Arslan: *Yakilacak Yazar,* Istanbul, 1988.
Yüzgün, Arslan: *Pembe Yolculuk,* Istanbul, 1988.
Yüzgün, Arslan: *It Tapinagi,* Istanbul, 1989

In Nicaragua:
Homosexuality Without a Gay World

Barry D. Adam, PhD

University of Windsor

SUMMARY. This paper addresses the social construction of homosexual relations among men in Nicaragua in the late 1980s. The political economy of a nation, subjected to a devastating war by the United States, created conditions where sexual relations among men have not become organized into a gay world which would be familiar to North Americans and Europeans. Rather, homosexually-inclined men remain fully integrated in family and neighborhood life where they are often "known about" but not "recognized," a condition which dissolves separateness but also suppresses the development of a gay culture beyond the bounds of heterosexist expectations.

Gay and lesbian studies in recent years has come to the realization that homosexuality is a many varied thing. A look through historical and anthropological records on sexual and affectional bonding between men and between women shows no lack of same-sex attraction but little of gay worlds or lesbian movements. Though it may be convenient to gather all of these examples together under the category of "homosexuality" (even if heterosexuals want us to claim the sexual but not the affectional as our

Barry D. Adam is Professor of Sociology at the University of Windsor. Correspondence may be addressed: Department of Sociology and Anthropology, University of Windsor, Windsor, Ontario, Canada N9B 3P4.

An earlier version of this paper was presented to the International Scientific Conference on Gay and Lesbian Studies in Amsterdam and appeared in *Out/Look* 1(4):74-82. Remarks here are based on participation in an east-side Managua social network in January and February 1986, May and August 1988, and November 1989.

171

own), homosexually interested people have at least as much in common with other people of their own culture as with homosexual people elsewhere. In societies where males marry their female cross-cousins–if they bond with other males at all–it tends to be in terms of warm or even sexual relationships with male cross-cousins rather than with other categories of men. Homosexual attraction and affection is not random, then, but tends to endorse standards of desirability and appropriateness already widespread in the culture. While modern gay and lesbian worlds have emerged primarily in advanced capitalist nations and in major cities of the former Soviet bloc and the third world, more traditional social arrangements of male homosexuality have typically relied upon age and gender differentiation as their organizing principles (see Adam 1985a, 1985b, 1987).

Nicaragua offers an important example of homosexuality in a society which has never had the accoutrements of a modern gay world, that is, commercial enterprises, voluntary organizations, or a social movement composed of self-identified homosexual people. In brief, the folk categories employed by Nicaraguan men in interpreting and organizing their "homosexual" experiences rely upon a gender-inscribed discourse common to most of Latin America (Lacey, 1979; Carrier 1971, 1976, 1977; Taylor 1986; Fry 1986; Parker 1984; Young 1972; Murray 1980; Arboleda 1980, 1981; Kutsche 1983, 1986).[1] At the same time, there is an awareness of gay definitions of homosexual experience developing among those Nicaraguans with more education and international contacts. Most people regardless of sexual orientation recognize the word 'gay' from the international press.

THE WAR AND THE ECONOMY

Even towns of 30,000 or 40,000 have loose networks of homosexually interested men, but the lack of a developed gay world in Managua, a city of about 750,000, is striking especially in comparison with the adjacent capital of San José, Costa Rica, with its bars and saunas and comparative prevalence of gay-defined homosexuality (Kutsche 1986).

An understanding of the current socio-economic conditions of the city and the nation can begin to throw light on the situation in Managua. A recent issue of *Envío* (Managua . . . 1986:37) describes Managua as:

> barely a capital and even less urban or sophisticated. In fact, it is an immense, sprawling rural town. . . . With its infrequent traffic

lights and even more infrequent sidewalks, the city is actually a knitted belt of neighborhoods wrapped around a wasteland made empty by the 1972 earthquake. . . . Transport and communication, already difficult before the war, are now nearly impossible. The steamy city lacks recreation or diversion centers, with the exception of some baseball lots and few badly air-conditioned theaters.

The rural atmosphere is reinforced by the goats grazing in the middle of major boulevards and the cacophony of roosters that is heard every morning throughout the city.

The 1972 earthquake destroyed much of the housing in the city and, with the second highest birthrate in the western hemisphere and an influx of rural migrants, most people in Managua live in very crowded circumstances. As well, the contra war, waged from 1980 to 1990 by the Reagan/Bush administration with U.S. taxpayers' money, bankrupted the country, forcing it to turn half of its national budget to defense and place on hold many social programs intended to improve the medical, educational, and nutritional standards of the people. Almost all Nicaraguans feel intense economic pressure. With salaries ranging from $35 to $45 per month for most blue collar and white collar workers and no more than $60-$70 for professionals, few are able to survive on the income from one job alone and, with wages controlled by the state while inflation topped 30,000% in 1987, few escaped a severe financial squeeze.

These conditions create a series of consequences inhibiting the growth of a public gay life beyond the current situation where homosexual men "hang out," "keeping their eyes open" in the central Plaza de la Revolución and in the most populated bars, streets, and cinemas of the eastern neighborhoods of Bello Horizonte. Meeting other gay people, then, is not especially easy or convenient.

These socio-economic conditions mean that very few are able to have control over personal space, being unable to find or afford housing of their own. This inability to avoid family supervision is compounded by the usual architecture of houses and commercial establishments. Except for the houses of the small middle class, most people live in houses that open directly onto the street permitting passersby to apprehend at a glance the activities of all the residents therein. Though there is a bar owned by two gay men, it is separated from the street by no more than a metal grill, in common with other cafes and bars in the neighborhood, obliging those of its patrons who are homosexual to observe the norms of heterosexist propriety. [2]

Managua consists of a set of loosely connected small towns in which most inhabitants spend a great deal of their lives where they know everyone and are, in turn, known by all. These living conditions fundamentally reorganize conceptions of public and private and of coming out as understood in northern societies. Privacy as such is largely unknown. Without privacy, homosexual people remain fully embedded in family life and involved in its rituals while they are at the same time held to the expectations of heterosexism. With the difficulty of getting around the city and lack of money, people spend a great deal of their lives in their home neighborhood so families and neighbors are rapidly apprised of the personal habits of all of its inhabitants including their homosexual inclinations. When I went with a friend to a town in the mountains where he grew up, we walked easily through the streets, looking in windows and stepping unannounced through unlocked doors into houses to talk to townsfolk who showed no surprise at our apparent intrusion. He was also able to let me know who was "interested" and who wasn't. Just as he knew about everyone else, little about him was not known to his kin and neighbors. The result is that coming out is not quite the issue, when everyone already knows, and ironically neighborhood gossip may be so efficient that it informs homosexual people about others in their area.

Despite being known about, however, there is no publicly recognized gay identity and men with homosexual interests are still regularly asked about their marital status and about girl friends. They are likely to be lectured on the virtues of family life, as are all other unmarried men.[3] Knowledge, then, does not entail any allowance or respect for alternative domestic arrangements. Rather, it is "unofficial" and in some sense unmentionable like a host of other personal habits and peculiarities known about other members of the neighborhood.

RELATIONSHIPS

Sexual relationships among men in Nicaragua typically participate in the gender-defined codes that have been observed elsewhere in Latin America. It is the "pasivos" who are usually equated with "homosexuales" by both "homosexuales" and the larger society, while "activos" are largely indistinguishable from the rest of the male population and generally escape unlabelled. Though there are few words of self-appellation, the Spanish language requires that all nouns show gender: pasivos share a sense of collective identity by inflecting a wide range of terms into the feminine when referring to themselves. It is the pasivos, as well, who appear to have well developed social networks and a culture of "queen talk" recognizable to anyone from a society with a gay world.

Among themselves, pasivos are "sisters." Sexual interests are believed to come about only across the "gender" line and everyone is slotted into one or other of the folk categories, though everyone knows that actual behavior is not always so easily categorized. Assignment to one or other of these categories is neither self-evident nor automatic as there is no necessary link between pasivos and effeminacy, and roles may have to be worked out between individuals.

The activos are, at least theoretically, ordinary men, and as such, have no identity or society apart from the mainstream. When I remarked to an activo that in North America, 'gay' refers to sexual orientation and includes both 'activo' and 'pasivo,' he concluded that everyone must be 'gay' for the entire gender complex depends on the machista ideology that men have the right to fuck anyone (sex of the partner being irrelevant), while those who are fucked are the subordinate/feminine. In this, Nicaragua shares a gender system and an understanding of homosexuality in common with other less urbanized regions of Latin America.

Sexual contact itself is limited by the general absence of privacy to vacant lots, parks, and dark recesses, which are also sought by young heterosexual pairs, and subject to invasion or interruption at any moment by passersby (not to mention the inconvenience of biting ants and poisonous snakes). Nevertheless, it must still be pointed out, that there are some male couples who have succeeded in living together in Managua, even though they may present themselves as cousins to their neighbors.

Overall, homosexual life in Nicaragua has been little influenced by official or expert discourses. There are no books on homosexuality in the National Library and but one antiquated Catholic text at the university. Medicine, it would appear, has been so preoccupied with pressing crises of infant mortality, malaria, and abysmal health conditions, that it has not thought to launch into more esoteric realms such as sexuality. Awareness of the gay world and political movements elsewhere tends to be confined to personal contact with foreigners.

OPPRESSION

Recognizable or "suspect" homosexual men may be subjected to harassment or assault, evicted from bars, or taunted in the street. In a city where youth gangs have become a problem, homosexual men feel especially vulnerable, as they do in so many other cities of the world. There is also entrapment, not by the police, but by machos who chat up the unsuspecting for blackmail. In any society as poor as this, economics intrude, either benignly in the young men who are attracted to successful men they hope to have become their sponsors, or malevolently through blackmail.

The primary perceived sources of oppression, then, are machismo, family, and the church. It must be emphasized here, that the revolutionary Sandinista government was generally looked upon as a progressive coalition working to break down the hegemony of machismo and Roman Catholicism and homosexual men and women are involved and even recognized to be involved in Sandinista organizations. In a country of three million, the rumor circuits keep everyone up to date on the scandals and foibles of the leadership and few heterosexual Nicaraguans have not heard persistent reports of certain homosexual male and female comandantes. Official spokespersons of AMNLAE, the Sandinista women's association, insist that there is no restriction by sexual orientation on membership in the mass organizations, that the work of gay men and lesbians for the revolution is respected, and that there are no laws about or against homosexuality, though the issue of gay rights is not a public topic or part of the political culture. Outside observers, mindful of the repressive roles of the Committees for the Defense of the Revolution (CDR) in Cuba, have questioned the role of the Sandinista Defense Committees (CDS) in Nicaragua, but in fact the CDS has steered away from examining personal morality or sexuality (Adam 1988). Indeed, the CDS as a political unit organized on a block by block basis could conceivably be the locus of gay organizing, but without a commercial or residential district, there has not developed any concentration of gay people who could form a majority of any city block.

There are both historical and national reasons for the difference. In seeking to throw U.S. exploitation off the island in 1959, the Cuban revolutionaries evicted the American corporate elite and the mob-run casinos and brothels. Homosexuality got lumped in as another "foreign vice" at the time. In Nicaragua, there had been no history of an American "sin industry" attracting local resentment. As well, both left and right wing ideologies of the 1950s agreed on the wickedness of homosexuality. Both McCarthyism in the United States and Stalinism in the Soviet Union had their campaigns of persecution against gay people. By the 1970s, gay liberation had entered on the side of the "good guys" among Eurocommunists and progressive movements of Europe and North America and the Sandinistas reflect the modern era.

Police harassment has been reported but this seems to stem more from machismo than any official policy. While I was in Managua, one of my friends after becoming very drunk, accosted a stranger in the street who reported him to the police. The police kept him overnight in the local station to dry out. He emerged next morning, without any charges having been laid, with a broad grin on his face to tell us about the "adventure" he had had with a fellow inmate during the night.

PUBLIC DEBATE

Though there has been very little public discussion of homosexuality in postrevolutionary Nicaragua, the topic did come into print during November of 1985 in the pages of the daily *El Nuevo Diario*. The issue surfaced at a time when the legalization of abortion was being debated and arose specifically in an editorial about Managua's perennial garbage problem, where homosexuals were referred to as garbage (*basura*) (Miranda 1985a:2). This was followed by an editorial page commentary by Pablo Juarez Calvo (1985a:2) who charged:

> The assertion is clearly defamatory for a minority, or not a minority, of humanity, for a group of human beings in any case. Is not this claim the product of education in a machista society? Is such a claim in accord with the future Constitution of Nicaragua where all discrimination is rejected against people for religious, racial reasons, etc? Will the Constitution of Nicaragua make an exception for homosexuals because they are "garbage"? [4]

After mentioning the homosexuality of indigenous peoples of Latin America and the founding of the Mexican gay movement in 1978, Juarez concludes:

> The dominant sexuality condemns this minority, paralyzed by the politics of secrecy and guilt, to a clandestine existence fed by repression over three centuries. The indigenous, the disabled, transvestites, prostitutes, and women share common problems in the face of heterosexist, hegemonic domination.

(None of these remarks occur in a news vacuum and the facing page of the newspaper carries the headline, "Rock Hudson's lover appears!")

Adolfo Miranda (1985b:2) who made the "garbage" remark, then responded that "if we accept homosexuality as natural, we will have to accept gay and lesbian clubs, gay marriage, men kissing in parks, or holding hands at the movies," trotting out the usual shopworn appeals to nature, reproduction, sickness, and the seduction of youth.

Better homosexuality than the many unwanted children being born, replies Juarez (1985b:2) and after several more letters, the paper closed the debate by granting the last word to Mario Gutierrez Morales (1985:2), who declared:

> The rejection of the procreative sex act is a rebellion against the limitation of sexuality to procreation and against the institutions which guarantee it, rebellion against a society which uses sexuality as a "means to an end." We are falling into a subversion which is plotting against a machista, racist, sexist, and classist system that is trying to perpetuate itself. Furthermore, it should be said that if humanity desires happiness, pleasure as such, as the end or principal objective of sexuality, then the human species in the current state of things, is highly subversive, even "perverted," in that happiness, love, is the main aim of humanity.

After denouncing the persecution of gay people by the Argentine dictatorship, Gutierrez concludes that homophobia is "an ultra-reactionary ideology. . . . denying democratic liberties, human rights, the right to participate in the construction of a pluralist, revolutionary and democratic society."

Since 1985, *Barricada* and *El Nuevo Diario* have as well printed regular news items on AIDS, usually direct translations of wire service reports without editorial comment. The first AIDS case was not reported until 1988 and blood has been refused from foreign donors as the antibody screening test remained unavailable. In December, 1985, an AIDS seminar was held for physicians and residents in Managua under the leadership of Dr. Rodolfo Rodriguez Cruz, National Director of Epidemiology in the Cuban Ministry of Health. There, Dr. Rodriguez cautioned the audience of the necessity of "taking preventive measures without falling into hysteria" against both heterosexual and homosexual transmission, and of developing "an educative campaign among groups with the highest incidence" ("Prevenir," 1985:5). In recent years, a small network mobilized in cooperation with the Sandinista Ministry of Health to begin to get the safer-sex message out and coincidentally to provide the first "above ground" face to gay-related issues.[5]

COMPARATIVE REFLECTIONS

It is noteworthy that the self-understanding of Nicaraguan homosexual men is remarkably similar to that reported by George Chauncey (1985) of gay society in Rhode Island in the 1920s. The role distinction between the "queers" and their "friends" and "husbands" parallels Nicaraguan folk categories and raises the question of how the relationship between the role-defined and gay constructions of sexuality has developed. We do know that a commercial gay world already existed in major U.S. cities in the 1920s; there seems to have been a slow evolution in North America where the role-defined code has diminished into a submerged "little" tradition, with gay definitions now taking precedence. The gay/lesbian cosmology has drawn away from the heterosexist imprint in personal relationships toward valuation of same-sex relations where exclusive homosexuality has become possible for both partners, age and gender roles have been displaced by egalitarian norms, and a self-conscious cultural and political entity has asserted a will toward collective change (Adam 1987:6).

In discussing these differences with Nicaraguans, I was impressed with the strong interest pasivos showed in gay ideas as they interpreted them as a way of counteracting widespread homophobia and of gaining respect, equality, and loyalty in relationships with activos who often treat them with the disdain characteristic of male privilege. It is worth noting that gay movements which have emerged in Spain, Greece, and Mexico, where genderized codes of homosexuality have been strong, have sought to challenge, rather than affirm, folk categories in the name of equality. Whether relationships among homosexually-inclined men in Nicaragua evolve towards the gay model widespread in Europe and North America or develop in new directions has yet to be seen. Machismo was being challenged by Sandinista reform in law, education, and television broadcasting. The fall of the Sandinista government and restoration of the church-business coalition under the UNO banner led to a break of the safer-sex network from the Ministry of Health and the new state is unlikely to offer any further reform.

NOTES

1. Because I met too few lesbians during my stay in Nicaragua to be able to comment intelligently, I am confining my remarks to the men.

2. I use the term 'gay' advisedly here.

3. Lacey (1979:24) notes the same dynamic in Mexico.

4. All translations from the Spanish are mine.

5. Nicaragua is not alone in having AIDS provide the impetus for the formation of the first gay-related groups (see Adam, forthcoming).

REFERENCES

Adam, B.D. (1985a). Age, structure, and sexuality. *Journal of Homosexuality,* *11*(3/4), 19-33.

Adam, B.D. (1985b). Structural foundations of the gay world. *Comparative Studies in Society and History,* *27*(4):658-670.

Adam, B.D. (1987). *The rise of a gay and lesbian movement.* Boston: G.K. Hall/Twayne.

Adam, B.D. (1988). Neighborhood democracy in Nicaragua. *Dialectical Anthropology* *13*(1), 5-15.

Adam, B.D. (Forthcoming). Sex and caring among men. In Kenneth Plummer (Ed.). *Beyond Homosexuality.* London: Routledge.

Arboleda, M. (1980). Gay life in Lima. *Gay Sunshine, 42/43*:30.

Arboleda, M. (1981). *Social attitudes and sexual variance in Lima, Peru.* Paper presented to the American Sociological Association, Toronto.

Carrier, J. (1971). Participants in urban Mexican male homosexual encounters. *Archives of Sexual Behavior, 1*(4):279.

Carrier, J. (1976). Cultural factors affecting urban Mexican male homosexual behavior. *Archives of Sexual Behavior, 5*(2):103.

Carrier, J. (1977). Family attitudes and Mexican male homosexuality. In C. Warren (Ed.). *Sexuality: Encounters, Identities, and Relationships.* Beverly Hills, CA: Sage Publications Inc..

Chauncey, G. (1985). Christian brotherhood or sexual perversion? *Journal of Social History, 19*(2):189.

Colburn, F. (1986). *Post-Revolutionary Nicaragua.* Berkeley: University of California Press.

Fry, P. (1986). Male homosexuality and spirit possession in Brazil. *Journal of Homosexuality, 11*(3/4):137.

Gutierrez Morales, M. (1985). Prejuición contra un (?) % de nicaragüenses. *El Nuevo Diario* (Nov 25):2.

Juarez Calvo, P. (1985a). Homosexualidad y basura. *El Nuevo Diario* (Nov 13):2.

Kutsche, P. (1983). Situational homosexuality in Costa Rica. *Newsletter of the Anthropology Research Group on Homosexuality, 4*(4):8.

Kutsche, P. (1986). *Gay male identity in Costa Rica.* Paper presented to the American Anthropological Association, Philadelphia.

Lacey, E.A. (1979). Latin America. *Gay Sunshine, 40/41*(Summer/Fall):22.

Managua's economic crisis. *Envío, 5*(66, Dec 1986):36.

Miranda Saenz, A. (1985a). Sensibilizar contra la basura. *El Nuevo Diario* (Nov 8):2.

Miranda Saenz, A. (1985b). Basura y homosexualidad. *El Nuevo Diario* (Nov 19):2.

Murray, S. (1980). Lexical and institutional elaboration. *Anthropological Linguistics, 22*(4):177.

Norman, C. (1987). Police in Nicaragua town question gay men. *Gay Community News, 14*(28):3.

Parker, R. (1984). A report from Rio. *Newsletter of the Anthropology Research Group on Homosexuality, 5*(1-2):12.

Prevenir el SIDA sin caer en la histeria. *El Nuevo Diario* (Dec 2, 1985):5.

Taylor, C. (1986). Mexican male homosexual interaction in public contexts. *Journal of Homosexuality, 11*(3/4):117.

Young, A. (1973). Gay gringo in Brazil. In A. Young (Ed.), *The Gay Liberation Book*. San Francisco: Ramparts.

Invertidos Sexuales, Tortilleras, and Maricas Machos: The Construction of Homosexuality in Buenos Aires, Argentina, 1900-1950

Daniel Bao, MA

Condom Resource Center

SUMMARY. The author discusses Argentinean construction of homosexuality from 1900 to 1950 in the context of the raging debate of the essentialists versus social constructionists. The history of sexual inverts is discussed with reference to early sexologists. After a broad exploration of sexual inversion, the author turns to the Argentinean doctors who distinguish between acquired and congenital inverts. There was much resistance to the medical and legal establishments as there were autobiographies written by inverts, who subverted the medical views of the day. Finally, Bao concludes that there was, indeed, an Argentine construction of homosexuality, and that there were similarities between Buenos Aires and other large European cities. It is also noted that at the beginning of the twentieth century, there was a developed Argentine subculture of inverts who had meeting places, fashion, sexual tastes, and customs.

INTRODUCTION

History is often both a blessing and a curse. In the context of current sexual politics, this is precisely history's position. By displaying a pano-

Daniel Bao is currently the Director of the Condom Resource Center, P.O. Box 30564, Oakland, CA 94604. Correspondence may be addressed to the address above or to: 21043 Christensen Drive, Cupertino, CA 95014.

ply of past sexual possibilities, it is a blessing, pointing out the range of possible sexualities. But, simultaneously, it undermines many people's cherished and entrenched views of the way things should be. Therefore, historical research in the currently politicized area of sexuality has been met by great resistance.

Yet, against these obstacles, the emergence of feminist and gay politics in their full diversity, has helped generate work in this generally obscure and often obscured part of history. The majority of research that has been undertaken has concentrated on the United States, Canada, and Western Europe, mostly as a matter of convenience. With research money scarce and the shortage of political and academic space in most non-Western societies lacking well organized gay and feminist political movements, not to mention language difficulties, it has made most sense to stick close to home. Now that a reasonable body of theory and research has been articulated and accumulated in the West, it is time to see if our paradigms and research can be extended to non-Western cases. [1]

I will examine the Argentine construction of sexual inversion, the precursor of our current categories of homosexuality, transvestism, and transexuality. Argentina's position as a country outside the United States, Canada, and Western Europe, yet, at the same time, a part of the "West" with comparatively few indigenous influences left, make it an interesting case on the outskirts of the already studied West.

First, I will look at the broad issues in academia labeled the "essentialism versus social constructionism" debate which lay out the context and directions for research and thinking on sexuality. The theorizing of the early sexologists on sexual inversion, especially Krafft-Ebing will establish a European and theoretical context on sexual inversion. Next, the U.S. and Western European invert subcultures from the late nineteenth and early twentieth centuries that have been studied and described will give us a basis from which to compare the Argentine invert subculture.

We will then be ready to move to Argentine definitions and conceptualizations of sexuality. Moving from theory to practice, the sexual invert stereotypes will give a flavor of how inverts were concretely perceived by doctors and, to some extent, by broader society. Since definitions are seldom accepted passively and undialectically, signs of resistance from inverts themselves will be explored. Finally, I will try to reconstruct the Argentine invert community, its language, fashion, and way of life.

ESSENTIALISM VERSUS SOCIAL CONSTRUCTIONISM

The emerging field of the history of sexuality has been afflicted, as new academic fields often are, with a debate over what its proper bounds should be. For years, sexuality has been conceived as an a-historical category, constant and unvarying across cultures and ages. This is, of course, not to say that people were blind to cultural differences in sexual customs. It is that sex was viewed uncritically as Sex, whether in the view of Protestant missionary position or the more expansive positions in the Kama Sutra. Categories such as heterosexual, homosexual, bisexual, transexual, and transvestite were used retroactively to redefine earlier historical categories such as sodomite, sexual pervert, tribadist, and sexual invert. Like Dante, who placed the virtuous pre-Christians in purgatory since, through no fault of their own, they could not be in paradise, historians and gay activists alike placed "famous homosexuals" in an unbroken chain from Socrates through Michelangelo and Leonardo, to Liberace.

Michel Foucault and his followers radically challenged this view. They viewed sexuality as being arbitrarily constructed in the power relations of societies. This liberatory view of sexuality, and especially its implications for homosexuality, were eagerly embraced by many. Yet, while Foucault's views were "liberatory" in the sense that they enabled gay liberationists to criticize the prevailing social culture as an arbitrary construction based on power, paradoxically, in the context of the liberal paradigm, it undercut one of the strongest claims that gay liberationists used, that homosexuality was "natural" since it occurred in all places at all times in the same proportions. At the same time, it seemed to play into the hands of reactionaries who argued that since categories such as "homosexual" were arbitrary, existing homosexuals could be "converted" or "cured" of their affliction or category.

In the academic world, in parallel to these political debates, there arose two competing "camps." One was labeled "essentialist" and the other "social constructionist." This was basically, a variation of the old nature vs. nurture argument. Essentialists, siding with nature, argue that homosexuality exists as a coherent historical category. The ancients may not have had a word like "homosexuality" but they knew what same-sex relations were. Constructionists, on the other hand, argue that sexuality is age and culture specific. Therefore, it is impossible to contain in one coherent category people as diverse as Socrates as represented in Plato's Symposium and the stereotypical diesel dyke.

For example, the Attic Greek conception of sexuality was constructed in such a way that sex between two women does not seem to have been a possibility. Sex was defined as occurring between a bearded male citizen and a boy, woman, or foreigner in a strict active/passive construction in sexual intercourse. Furthermore, boys, who partook of the passive role as youth, were expected to marry (women) when they grew up, raise families, and have sexual relations with boys.

John Boswell, a leading gay historian, has put it well:

> Nominalists ("social constructionists" in the current debate) in the matter aver that categories of sexual preference and behavior are created by humans and human societies. Whatever reality they have is the consequence of the power they exert in those societies and the socialization processes that make them seem real to persons influenced by them . . . Realists ("essentialists") hold that this is not the case. Humans are, they insist, differentiated sexually. Many categories might be devised to characterize human sexual taxonomy, some more or less apt than others, but the accuracy of human perceptions does not affect reality. The heterosexual/homosexual dichotomy exists in speech and thought because it exists in reality: It was not invented by sexual taxonomists, but observed by them.[2]

Boswell, the main (and perhaps the only) exponent on the essentialist side was met by Foucault, Weeks, Katz and others on the constructionist side. The above discussion, of course, is rather a simplistic view of the issues; I've simplified the sides to be able to draw them more clearly. As in the nature versus nurture debate, everyone agrees that both sides are right, the critical question is not who is correct, but what the balance between the two should be.

Lately, a view that encompasses the essentialist and constructionist debate has emerged.[3] Bolstered by studies from cultures around the word, the new view argues that "homosexuality" has historically been organized in three basic patterns. One is a construction based on class/age differences as with the ancient Greeks, and many Asian, African, and Middle Eastern cultures. The second is a construction based on gender difference, as in Latin America and Western Europe and North America before the 1950s. The third and most modern category is the egalitarian one, based on a perceived equality between partners, as in post-1960 North America and Western Europe.

The class/age construction of homosexuality usually posits two separate types of sexual beings, the higher class/older male, and the lower class/younger male. Unlike the other categories, the first category is usually transitory so that one shifts from one type to another as one matures. The older/higher class male is usually conceived of in a ritual or mentoring capacity to the younger/lower male and none of these activities precludes sexual contact with women in a marriage situation. The Greek example cited above fits this category.

The gender construction usually posits two or three sexual categories:

male, female, and other. Sex is conceived as relations between a person in one category and another in the same category or in a "third" or "intermediate" category. This construction, compared to the class/age one, is more likely to construct specific sexual categories. This occurs because, unlike the class/age construction which tends to construct transitory categories, the gender construction is often based on biological or deep psychological origins, thereby lending permanence to these categories.

The egalitarian construction posits two equal beings. This is the category most intelligible to us in the U.S. and Western Europe now and it originated in gender constructed homosexuality. The theory is that as current explanations of gender creation have moved away from biological or deep psychological origins, gender stereotyping has weakened dramatically. Therefore, the non-transitory gender construction model's sexual categories which originally were constructed on the same bases, have been separated from unequal gender conceptions and have paralleled heterosexual gender movements toward a more egalitarian sexual ideal.

With this construct in mind, the work of the early sexologists can be better placed. Living in Europe in the latter half of the nineteenth century, their work reflected the gender based construction of sexuality of their cultures. And, though we often now view them as conservative, controlling, and confused, their creation and popularization of "sexual inversion" as a medical category undoubtedly comforted many isolated inverts even as it classified them as ill.

EARLY SEXOLOGISTS AND KRAFFT-EBING

Before I begin discussing the inversion theories of the early sexologists, let me make clear that in looking at theory, I do not mean to imply that early sexology theory literally "created" the invert. In many ways, early sexologists described and reacted to what they observed. On the other hand, inverts did not "create" themselves out of whole cloth. They often reacted to what they read and experienced in their everyday lives. My working hypothesis is that a complex set of interactions centered on societal views of gender, the sex/gender system in Gayle Rubin's parlance, was what created the circumstances around which "sexual inversion" was defined. These sociological and sexological texts are among the few sources of information available for this time period on sexual inversion (especially in Argentina).

At the turn of the last century, the prevailing sexual ideology in the West spoke about sexual inversion rather than homosexuality. As George

Chauncey Jr. explains, "'Sexual Inversion' referred to a broad range of cross-gender behavior (in which males behaved like women, and vice-versa), of which homosexual desire was only a logical but indistinct aspect, while 'homosexuality' focused on the narrower issue of sexual object choice."[4] Inversion was viewed as literally a reversion of the sexual personality of a person. The common metaphor of the time was a female brain (or mind) in the body of a male, and vice versa. Since gender roles were rigid, well-defined, well-separated, and generally believed to be inherently biological in origin, there existed an entire constellation of stereotyped gender qualities which formed inversion, among these were clothing, mannerisms, and personality traits.

Havelock Ellis and Sigmund Freud were the first major theorists to clearly separate gender from sexual object choice. Freud published his groundbreaking essays on sexuality in 1905. They posited a separation between what was viewed as biological gender and psychological sexual object choice. Though some of the invert theorists also gave importance to psychological concerns, Freud was the first to posit this separation at a basic theoretical level. Now, the "homosexual" was a person identified not by a constellation of feminine or masculine qualities, but by the gender of his/her sexual object choice. In the U.S. by the 1920s and 30s, under Freud's influential differentiation, the present day categories of homosexual, heterosexual, bisexual, transvestite, and transexual, became established. In Argentina, these developments occurred later than in Europe and the U.S. The "invert," in its non-scientific guise, the *maricon*, persists to this day, the "homosexual" seems to have only strongly emerged in the early 1960s, and the explicitly political "gay and lesbian," introduced from the U.S. and Europe, in the early 1970s. Most likely, these divergences from the U.S. and Europe are best explained in the context of broader social change. Argentina did not experience the 1960s feminist movement in the same manner, form, or extent as the U.S. and Europe. Sexism is far more prevalent in all of Latin America and the gender constructed homosexuality in all of the region is likely to remain and not evolve into the egalitarian model as long as gender stereotyping and sexism remains strong.

It is instructive to take a closer look at the most prominent of the early sexologists, Richard von Krafft-Ebing, since he was the most prominent sexual invert theorist. Furthermore, his theory of sexual inversion is closest to our modern views of homosexuality, therefore, the differences in his conceptions of homosexuality and sexual inversion are very instructive. Early sexologists generally spoke of "homosexuality" as a trait but did not usually identify a "homosexual" as a unique individual. Krafft-

Ebing, unlike most of the early sexologists, did argue for the existence of the "homosexual." However, Krafft-Ebing's homosexual was a lesser version of the full sexual invert. Krafft-Ebing argued that there were two types of sexual inversion, congenital and acquired. His construction of congenital sexual inversion was in four categories. Category four was the "ideal" case of congenital sexual inversion, while categories one to three were less advanced forms:

1. Traces of heterosexual, with predominating homosexual, instinct (psycho-sexual hermaphroditism).
2. There exists inclination only towards the same sex (homosexuality).
3. The entire mental existence is altered to correspond with the abnormal sexual instinct (effemination and viraginity).
4. The form of the body approaches that which corresponds to the abnormal sexual instinct. However actual transitions to hermaphrodites never occur, but, on the contrary, completely differentiated genitals; so that, just as in all pathological perversions of the sexual life, the cause must be sought in the brain (hermaphroditism and pseudo-hermaphroditism).[5]

The stages of acquired sexual inversion (we will see later why this distinction between congenital and acquired inversion was important) were similar. However, while the four categories of congenital sexual inversion appear to have been constructed as categories by which different individuals could be classed, the categories of acquired sexual inversion could progress depending on the individual's environment or actions:

1. Simple Reversal of Sexual Feeling
2. Eviration and Defemination
3. Stage of Transition to Change of Sex Delusion
4. Delusion of Sexual Change[6]

Notice that congenital stage #2 and acquired stage #1 (a "reversal" of feeling) were what we would now identify as a homosexual, someone identified solely by his/her same sex sexual attraction. Congenital stage #3 and acquired stage #2 continue the progression of inversion to the entire personality, i.e., men became feminine and women masculine. Congenital stage #4 identified a physical change such as shrunken testes, high voice, small waistline, and a wide pelvis in men and low voice, shrunken breasts, and narrow pelvis for women. This explains why early sexologists searched for physical body changes as signs of inversion. In

Krafft-Ebing's formulation, physical change or mental change, necessarily implied homosexuality. In other inversion theories, all of these changes (sexual, mental, physical) were usually seen as coeval.

Inversion theory showed two major theoretical and practical flaws. One is that since gender was conceived of as biologically based, people should show signs of inversion early in childhood. Inversion that occurred later in life, especially after a "successful" "normal" sexual life, implied that gender might not be biologically based. The second problem is "Who sleeps with inverts?" For male inverts, "normal" men should want to have sex with women, women should desire it with men, and male inverts with men too. The only category which should theoretically desire to have sex with male inverts is female inverts (and vice versa)!

The first problem, the late first occurrence of signs of inversion, was dealt with by Krafft-Ebing and the early sexologists in a similar way. They posited that an invert showing early signs of inversion was a congenital invert. On the other hand, inverts who had begun their lives "normally" with marriage, prostitutes, or other women, must have acquired the inversion. For Krafft-Ebing, the disease did not run its course in the same manner in both the congenital and acquired versions. Only congenital inverts showed the physical changes that accompanied true inversion (congenital stage #4), acquired inverts only were deluded into believing they were undergoing physical changes (acquired stages #3 and #4). Later on, we will see how this question was handled in Argentina.

The second problem of who sleeps with inverts was a bit tougher. Here, the acquired/congenital distinction was often brought in. The argument was that since acquired inverts were not congenitally formed, they might retain some sexual feeling towards members of their own sex. Having a hermaphroditic desire, they would therefore desire inverts. This explanation was rather weak and many theorists realized it. Krafft-Ebing, as we have seen, constructed a continuum of categories which explained this behavior. By establishing a continuum, however, Krafft-Ebing pointed to the complete separation of gender and sexual object choice which Ellis and Freud were to establish in the early 1900s.

INVERT SUBCULTURES

Inverts did not exist in isolation, invert subcultures were present in major cities across Europe and the United States in the late nineteenth and early twentieth centuries. In cities such as Chicago, New York, Philadelphia, San Francisco, Paris, Berlin, and London, inverts congregated in public and private areas, attending drag balls, avoiding police harassment (especially the economically worse off who engaged in prostitution), and forming their own customs and traditions. According to La Forest Potter, for example:

> there is no other city in the world in which there are as many social unions of urnings, as there are in Berlin. In addition to lavish private parties, they give dinners, suppers, teas, dances, picnics and festivals–all arranged and attended by the urnings and their lesbian friends.[7]

While the middle and upper classes were thus occupied, among the lower classes, according to Potter:

> There is a certain infestation of 'aunties', who give themselves for payment to well-to-do homosexuals, or who set out to make conquests of heterosexuals. These individuals are practiced in the art of make-up and coquetry, just as is a courtesan. However, in the Germanic countries solicitation and the seduction of heterosexuals are severely frowned upon.[8]

Similar descriptions can be found for the U.S. In New York, circa 1890, for example:

> There were several resorts called beer gardens in those days on the Bowery and lower east side in which male perverts, dressed in elaborate feminine evening costumes, "sat for company" and received a commission on all the drinks served by the house to them and their customers.[9]

Again, in Philadelphia:

> Sexual perversion was just as rife in Philadelphia as in any city of the east. These creatures solicited on the streets on very much the same terms as elsewhere. Between Chestnut and Walnut Streets (late at night) we were accosted by an over dressed male pervert who began his solicitation in the usual way which was more or less inferential. His mannerisms and speech were, of course, exaggeratedly feminine and his face was clean shaven and highly decorated with cosmetics.[10]

Buenos Aires at the turn of the last century was a growing immigrant metropolis, the capital port city of a country blessed with abundant fertile land. Between 1897 and 1906, Buenos Aires saw its population grow from 738,484 to over 1 million inhabitants, a fifty percent increase in little over a decade.[11] Cosmopolitan and urbane, Buenos Aires shared many characteristics with other large European and U.S. cities of the time, including a large population of "sexual inverts," many brought along in the immigrant tide. The medical literature on sexual inversion cases shows that many of the inverts of Buenos Aires were immigrants; and reformers often pinpointed immigration as being the source of social problems:

> Buenos Aires, lo mismo que toda la República, abierta de par en par á quien quiere venir á ella, recibe por fuerza, dentro de la corriente inmigratoria normal, buena parte de la escoria antisocial del los demas países.[12]

Another telling bit of information (indicating that Buenos Aires was also exporting inverts) is an account of the life of a certain traveler who, according to the book, *La Mala Vida En Barcelona:*

> Citaré el caso de un *cocoto*, que relató la prensa local. Se trata de *La Teresita*. Expulsado de Buenos Aires, Chile, Bolivia y otros estados americanos, desembarcó en La Coruña en marzo de 1911. Su verdadero nombre es Rojo. Tiene 30 años y es hijo de un antiguo comerciante; es afeminado y no mal parecido. Disfrazado de mujer y vistiendo elegantísimos trajes, se dio maña para conquistar a no pocos americanos, recibiendo cuantiosos regalos . . . En Buenos Aires, se instaló fastuosamente en la calle de Belgrano y daba grandes fiestas y saraos, en los que se presentaba vistiendo trajes femeninos de un lujo escandaloso.[13]

The mobility shown by La Teresita hints, and the sheer number of immigrants in Buenos Aires at the turn of the century implies that there was exchange and contact between the invert culture in Buenos Aires and those in Europe.

ARGENTINE DEFINITIONS

"Los médicos y los procuradores siempre le han de inventar nombres raros a las cosas más sencillas . . . En mis tiempos se les llamaban mariquita, no más, o maricón, que es más claro . . ."[14]

This quote, spoken in José González Castillo's play, *Los Invertidos*, by Petrona, a lower-class maid, probably represents the view of many in the lower classes who did not see much of a social problem inherent in "maricones." Not that it was not a problem in any way, for Petrona also comments that, "¡Casi todos los mariquitas que yo he conocido o he oído decir, han muerto lo mismo (suicide) . . . , como si juera [sic] un castigo de Dios!"[15] Others, as Petrona points out, in the medical and legal establishments, were more interested in "inventing strange names for simple things." Her social reality is very difficult to investigate for what we do have access to is mainly the views of respected doctors and lawyers, an aspect of reality but not the entire story.

Dr. Francisco De Veyga was a professor of legal medicine at the University of Buenos Aires, Director of services to the insane with the Buenos Aires police, and, incidentally, a member of the editorial committee of the *Archivos de Psiquiatría y Criminología*. Dr. Veyga's medical articles are the earliest I have found of the post-colonial period in Argentina and only seem to have been predated in Latin America by Brazilian medical texts. They date from 1902 to 1903 and were published as articles in the *Archivos de Psiquiatría y Criminología*. The articles include, *Inversión Sexual Congénita, Invertido Sexual Imitando La Mujer Honesta, La Inversión Sexual Adquirida, El Amor En Los Invertidos Sexuales,* and *La Inversión Sexual Adquirida, Tipo profesional: un invertido comerciante.* As a doctor connected with the police, he examined many inverts, and was considered the most knowledgeable neurologist in Argentina at the turn of the century. His set of examples is relatively skewed, since his connection to the police led to many of his cases being inverts who had been arrested, often for prostitution, and were consequently members of the lower classes. Educated at the Pasteur Institute in Paris, Dr. De Veyga's writing seems relatively untouched by his personal views, especially in comparison to that of other social reformers of the time.

Dr. De Veyga espouses a relatively straightforward view of inversion, though he does not explicitly state which inversion theories he is using. His main difference from classic inversion theory is that though "congenital inverts" were "true" inverts, that is, they were really women in men's bodies, "acquired" inverts were not. Acquired sexual inversion was not true inversion since it arose because of mental decay in one form or another. De Veyga also always uses "homo-sexual" as an adjective and never a noun. He speaks of "el aparato homo-sexual del invertido,"[16] or "la fornicación homosexual,"[17] and even, "tendencias homosexuales." [18]

Another Argentine to discuss sexual inversion is Eusebio Gómez in his book, *La Mala Vida en Buenos Aires*, published in 1908. Gómez was a lawyer with the Instituto de Criminología and his book, similar to other social reform books of the time, was intended as a popular presentation of the urban problems of Buenos Aires. Gómez, like many people of his time, also believed in the power of genes:

> Anteriormente hemos insinuado que la calidad de las corrientes inmigratorias que llegan al país contribuye en gran parte al desarollo de la criminalidad.
>
> Ocupándose de este problema, el doctor Moyano Gacitúa llega á afirmar que esas corrientes llevan en sí el sello de la criminalidad más alta de la tierra, en razón de las razas que las constituyen. [19]

Gómez defines sexual terms in this way:

> Consiste la homosexualidad en la inclinación hacia las personas del mismo sexo, para el cumplimiento y satisfacción de los apetitos carnales. Cuando la inclinación indicada es de hombre á hombre, se llama uranismo ó pederastía; safismo ó tribadismo cuando es de mujer á mujer.
>
> La sodomía es el término que sirve para distinguir á las relaciones sexuales caracterizadas por la *inmissio membri in anum*, sean esas relaciones entre personas de distinto sexo ó pertenecientes ambas al mismo.
>
> La pederastía reviste formas diversas: la masturbación recíproca, el coito anal y la *inmissio penis in os alterius*. (Coito bucal)[20]

Gómez's definitions appear to be very similar to modern ones (except for the use of Latin in particular areas), especially his definitions of homosexuality and sodomy.[21] His definition of pederasty differs from the current definition of contact between man and boy, not man and man. He uses sexual inversion and homosexuality more synonymously than De Veyga does but in an ambivalent, almost synonymous way. For example, Gómez uses "Los Homosexuales" as a chapter title, but his subchapter titles are, "Los invertidos sexuales; La moral de los invertidos sexuales; Invertidos aristócratas é invertidos plebeyos; El sarao de los uranistas." He also refers to the "inversión de los homosexuales"[22] Additionally, of the four photos in the chapter on homosexuals, three are labeled "invertido sexual" and one "pederasta pasivo."

Additionally, his explanation of a theory of the origins of homosexuality, which he offers as a possible explanation but implies is his own states:

si entonces sucede que en el desarrollo posterior del feto los dos
sexos se reducen á uno solo, y si al mismo tiempo se atrofia el
sistema psíquico opuesto á los órganos sexuales que desaparecen,
se tendrá un individuo con inclinaciones sexuales opuestas a la
naturaleza de sus órganos; el dotado aparentemente como hombre,
se sentirá hembra, será un andrógino, un pederasta pasivo; mientras
que el individuo dotado anatómicamente como mujer, se sentirá
macho, y deseará unirse con un individuo del sexo femenino para
entregarse al amor lésbico.[23]

This theory appears to be invert theory, a female mind in a male body or
a male mind in a female body.

An interesting point in the separate histories of male and female
sexualities is the almost complete absence of inverted women in these
documents. Gómez refers to women in the above quote, defining female
same-gender sex as sapphism or tribadism. De Veyga too, mentions the
possibility of female same-gender sexual behavior in a passing reference
to male frottage, "imitación de lo que hacen las mujeres invertidas en
semehantes casos." [24] Though he seemed aware of how inverted women
had sexual relations, none of his case examples, or Gómez's is of a woman. Other than these passing references, women in the context of inversion are not dealt with at all. Though there may have been fewer female
inverts, economic and social gender discrimination probably played a
large role in their absence. Since most of Dr. De Veyga's cases originated in police arrests, this implies that inverted women were less likely to
be arrested. Probably in the context of the male-centered Argentine
world, they were not considered as a problem.

Dr. De Veyga tries to answer the two major ideological flaws in the
theory of inversion, aside from the fact that female inversion seemed to
be more hypothetical than real. The first theoretical problem was that
inverts, if they were really women in men's bodies, should show their
proclivities at an early age by playing with dolls, being quiet, in general,
acting like little girls. Some inverts, however, became inverts later in life
having shown few or no signs of their future inversion in their youth. In
similar fashion to the above, De Veyga, following Krafft-Ebing and other
major theorists, solved this problem by looking at the causes of acquired
sexual inversion and concluding that it was caused either by desire for
money, suggestion exacerbated by mental weakness, or mental derange-
ment. This differentiation between acquired and congenital, however, was
not as easy to make in the real world as he himself admitted:

A decir verdad, la clasificación que se basa en la naturaleza de orígen de esta desviación psicorgánica es puramente artificial, no existiendo en la clínica un rasgo determinado que distinga al invertido nato del que se convierte en tal por cualquier motivo. La influencia que ejerce el sello de orígen sobre el sujeto, consiste unicamente en el modo de aparición de las primeras manifestaciones y aún en ese mismo fenómeno hay algunas veces tal semejanza de detalles, que bien pueden identificarse unos casos con otros.[25]

Here he admits, that the difference between congenital and acquired inversion is "purely artificial." The only difference he could discern between congenital and acquired inversion rested on the timing of the first manifestations and even here, it was extremely difficult to separate the two.

The second major problem was the question of who would have sex with these male inverts. Being male inverts, under the prevailing sexual ideology, they should be pasivos. Who would fill the activo role? Other inverts were pasivos while non-inverted men should desire women. The theoretical possibility of inverted women (who were really men) assuming this position never appears in these documents. De Veyga has two explanations for this problem. One is that in some men with acquired sexual inversion, their "normal desires" might not be completely altered. He even identified a term for them:

Eso explica la singular contradicción que ofrecen algunos sujetos que son invertidos y al mismo tiempo frecuentan mujer, ya sea que la encuentren ocasionalmente ó que la tengan de fijo. Hay ejemplos de invertidos casados que continúan haciendo vida marital y procreando . . . La presencia de estas tendencias explica tambien los casos en que se acoplan momentáneamente á un tiempo dos invertidos y las propensiones que tienen algunos á hacer papel de hombres en medio de sus devaneos homo-sexuales. A estos tipos, el azote de los invertidos, les ha dado el título sugestivo de *maricas machos* (!)[26]

This answer was only partially satisfactory, for what was one to think of the seemingly sane *non-inverted* men who were found with male inverts? These men required a more complicated answer:

En cuanto á los cómplices de esta singular pantomina mórbida, avancemos esta conclusión general, que puede servir de principio etiológico para el estudio y comprensión de todos estos fenómenos de aberración sexual en el hombre: existen al lado de los invertidos, para determinar ó fomentar las tendencias homo sexuales, tipos previamente inclinados al goce corporal dentro de su sexo. La idea de aceptarle con un ser de idéntico género, temporario ó permanentemente, no puede tener por orígen exclusivo la degeneración mental ó la locura; por más extraviadas que sean las concepciones de la mente enferma, siempre hay en el mundo ambiente una base que les sirve de pié, y en este caso, lo de "convertirse en mujer", sea de tipo libertino ó casto, responde á la existencia de una clase especial de sujetos, más numerosos quizás que la de aquellos, ó por lo menos tanto, que busca de satisfacer las impulsiones viriles sobre un individuo de su sexo forjándose la ilusión de que es mujer. De todos modos, al lado del invertido se encuentra siempre el sodomita más ó menos enviciado, sirviéndole de complemento y de estímulo.[27]

Here we see Dr. De Veyga struggling with the entire concept of inversion. While Krafft-Ebing solved this problem by positing a category of homosexuals, De Veyga comes close. Instead, he posits a type of man, as numerous or more numerous than inverts themselves, who sexually desires other men acting as women. Not having a good word to describe this person, he uses the word sodomite, not technically the correct word since sodomites, as Gómez points out, seek a particular sexual act with either males or females.

As we have seen, sexual inversion was theorized on the basis of gender constructs and gender stereotypes were biologically based and very strong. Though we now view many of these stereotypes as quaint and absurd for men and women of whatever sexual orientation, it is interesting and instructive to see how many have persisted in one way or another.

STEREOTYPES

De Veyga in his articles mentions quite a number of features he attributes to inverts. Some seem to have persisted down to the present, such as areas of employment for inverts, "El arte de peinador de señoras, sea dicho de paso, es frecuentemente ejercido por invertidos."[28] In discussing an unusual case in which one individual preferred men of his own age, De Veyga points out that most inverts prefer the young, "Contra el gusto dominante entre los demás invertidos, prefiere hombres de edad á los jóvenes."[29] Dr. DeVeyga, in discussing another case of an invert willing to do anything for money, also strongly implies that male inverts are supposed to assume the *pasivo* role:[30]

> En su comercio carece igualmente de signos especiales, prestándose todo lo que se le exije, según el caso. Hace hasta de *activo* si las circunstancias lo obligan, pues andando á la pesca de solicitantes, si encuentra algún sujeto que anda en la misma aventura pero prometiendo paga, se ofrece á satisfacerlo sin mayor dificultad.[31]

This distinction between activo and pasivo also appears in *Los Invertidos*, in a scene from Act III where Clara is interrogating Benito, Florez's servant. She asks about why Perez's house is called a club and Benito answers, "Y . . . será porque tiene socios, ativos y pasivos."[32]

The stereotype of the seduction into the self-indulgent life of pleasure is evident in these quotes, "Un día encontró un sujeto que lo abordó de lleno el seductor de siempre, el agente inicial de estas desviaciones que parecen obra exclusiva de la naturaleza . . . "[33] and, "Todos ellos [los invertidos] se caracterizan por la extravagancia y la niñería."[34]

The most prominent features of male inverts, of course, were their "female characteristics." In interviewing Aurora, an acquired invert, Dr. De Veyga says, "No le [a Aurora] han faltado tentaciones de simularnos una novela sobre la iniciación á su vida de marica y contarnos, como cosa seria, sus 'inclinaciones femeniles', sus 'gustos artísticos',· su 'sensibilidad exagerada', su 'alma de mujer', que es el fuerte de todos ellos; pero optó por la franqueza, evitándonos mayor pérdida de tiempo."[35] This quote not only shows the beliefs that "true" congenital inverts had female inclinations, artistic tastes, exaggerated sensibilities, and the soul of women, but also shows how some were playing with these stereotypes, an act which I, following Jonathan Katz, call resistance. Additionally, as we saw with Krafft-Ebing, physical features were important. Cione, in his novel, *Luxuria*, describes a sexual invert in this way, "Paquillo, el peinador y sus corifeos, que lo admiraban y envidiaban, era un andaluz que vestía a lo chulo y tenía especial placer en mostrar las curvas de sus caeras, sus muslos femeninos y su cintura de avispa."[36]

Of course, not all the stereotyping was neutral, Gómez has this to say:

> Al rasgo que acabamos de indicar en los invertidos, la venalidad, ó mas bien dicho, el parasitismo, únese su caracter caprichoso, sus envidias, la ruindad de todos sus procederes, su deseo de venganza, y sus rencores ilimitados. Tarnowski dice que reunen en sí todos los defectos de las mujeres sin tener nunguna de sus cualidades, careci-

endo, además, de las condiciones que hacen amable el carácter viril.[37]

Even worse, "Son celosos y esta pasión los lleva hasta el crimen. Un sensacional proceso recientemente debatido ante la justicia militar, acaba de dar la prueba al respecto." [38]

RESISTANCE

There is interesting evidence in these documents that inverts were not behaving in the way that they were supposed to according to medical experts and were, in fact, subverting categories. For example, in the just mentioned case of Aurora, an acquired invert, Dr. De Veyga observes that:

> El concepto que todos ellos [invertidos adquiridos-DB] se forman de la sexualidad femenina, á cuya imitación dedican todo su afán, –es, por lo pronto, completamente erróneo. Esa 'alma de mujer' que tantos de entre ellos pretenden poseer y en cuya existencia han llegado á hacer creer á muchos observadores dignos de la mayor consideración, no es sinó una pura fantasía, una ilusión delirante en la verdadera acepción de la palabra. [39]

Here there is the clear implication that inverts are claiming to have the soul of women (i.e., being "congenital inverts"), instead of the acquired inverts that De Veyga believed they were. Ideologically, the reason seems to be relatively straightforward. Being born an invert was a better position than becoming one through prostitution, a bad environment, or mental decay (which were the possible causes of acquired inversion).

A clearer example is provided by Gómez, who not only shows that some inverts tried to justify their lives within the context of femininity but that they also followed scientific journals written on their condition. "Tratan de justificarse [los invertidos], alegando la feminidad de sus sentimientos y es curioso observar el interés con que siguen la literatura científica que les concierne."[40]

The most fascinating resistance document is an autobiography written by "La Bella Otero" who straightforwardly and even proudly speaks about his/her life and experiences. Dr. De Veyga introduces La Bella Otero's autobiography in this way:

Su psicología mórbida, combinacíon curiosa de vanidad, mentira é ideas sexuales paranoides, revélase en la siguiente página, que nos entregó como *autobiografía*, junto con los retratos anexos, sin disimular mucho su deseo de figurar como caso clínico en el libro que preparamos sobre los invertidos sexuales.

(*Autobiografía*)

He nacido en Madrid, en el año de 1880. Siempre me he creído mujer, y por eso uso vestido de mujer. Me casé en Sevilla y tuve dos hijos. El varón tiene 16 años y sigue la carrera militar en París. La *niñita* tiene 15 y se educa en el 'Sacre-Coeur' de Buenos Aires. Son muy bonitos, parecidos á su papá.

Mi esposo ha muerto y soy viuda. A veces quiero morir, cuando me acuerdo de él. Buscaría los fósforos ó el carbón para matarme, pero esos suicidios me parecen propios de gente baja. Como me gustan las flores, me parece que sería delicioso morir asfixiada por perfumes.

Otras ocasiones me gustaría tomar el hábito de monja carmelita, porque soy devota de Santa Teresa de Jésus, lo mismo que todas la mujeres aristocráticas. Pero como no soy capaz de renunciar á los placers del mundo, me quedo en mi casa á trabajar, haciendo costuras y bordados para dar á los pobres.

Soy una mujer que me gusta mucho el placer y por eso lo acepto bajo todas sus fases. Algunos dicen que por todo ésto soy muy viciosa, pero yo les he escrito el siguiente verso, que se lo digo siempre á todos.

Del Buen Retiro á la Alameda
los gustos locos me vengo á hacer,
Muchachos míos ténganlo tieso
que con la mano gusto os daré.

Con paragüitas y cascabeles
y hasta con guante yo os las haré,
y si tú quieres, chinito mío,
por darte gusto la embocaré.

Si con la boca yo te incomodo
y por la espaldas me quieres dar,
no tengas miedo, chinito mío,
no tengo pliegues ya por detrás.

Si con la boca yo te incomodo
y por atrás me quieres amar,
no tengas miedo, chinito mío,
que pronto mucho vas á gozar.

He estado en París, donde bailé en los cafés-conciertos dándole mucha envidia á otra mujer que usa mi mismo nombre para pasar por mí.

Muchos hombres jóvenes suelen ser descortes conmigo. Pero ha de ser de gana de estar conmigo, y ¿por qué no lo consiguen? porque no puedo atender á todos mis adoradores.

No quiero tener más hijos, pues me han hecho sufrir mucho los dolores del parto, aunque me asistieron mis amigas "Magda" y "Lucía", que no entienden de parto, porque nunca han estado embarazadas, porque están enfermas de los ovarios.

Me subyuga pasear en Palermo, porque el pasto es más estimulante para el amor que la mullida cama.

Esta es mi historia, y tengo el honor de regalarle al doctor Veyga algunos retratos con mi dedicatoria–"La Bella Otero." [41]

The autobiography is an amazing example of someone thumbing their nose at respectable society, especially the poem that she has written. As an interesting side note, when Gómez reprinted La Bella Otero's autobiography in his book, *La Mala Vida en Buenos Aires*, he omitted the poem entirely and without any explanation. The sexual paranoia that De Veyga sees is probably connected to La Bella Otero's claim to have physically given birth. Though she is delusional, I read it as a way of inadvertantly subverting the category of invert. After all, there are two main ways of subverting categories. One is to reject them and construct new ones and the other is to take existing ones to their logical (and usually irrational) extremes. Birth was the main biological difference that kept inverts from being women. González Castillo presents a similar scene when Petrona describes Lilí, the cousin of Dr. Perez, who when his aunt had a child, he " . . . se echó en cama y se puso a gritar también como si lo estuviera degollando . . . Al muy chancho se le había antojado tener hijos también." [42]

La Bella Otero distinguished herself in another way too, she was very frank not only about her sexual desires for men, but also her individual sexual tastes:

Contra el gusto dominante entre los demás invertidos, prefiere hombres de edad á los jóvenes; explica su gusto porque los viejos prolongan el coito y le pagan puntualmente, mientras que los jóvenes lo practican rápidamente, y en lugar de pagar le exigen dinero ó lo maltratan. Entre los viejos prefiere los "barrigones y peludos"; barrigones porque la intromisión del pene es menor y toda la excitación se localiza en el esfínter; peludos porque le producen gratas cosquillas en la espaldas y las regiones glúteas. [43]

This certainly does not sound like a person agonizing over his/her psychological problems. The quote also points out another stereotype of male inverts, that their sexual satisfaction resided in the anus and sphincter, not in their biological gender genitalia which would make sense if these male inverts had some biological changes, as in Krafft-Ebing's congenital inversion #4. In the case of Manón, a congenital sexual invert, Dr. De Veyga notes that he feels sexual pleasure but that, "sin embargo su sensación de voluptuosidad física no se localiza en el recto; este sitio parece ser el punto de excitación de sensaciones voluptuosas perfectamente localizada en sus órganos genitales y que se terminan por la eyaculación."[44]

La Bella Otero was able to support herself and lead her life independently as was another one of De Veyga's cases who, "Abandonó su casa y su familia al poco tiempo, constituyendo aparte, con un solicitante activo que encontró, una unión conyugal que duró largo tiempo y que hizo hablar á sus congéneres por el lujo que gastaban y la generosidad con que trataban á todas sus relaciones."[45] This invert seems to have been able to achieve some life for himself apart from his family, with a non-inverted male "husband."

Resistance is also shown by the character of Paquillo in the novel *Luxuria*. Though Paquillo is a fictional character, he mirrors reality, reiterating the themes of being like a girl when young and like a woman now, both physically and psychologically. He justifies himself by arguing that he's been this way since he was young, he insists on being called by the feminine version of his name, and, like the Bella Otero, claims a physiological female fact, menstrual pains:

> El [Paquillo] decia para justificar su morbosidad sexual:
> - Ende que nací a mí me dió po las labores del sexo femenino. Yo prendí a vestí muñecos y a hacé croché ante que a leer. Y cuando jugábamos a casarnos con otros chicos, yo era siempre la novia.
> Todo el dinero que ganaba en su oficio el peinador lo invertia en regalarlo a sus favoritos. Si se le llamaba Paquillo enojábase de veras y contestaba:
> - Yo so Paquilla y no sé por qué a nosotras las mujeres nos han de llamar con nombres masculinos. ¡Ah! por la virgen santísima, cuando a mí me "viene el mes" me pegaria un tiro si tuviera való!
> Varios tipos como él, la escoria de la inversión sexual, le acompañaban con verdadera admiración, melancólicos y tímidos.[46]

Another example of behavior which shows inverts not being ashamed of themselves is the response that Gómez received to a question, "Los hombres nos pagan, decía un profesional, contestando á preguntas que le dirigíamos, porque han llegado á comprender que solamente *nosotras* les podemos dar el *amor verdadero.*" Here, invert sex is touted as "true love."[47] In a similar fashion, Manón "Considera que el placer sexual puro debe ser el único objetivo del amor y que el amor con mujeres deja de ser un medio de placer puro, por cuanto se convierte en simple medio de reproducción de la especie."[48]

Another short autobiography that exists is one by Myosotis, who is classified by Gómez as, "invertido congénito, joven, y de la clase que llamaremos 'aristócrata'."[49]

> Es ridícula su exigencia de que le cuente, en la forma comprometedora de la carta, los detalles de mi vida; pero como soy *atenta*, y nunca fuí descortés con un hombre, allá van estas líneas, para que las guarde y sea discreto. *Noblesse oblige,* como dicen los caballeros.
>
> Yo soy así por que así he nacido; y de todos modos tendría que serlo, porque, para mí, la belleza no tiene sexo, ni el amor lo reconoce.
>
> Yo no hago nada de extraordinario: me gustan los hombres y por eso tengo *expansiones* con ellos.
>
> Los trato con exquisito *savoir faire*, como dice una de las de la *cofradía*, que escribe la crónica social de cierto diario; pero no los busco, por que soy *hermosa* y ellos son quienes me deben buscar.
>
> No podría decirle que clase de hombres prefiero: el amor es ciego. ¡Bendito sea el amor!
>
> No tengo *querido*, porque me considero incapaz de serle fiel. Au revoir MYOSOTIS
>
> P.D.–Rompa esta carta después de leerla.–Vale.[50]

Though not as detailed as La Bella Otero's words, Myosotis does make some interesting points. Clearly Myosotis was worried about disclosure, the first and especially the last paragraphs show this clearly. Gómez's callousness is also evident since he published the letter instead of destroying it.

Another area of resistance is the relationships that inverts tried to sanctify publicly through a quasi-marriage ceremony. Dr. De Veyga comments that:

El "casamiento" de invertidos sexuales no es un hecho raro, por cierto, pero esta ceremonia no se realiza ordinariamente

sino como acto de ostentación escandalosa, para hacer público un amancebamiento existente ó meditado, siendo siempre gente corrida en el ageno quien la practica.[51]

He goes on to describe an actual ceremony:

El acto se realizó con el aparato convencional de una boda real; *ella*, vestida de blanco, adornada la cabeza de azahares; él de frac y guante blanco, como si fuera á recibir la santa unción del sacerdote. . . . Pocos festejos hubo, no permitiendo la timidez de la novia darle la repercusión deseada. Una modesta pero bien arreglada casita (puesta probablemente por *ella*) les recibía bajo su techo y debía guardarles por todo el tiempo que había de durar la unión.[52]

Along with these individual acts of resistance, there existed in Buenos Aires at the turn of the century, what appears to be (seen through doctor's and lawyer's accounts) a large and well developed community of inverts.

COMMUNITY

Recently, there has been much controversy over whether the medical and legal establishments invented inversion as a category and thereby also invented inverts or whether inverts already existed and doctors merely responded to the phenomena that they saw and experienced. I argue that both points of view are correct. In Buenos Aires at this time, doctors like Francisco De Veyga were both responding to a community they saw and also applying their sexual ideology to interpret what these inverts were doing. Both inverts and doctors were responding to a rigid gender role system which posited opposing poles for males and females. Since one had to be at one pole or the other, inversion is a logical category in the system. Once the categories were established, they could be both used and subverted and a community of people created from them:

Ofrecen los homosexuales de Buenos Aires una particularidad digna de ser señalada: es la tendencia á asociarse, formando una especie desecta, designada por ellos con el pintoresco nombre de 'cofradía'. Cuando un invertido ha *'tirado la chancleta'*, frase que en la jerga quiere significar que se han perdido los miramientos y que no hay escrúpulo alguno en practicar el vicio profesionalmente, ingresa á la cofradía; entonces viste de mujer, se pinta, adopta un nombre femeninio, comienza á 'girar' es decir, á recorrer las calles en busca de clientes y frecuenta los bailes que, periódicamente se organizan para *estrechar los vínculos de solidaridad.*[53]

DeVeyga corroborates much of this information (Though, since De Veyga published first and Gómez clearly knew De Veyga's work well, it is quite possible that Gómez was using De Veyga's information). He mentions parties in conjunction with a case of acquired sexual inversion by "mental decadence," "pero la ocasión quiso que sus compañeros de entonces lo llevaran á una fiesta de *maricas*, hablándole con entusiasmo de las novedades que allí había de encontrar."[54] Also in the case of Maón, "así ataviado [as a woman] da rienda suelta á sus sentimientos de invertido, asistiendo á tertulias y bailes de invertidos, en que junto con otros congéneres desempeña el rol de dama."[55] Dr. De Veyga also mentions cofradías when he says, "Estaba muy ageno, por cierto, á suponer que en Buenos Aires había toda una 'cofradía' que ejercitaba este comercio."[56]

It is difficult to establish much about the parties and dances. One thing we do know is that they were subject to police harassment. The following is an account from the city of Rosario, another major metropolitan area of Argentina, from a little before 1930:

estos individuos marginados de la sociedad de entonces (y de la de ahora), encontrarán un lugar para sus expansiones de clan: una casa en Avenida Corrientes al 200 . . . El más conocido entre lo habituales concurrentes, era un homosexual apodado *La Renée*, Allí, en los altos de la tienda *La Vendedora*, celebraban sus encuentors y fiestas, que termindaban muchas veces con la irrupción imprevista de la policía, sobre todo en la época en que era más urgente la limpieza peródica de los vidrios de la Jefatura, menester para el que los vigilantes elegían siempre a los *maricas*, obligados entonces a entregarse con trapo, jabón, y agua a la muy femenina pero nada agradable tarea.[57]

In terms of language, all the works mention inverts referring to themselves with feminine pronouns and even giving themselves feminine names like Aurora, Rosita de la Plata, La Bella Otero, etc. There is also a mention of the *gremio* and a strong indication that alternative vocabularies were constructed when De Veyga states, "Hay toda una clase especial que se distingue en el gremio con el nombre de *tortilleras* (!) que buscan el placer venéreo por medio del frotamiento cuerpo á cuerpo juntando las partes homólogas, imitación de lo que hacen las mujeres invertidas en semehantes casos. De ahí su nombre, según parece."[58]

Castillo also corroborates Gómez's information about 'tirar la chancleta' though I view it in a very different light from Gómez. In a scene from Act II of *Los Invertidos*, Emilio, Juanita, and Princesa are talking about Florez (the doctor):

> JUANITA.–¡Bah! Y a mí qué me importa de Florez . . . El hombre serio . . . ¡Hipócrata! . . . No hace más que andar disimulando con su aspecto de sabio en conserva una cosa que todo el mundo sabe . . ¡Rico tipo el Florez ese! Yo, ya hace tiempo que 'tiré la chancleta'!
>
> EMILIO.–Pero tiene razón, hombre . . . Es un individuo de posición social, de vinculaciones, casado, con hijos . . . ¿Qué ande como vos por la plaza Mazzini[59] o los kioscos de la calle Callao, buscando aventuras? . . .
>
> JUANITA.–Che . . . Che . . . Ya te pasaste . . . Yo no ando por la plaza Mazzini . . .
>
> PRINCESA.–Tiene razón Juanita . . . Se es o no se es . . . Para qué tanta hipocresía . . . yo también he 'tirado la chancleta.'[60]

This dialogue presents some very complex issues. The obvious one is the question of what we would now call "coming out." Amazingly, Castillo presents the discussion in very modern terms. Juanita and Princesa argue that Florez is being a hypocrite for not "coming out," after all, either "one is or one is not " (an invert). It is also very interesting that the two critics of Florez, Juanita and Princesa, are less likely to be able to "pass" in Argentine society. After all, they both use female names and clothing. Emilio the defender, on the other hand, is more "masculine" from his name to his attire. In fact, Juanita and Princesa mock fight over him with Princesa claiming Emilio as his "maridito" while Juanita responds that, "Este es mio."[61] In the dialogue one also senses that there is a hierarchy of social acts with marriage and children on one end and going to the plaza Mazzini "looking for adventure" on the other.

Paco Jamandreu's autobiography, *La Cabeza Contra el Suelo* corroborates the "tirar la chancleta" quote. Writing in 1975 in reference to a time circa 1948, he talks about an episode immediately after he has lost his virginity to another (male) youth where his friend, El Gordo and his brother, Jorge, taunt him in jest by singing:

> Lo corrieron de atrás
> lo corrieron de atrás
> le metieron un palo en el culo
> no se lo pudo sacar
> no se lo pudo sacar
> lo tuvo que dejar como pudo

Yo me enojé pero terminé por reir. El Gordo, teatralmente, decía: –¿No respirás distinto, Jorge? Aquí vivia alguien virgen, contenido, histérico; ya ves, largó la chancleta. ¿Adónde, adónde irá a parar esa chancleta? Cuando más tarde se la tira, más lejos se va. Esta va a dar mucho que hacer, ya lo verás. [62]

Jamandreu also writes about attending a party of "maricones" which in Jamandreu's terminology means invert. He remembers back to circa 1948,

cuando me invitaron a una fiesta de maricones. No pude soportarlo. Me hirio–en lo más profundo de mi pudor ver a los tipos bailando juntos, maquillados y vestidos de mujer. Eso es distinto del arte del travesti. En cambio me ofende el travesti como tipo que se siente mujer no el travesti como arte que se remite a las primeras manifestaciones del teatro del mundo. La gente no entiende este problema y cree que todo forma parte de una misma madeja.

Nunca pude apartar de mi memoria esa primera fiesta de maricones a la cual me llevó El Gordo, los grititos, histéricos, el ambiente lleno de humo. [63]

Along with these "fiestas" and language there clearly existed various streets and other places in Buenos Aires where "giras" commonly took place. Emilio in the quote from *Los Invertidos* mentions "la plaza Mazzini" and "los kioskos de la calle Callao." De Veyga also mentions offhandedly when discussing the invert "Aurora" that, "Hay que decir, entre paréntesis, que su hotel quedaba en el paseo de Julio y que se encontraba ya muy próximo á él; cualquiera creería que ha sido una predestinación!"[64] Clearly, "el paseo de Julio" must have been a well known street for inverts.

Finally, this community also had fashions both in clothing and photo taking, "*Ella* [Rosita] ha impuesto la moda de varios trajes y de estos retratos disparatados que parecen ser una especialidad de esta gente, tan personales les son."[65] And even sexual standards, as the La Bella Otero's abilities attest to, "entre sus congéneres es alabado por esta última 'habilidad' [oral sex]."[66]

CONCLUSION

Having taken a close look at the Argentine construction of inversion, we have noted the similarities between Buenos Aires and the other large European cities. At the turn of the century, a developed Argentine subculture of inverts had meeting places, their own argot, fashion, and sexual tastes and customs. They held balls and dances, got married to each other, and engaged in prostitution. Yet, many unanswered questions remain. It is unclear whether the phenomenon of invert subcultures extended to other Latin American countries or other continents. Here, I will posit a preliminary hypothesis that at the turn of the last century, other major cities located in gender constructed cultures and having some contact with Europe and/or the U.S. also contained invert subcultures.

What is more unclear from these documents is how daily life was organized for the inverts themselves. Were there organizers and leaders as the name implies or was it a loosely knit community? What about female inverts? Did class and race function in the same manner as in broader society? What did inverts really feel about themselves?

Though we now know a great deal about what sexologists and social reformers were doing, we have little unfiltered information from inverts themselves. The road ahead is clear, as George Chauncey, Jr., has written:

> As in other new fields of social history, historians of homosexuality first considered the literature of the elite before grappling with the more elusive evidence of the ordinary. It is to that more difficult project that we must now turn.[67]

NOTES

1. For some preliminary looks at non-Western sexuality history texts, see *The Construction of Homosexuality*, Rosenberg, 1989, a large tome in the anthropological tradition and also *Hidden From History: Reclaiming the Gay and Lesbian Past*, Duberman, Vicinus, and Chauncey, Jr., eds., 1989, a collection of essays.

2. Boswell, John, "Revolutions, Universals, and Sexual Categories," in *Hidden From History: Reclaiming the Gay and Lesbian Past*, Martin Duberman, Martha Vicinus, and George Chauncey, Jr., eds., New American Library, New York, 1990, p. 19.

3. For more on this new view, see the foreword of *Hidden From History*; Rosenberg, *The Construction of Homosexuality*; and Murray, *Social Theory, Homosexual Realities*.

4. Chauncey Jr., George, "From Sexual Inversion to Homosexuality: The Changing Medical Conceptualization of Female 'Deviance'," in *Passion and Power*, Kathy Peiss and Christina Simmons, eds., Temple University Press, Philadelphia, 1989, p. 88.

5. Krafft-Ebing, Richard von, *Psycopathia Sexualis*, trans. by Franklin Klaf, Stein and Day, New York, 1965, p. 221-222.

6. *Ibid.*, taken from p. 190-216.

7. Potter, La Forest, *Strange Loves*, The Robert Dodsley Company, New York, 1933, p. 72.

8. *Ibid.*, p. 73.

9. Nesbitt, Charles Torrence, as quoted in *Gay/Lesbian Almanac* by Jonathan Katz, Harper & Row, New York, 1983, p. 219.

10. Nesbitt, Charles Torrence, *ibid.*, p. 221.

11. Gómez, Eusebio, *La Mala Vida En Buenos Aires*, Juan Roldan Editor, Buenos Aires, 1908, p. 46. According to Gómez, the precise figure was 1,084,113.

12. Ingegnieros, José, from the foreword of *La Mala Vida En Buenos Aires* by Gómez, p. 30. "Buenos Aires, the same as in all the Republic, open to anyone who wishes to come, receives by force, within the normal immigration wave, a good part of the antisocial dross of the rest of the countries."

13. Max-Bembo, *La Mala Vida en Barcelona*, quoted in *Prostitucion Y Rufianismo*, by Rafael Ielpi and Hector Zinni, Editorial Encuadra, Buenos Aires, May 1974, p. 81-82. "I will cite the case of a *cocoto*, which the local press covered. It concerns *La Teresita*. Thrown out of Buenos Aires, Chile, Bolivia, and other american states, he disembarked in *La Coruña* in March, 1911. His real name is *Rojo*. He is 30 years old and is the son of an old businessman; he is effeminate and not bad looking. Disguised as a woman and dressed in very elegant suits, he conquered not a few americans, receiving innumerable gifts . . . In Buenos Aires, he ostentatiously installed himself on Belgrano Street and gave large parties and get-togethers, in which he presented himself dressed in feminine costumes of scandalous luxury."

14. Castillo, José González, *Los Invertidos*, Argentores Ediciones del Carro de Tespis, Buenos Aires, 1957, p. 10. José González Castillo was a well-known playwright connected to the famous Compañía Podestá-Ballerini. *Los Invertidos* opened on September 12, 1914 and was banned after 90 performances. The play apparently still retained its power approximately forty years later, for when it was revived at the Teatro Lasalle, with the Compañía de Homero Cárpena producing the play, it was banned again. Though a fictional play, José Gonzalez Castillo

seems to have known about the Buenos Aires invert subculture, much of the information in Los Invertidos is quite accurate (see later footnotes).

"The doctors and lawyers always invent strange names for the simplest things. . . In my time, they were called *mariquita*, no more, or *maricón*, which is clearer."

15. Castillo, José González, *ibid.*, p. 11. "Almost all of the 'fags' that I have known or have heard of have died in the same way [suicide] . . . as if it were punishment from God!"

16. De Veyga, Dr. Francisco, "El Amor en los Invertidos Sexuales," *Archivos de Psiquiatría y Criminología*, Buenos Aires, May 1903, p. 341.

17. De Veyga, Dr. Francisco, "La Inversión Sexual Adquirida, Tipo profesional: un invertido comerciante," *Archivos de Psiquiatría y Criminología*, Buenos Aires, August 1903, p. 493.

18. De Veyga. "La Inversión Sexual Adquirida," *Archivos de Psiquiatría y Criminología*, Buenos Aires, April 1903, p. 202.

19. Gómez, *op. cit.*, p. 29. "Before, we have insinuated that the quality of the immigration waves that reach this country contributes, in great part, to the development of criminality.

Occupying himself with this problem, Dr. Moyano Gacitúa comes to affirm that these waves contain in themselves the highest rate of criminality in the world, because of the races that constitute it."

20. Gómez, *op. cit.*, 1908. p. 177. "Homosexuality consists of the inclination towards people of the same sex, for the completion and satisfaction of the carnal appetites. When the indicated inclination is man to man, it is called uranism or pederasty; saphism or tribadism when it is woman to woman. Sodomy is the name that serves to distinguish the sexual relations characterized by *inmissio membri in anum*, whether these relations are between people of different sexes or the same. Pederasty exists in many forms: mutual masturbation, anal coitus, and *inmissio penis in os alterius* (oral coitus).

21. Gómez was also quite prudish in comparison to Dr. De Veyga. Not only does he use Latin and alter information he feels is inappropriate (see later re: Gómez's reprinting of La Bella Otero's autobiography), but the following quote should give a sense of his attitude towards sexual inversion:

Hemos asistido á uno de esos bailes. Nuestra débil pluma se resiste á trazar los rasgos descriptivos de tan extraña fiesta, en la que uno no sabe contra que ha de protestar con major vehemencia. (Gómez, p. 192)

We have attended one of those dances. Our weak pen resists the outlining of the descriptive characteristics of such a strange party, in which one does not know what to protest with greater vehemence.

22. *Ibid.*, p. 180.

23. *Ibid.*, p. 179. " . . . if then it occurs that the posterior development of the fetus both sexes are reduced to just one, and if, at the same time, the opposite psychic system in reference to the sexual organs atrophies, there will be an individual with sexual inclinations opposite to his organs' nature; the apparent man

will feel himself female, he will be an androgyn, a passive pederast; while the individual anatomically a female, will feel male, and will desire to unite with an individual of the female sex to give herself to lesbian love."

24. De Veyga, "El Amor . . . ," p. 340-341.

25. De Veyga, "La Inversión . . . ," p. 193. To tell the truth, the classification that is based on the origin of this pychorganic deviation is purely artificial, no clinical marker exists which distinguishes the congenital invert from the one who converts into one for whatever reason. The influence that the seal of origin exercises over the subject, consists only on the mode of appearance of the first manifestations and even in that same phenomenon there are sometimes such similar details, that one case can be identified as another."

26. De Veyga, "El Amor . . . ," p. 340. "That explains the singular contradiction of some subjects who are inverts and, at the same time use women, be it occasionally or permanently. There are examples of married inverts who continue marital life and procreation . . . The presence of these tendencies also explains the cases of two inverts having sex and the propensities that some have in playing the male role in his homosexual encounters. To these men, the scourge of the inverts, has been given the suggestive title of maricas machos(!)" [lit. macho fags].

27. De Veyga, "Invertido Sexual Imitando La Mujer Honesta," *Archivos de Psichiatría y Criminología*, Buenos Aires, 1902, p. 373-374), "In regards to the accomplices of this morbid pantomine, we put forward this general conclusion, that can serve as an etiological principle in the study and comprehension of all of these phenomena of sexual aberrations in the male: there exists, at the side of inverts, to determine or foment homosexual tendencies, a type of person previously inclined towards physical pleasure within his sex. The idea of accepting this type as an identical type, temporarily or permanently, cannot have as an exclusive origin mental degeneration or craziness; for no matter how disorderly the conceptions of mental illness are, there are always in the world a base that serves them on foot, and in this case, the 'converting oneself into a woman', of either a libertine or chaste type, responds to the existence of a special class of subjects, perhaps more numerous than the former, or at least as numerous, who searches for satisfaction of his virile impulses upon an individual of his sex forging an illusion that he is a woman. Be that as it may, at the side of inverts, one always finds the sodomite, more or less corrupted, serving as a complement and a stimulant."

28. De Veyga, *ibid.*, p. 199. "The art of female hairdresser, it is said in passing, is frequently occupied by inverts."

29. De Veyga, "La Inversión . . . invertido comerciante," p. 494. "Against the dominant tastes of the rest of the inverts, he prefers men of age instead of youngsters."

30. The activo/pasivo distinction is one that continues to this day in Latin America. The activo is defined as the "male" role of insertor in anal intercourse while the pasivo is the "female" role of insertee. For further information, see studies in Brazil (Parker, Fry), Nicaragua (Lancaster), and Mexico (Carrier, Taylor).

31. De Veyga, "La Inversión . . . ," p. 200-201. "In his job he lacks specialties, doing whatever is asked of him. He even does the activo if the circumstances oblige him, for at the whim of buyers, if he finds someone who is in the same line but promising pay, he offers to satisfy without major difficulty."

32. González Castillo, *Los Invertidos*, p. 51. "It would be because it has members, actives and passives."

33. De Veyga, "La Inversión . . . ," p. 203. "One day he found a person who [introduced him], the perpetual seducer, the initial agent of these deviations that appear to be the exclusive work of nature."

34. De Veyga, "El Amor . . . ," p. 334. "They [sexual inverts] are all characterized by extravagance and childishness."

35. De Veyga, "La Inversión . . . ," p. 197. "He/She hasn't lacked the desires to simulate a novel over his initiation into the life of the *marica*, and tell us, seriously, his 'feminine inclinations', his 'artistic tastes', his 'exaggerated sensibility', his 'female soul', which are strong in all of them, but opted to speak frankly, avoiding a major waste of time."

36. Cione, Otto Miguel, *Luxuria: La Vida Nocturna de Buenos Aires*, Editorial Ercilla, Santiago de Chile, 1936, p. 134. This is an interesting work by a (then) well-known writer. The soft-porn cover of a drawn naked woman is weakly balanced by the foreword claiming that the work is in no way intended to titilate. The novel, itself, however, fulfills the spirit of the cover much more faithfully than the foreword. Filled with subplots about dark nubian women and cocaine addicted lesbians, the novel does have a few tidbits of information.

"Paquillo, the hairdresser and his followers, who admired and were envious of him, was from Andalucia, who dressed to the hilt, and took special pleasure in showing the curve of his calves, his feminine thighs, and his waspish waist."

37. Gómez, *op. cit.*, p. 183. "In the outline we have indicated in inverts, the venality, or better said, the parasitism, unites his capricious character, his jealousies, the baseness of all his actions, his desire for vengeance, and his unlimited hates. Tarnowski says that they combine in themselves all of the defects of women without having a single of her qualities, missing, also, the characteristics that make the virile character lovable."

38. *Ibid.*, p. 189. "They are jealous and this passion takes them to crime. A recent scandal debated under military justice, proves this."

39. De Veyga, "La Inversión . . . ," p. 194. "The concept that all of them [acquired inverts-DB] form of their feminine sexuality, towards which imitation they dedicate all their energies, is completely incorrect. That 'female soul' that so many of them pretend to possess and in whose existence they have come to convince respected people, is no more than pure fantasy, an illusion contradicting the true meaning of the word."

40. Gómez, *op. cit.*, p. 183-184. "They try to justify themselves, alleging the femininity of their feelings and it is curious to observe the interest with which they follow the scientific literature that concerns them."

41. De Veyga, "La Inversión . . . invertido comerciante," p. 494-496. "His morbid psychology, a curious combination of vanity, lies, and sexual paranoia, revealed in the following page, that was given to us as an autobiography, along with the portraits, without hiding very much his desire to appear as a clinical case in the book we are preparing on sexual inverts."

Autobiography

I was born in Madrid, in 1880. I have always believed that I was a woman and that is why I dress as one. I married in Sevilla and had two children. The boy is 16 years old and is following a military career in Paris. The little girl is 15 and is studying at the "Sacre-Cour" in Buenos Aires. they are very beautiful, like their father.

My husband is dead and I am a widow. Sometimes I would like to die when I think of him. I would look for matches or charcoal to kill myself, but these suicides appear to me to be the type for lower class people. Because I like flowers, I think it would be wonderful to die asphyxiated by perfume.

At other times, I would like to take the habit of a carmelite nun, because I am a follower of Saint Terese de Jésus,the same as other aristocratic women. But I cannot renounce the pleasures of the world, I stay in my house to work, sewing for the poor.

I am a woman who enjoys pleasure and that is why I accept it in all its manifestations. Some say that because of this I am vice-ridden, but I have written the following poem, that I always tell everyone.

> From the Buen Retiro to the Alameda
> the crazy pleasures I have come to make
> Young men, hold them stiffly
> for with my hand pleasure I will give you
>
> With little umbrellas and castanets
> and even with gloves I will give you
> if you'd like, my dearest,
> to give you pleasure I will mouth it [use my mouth]
>
> If with my mouth makes you uncomfortable
> and from the back you'd like to give it to me,
> Don't be afraid, my dearest,
> I have no wrinkles from behind
>
> If with my mouth makes you uncomfortable
> and from behind you'd like to love me,
> Don't be afraid, my dearest,
> for soon you will enjoy much

I have been in Paris, where I danced in the cafe-concerts, causing that other woman who uses my name to pass as me much envy.

Many young men are rude to me. But it is because they want to be with me. And why do they not get what they want? because I can't attend to all of my admirers.

I don't want to have any more children, because they have given me strong birth pains, even though my friends "Magda" and "Lucía" helped me, they don't understand childbirth because they have never been pregnant, because they have a sickness in their ovaries.

I like to walk in Palermo, because the grass is more stimulating for love than the humid bed.

This is my history, and I have the honor to present to the Doctor Veyga some portraits with my dedication.–"La Bella Otero"

42. Gonzales Castillo, *op. cit.*, p. 11. "He threw himself on the bed and also started shouting as if he were giving birth . . . the pig had decided that he wanted children too."
Also see the quote from *Luxuria* below in reference to menstruation.

43. De Veyga, " . . . invertido comerciante," p. 494. "Against the dominant tastes of the rest of the inverts, he prefers men of age instead of youngsters; he explains his taste because older men prolong coitus and pay punctually while youngsters practice it quickly and instead of paying, ask for money or mistreat him. Among the older men, he prefers the 'barrigones y peludos'; with stomachs because the insertions of the penis is less and all the stimulation is localized in the sphincter; hairy because they produce nice feelings on his shoulders and gluteal regions."

44. De Veyga, "Inversión Sexual Congénita," p. 45, " . . . nevertheless, his sensation of physical pleasure is not localized in the rectum; this site seems to the the point of excitement of pleasurable sensations perfectly localized in the genital organs and which end in ejaculation."

45. De Veyga, "La Inversión . . . ," p. 207. "He abandoned his house and his family soon thereafter, living somewhere else, with an *activo* solicitant he found, a conjugal union that lasted a long time and that made his (congeneres) [i.e., other inverts] talk because of the large amount of money they spent and the generosity with which they treated all of their relations."

46. Cione, *op. cit.*, p. 134. "To justify his morbid sexuality, he said, 'Ever since I was born, I had an affinity for the labors of the female sex. I dressed dolls and crocheted before I could read. And when we played by "marrying" other boys, I always played the bride.'

All the money that he earned as a hairdresser he gave to his favorites as gifts. If one called him Paquillo, he got very mad and said, 'I am Paquilla and I don't understand why we women are called by male names. Ah! By the Virgin Mary, when "my time of the month comes" I would shoot myself if I were brave!'

Various types like him, the dross of sexual inversion, accompanied him with true admiration, melancholic and timid."

47. Gómez, *op. cit.*, p. 182-183. "The men pay us, said a professional, an-

swering a questions we asked him, because they have come to understand that only *we* can give them *true love.*"

48. De Veyga, "Inversión Sexual Congenita," p. 45. "[He] considers that pure sexual pleasure should be the only objective of love and that love with women stops being an act of pure pleasure when it is converted into the simple act of the reproduction of the species."

49. Gómez, op. cit., p. 184. "congenital invert, young, and of a class that we shall call 'aristocratic'."

50. *Ibid.*, p. 184-185. "Your demand that I tell you, in the compromising form of a letter, the details of my life, is ridiculous; but as I am very much at your service and I have never been rude with a man, here come these lines, that you may guard them and be discreet. *Noblesse oblige*, as the gentlemen say.

I am this way because I was born this way; and anyway, I'd have to be this, because, for me, beauty does not have a sex, nor does love recognize it.

I don't do anything extraordinary: I like men and that is why I have *expansiones* (lit. extensions) [a pseudonym for sex? -DB] with them.

I treat them with exquisite *savoir faire*, as one from the *cofradía* says, one who writes the social diary of a certain newspaper; but I don't search for them, because I am beautiful and they are the ones that should come after me.

I couldn't tell you what type of men I prefer: love is blind. Blessed be love!

I don't have a paramour, because I consider myself incapable of being faithful. Good Bye,
MYSOTIS.

P.S. Destroy this letter after reading it, Bye."

Though it may seem callous of me to have reprinted this letter here, I have done so for two reasons. The first is that it is very instructive, though, the ends don't necessarily justify the means. The second reason is that Mysotis clearly wished the letter destroyed not for its contents, but because it could have been used to identify her at the time.

51. De Veyga, " . . . Imitando la mujer honesta," p. 371. The "wedding" of sexual inverts is not rare, for sure, but this ceremony is not normally done unless as an act of scandalous ostentation, to make public an existing or planned concubinage, being always people who run in the stream who practice it."

52. *Ibid.*, p. 371-372. "The act was realized with the conventional apparatus of a real wedding; *she*, dressed in white, with a head adorned with blossoms; he with a dress coat and white gloves, as if he were to receive the holy benediction of the priest . . . There were few guests, the timidity of the bride did not permit the desired repercussions. A modest but well tended little house (furnished, most likely, by *her*) received them beneath its roof and would house them for all of the time the union was to last."

53. Gómez, *op. cit.*, p. 191-192. "The homosexuals of Buenos Aires have a particular quality that should be mentioned; it is the tendency to associate, forming a differentiated species, designated by them with the picturesque name of

'cofradía'. when an invert has 'thrown the slipper', phrase that in the argot means that they have lost the naivete and that they have no scruples whatsoever in practicing the vice professionally, he enters a cofradía; then he dresses as a woman, he paints himself, adopts a feminine name, begins to 'girar', that is, to walk streets in search of clients and frequents dances that, periodically, are organized to *stretch the bonds of solidarity.*"

54. De Veyga, "La Inversión . . . ," p. 207, " . . . but the occasion occurred where his friends at the time took him to a party of maricas, telling him enthusiastically the novelties he would find there. That party would decide his situation permanently."

55. De Veyga, " . . . Imitando la Mujer Honesta.", p. 46, "..dressed as this [as a woman], he gives in to his inverted feelings, going to parties and dances for inverts, in which, along with other inverts, he plays the role of the lady."

56. De Veyga, "La Inversión . . . ," p. 198. "He was too new, for sure, to think that in Buenos Aires there was an entire 'cofradía' that engaged in that commerce."

57. Ielpi, Rafael, and Zhill, Hector, *Prostitución y Rufianismo*, Editorial Encuadra, Buenos Aires, May 1974, p. 80:
        "these marginalized individuals of that time (and of now), will find a place for the expansiones (lit. extensions, see footnote # 50) of their clan: a house on Corrientes Avenue at 200 . . . The best known of the regular participants was a homosexual named *La Renée.* there, above the store, *La Vencedora,* they celebrated their encounters and parties, that often ended with the unforseen eruption of the police, above all when the periodic cleaning of the windows of police headquarters was most urgent, work that the police always chose the *fags* for, obligated then to work with rag, soap, and water at the very feminine but not agreeable task."

58. De Veyga, "El Amor . . . ," p. 340-341. "There is a special class that is distinguished in the union [i.e., community] with the name 'tortilleras' (!) who search for sexual pleasure by the rubbing of body against body joining the homologous regions, imitating what inverted women do in similar cases. From there came the name, it appears."

59. In another interesting real-life corroboration of González Castillo's play. There is a reference to the plaza Mazzini in the book, *Buenos Aires, La Ribera y Los Prostibulos en 1880,* by Adolfo Batiz, n.d. but reprinted from a printing in Paris, 1908:
        Referring to a walk taken circa 1885, Batiz says, "A los jardines del Paseo 9 de Julio le había tomado antipatía porque era el refugio de los pederastas pasivos que se juntaban alrededor de la estatua de Mazzini, el revolucionario y hombre de las libertades itálicas," or, "I had come to dislike the gardens of the Street 9 of July because it was the refuge of the passive pederasts who would congregate around the statue of Mazzini, the revolutionary and man of the Italic freedoms."
        Therefore, we have a continuity from 1885 to 1914 in reference to the plaza Mazzini and from 1908 to about 1948 in reference to the term "tirar la chancleta."

60. Castillo, *op. cit.*, p. 30:

JUANITA.- ¡Bah! And what do I care about Florez. . The serious man. . . Hypocrite! . . He does no more than dissimulate with his wise man face hiding something the entire world knows. Rich guy Florez is! I, have 'thrown the slipper' for quite some time now.

EMILIO.- But he is right, man . . He is an individual with a social position, with relations, married, with children . . Do you want him to be like you and go by the plaza Mazzini or the kiosks on Callao, looking for adventures?

JUANITA.- Hey . . . Hey . . . You've gone too far. I don't go by the plaza Mazzini

PRINCESA.- Juanita is right. One is or one is not . . . Why so much hypocrisy . . . I also have 'thrown the slipper'.

61. *Ibid.*, p. 28, "This one is mine."

62. Jamandreu, Paco, *La Cabeza Contra El Suelo*, Ediciones de la flor, Buenos Aires, 1975, p. 28. This autobiographical work, even though it is quite episodic in nature, provides personal information on the homosexual community in Buenos Aires in the late 1940s through the early 1970s. In this sense it is quite valuable since diaries and other unfiltered autobiographical information is critical (and rare) in looking at how inverts viewed themselves and their conditions:

> They ran behind him
> they ran behind him
> they put a stick up his ass
> he could not remove it
> he could not remove it
> so he had to leave it as he could

I got mad but finished by laughing. El Gordo, theatrically said,–Don't you breathe something different, Jorge? Here lived a virgin, contained, hysterical; You'll see, he 'threw the slipper'. Where, where will the slipper stop? The later one throws it, the further it will go. She will be a handful, you'll see.

63. *Ibid.*, p. 147-148:

> when they invited me to a "fag" party. I couldn't stand it. It hurt my modesty–in the most profound way–to watch those men dancing together, with make-up and dressed as women. This is different from the art of transvestism. On the other hand, the transvestism as the type who feels himself a woman offends me, not the transvestism that refers to the origins of world theater. The public doesn't understand this problem and believes that all forms part of the same thing.
>
> I could never forget that memory of that first fag party that El Gordo took me to, the little shouts, hysterical, the room filled with smoke.

Though this quote from Jamandreu is relatively late, it seems to clearly refer to an invert party. The reference to men dressed as women, the effeminacy, and a later reference to the use of women's perfume all point to this. Throughout the entire book, Jamadreu emphatically differentiates between "maricones" and "homosexuales." To Jamandreu, maricones are effeminate, bitchy, men who dress as women, i.e., inverts, while homosexuals are masculine men who dress as men. This, of course, is the very difference I have been emphasizing between sexual inverts and the modern homosexual.

64. De Veyga, "El Amor . . . ," p. 197. "It must be said, offhandedly, that his hotel was in the paseo de Julio and that he found himself very close to there; anybody would think that it was fate."

65. *Ibid.*, p. 203. "She has set the fashion in various outfits and in those stupid portraits that appear to be a specialty of these people, so personal they are." This quote helps explain the portraits that frequently accompanied Dr. De Veyga's articles and Gómez' book which almost all appear to be professionally taken in studios. For another reference to portraits see the translation of La Bella Otero's autobiography in footnote 41.

66. De Veyga, "La Inversión . . comerciante," p. 493-494. "Within his mates [friends?] he is honored for this last ability"[oral sex].

67. Chauncey, Jr., George, *op. cit.*, p. 109.

REFERENCES

Batiz, Adolfo (1908). *Buenos Aires, La Ribera y Los Postibulos en 1880*, Paris.

Chauncey Jr., George (1989). From Sexual Inversion to Homosexuality: The Changing Medical Conceptualization of Female 'Deviance'. In Kathy Peiss and Christina Simmons, eds., *Passion and Power*. Philadelphia: Temple University Press.

Cione, Otto Miguel (1936). *Luxuria: La Vida Nocturna de Buenos Aires*, Santiago, Editorial Ercilla.

De Veyga, Dr. Francisco (1902). "Inversión Sexual Congénita." *Archivos de Psiquiatría, Criminología y Ciencias Afines.* p. 44-48. Buenos Aires.

_____, (No.1, 1902). "Invertido Sexual Imitando La Mujer Honesta." *Archivos de Psiquiatría, Criminología y Ciencias Afines.* p. 368-374. Buenos Aires.

_____, (April 1903). "Inversión sexual adquerida; Tipo profesional." *Archivos de Psiquiatría, Criminología y Ciencias Afines* 4:3 (abril 1903), p. 193-208.

_____, (May 1903). "El amor en los invertidos sexuales." *Archivos de Psiquiatría, Criminología y Ciencias Afines.* 2:6 (mayo 1903), p. 333-341.

_____, (August 1903). "La inversión sexual adquerida; tipo profesional: un invertido comerciante." *Archivos de Psiquiatría, Criminología y Ciencias Afines.* 2:8 (agosto 1903), p. 492-496.

Gómez, Eusebio (1908). *La Mala Vida En Buenos Aires*. BA: Juan Roldan Editor.

González, José Castillo (1957) (originally 1914). *Los Invertidos*, BA: Argentores Ediciones del Carro de Tespis.

Ielpi, Rafael, and Zhill, Hector (1974). *Prostituctión y Rufianismo*. BA: Editorial Encuadra.

Jamandreu, Paco (1975). *La Cabeza Contra el Suelo. Memorias*. BA: Flor.

Katz, Jonathan (1983). *Gay/Lesbian Almanac*. New York: Harper & Row Pub., Inc.

Krafft-Ebing, Richard von (1965). *Psycopathia Sexualis*, trans. by Franklin Klaf. New York: Stein and Day.

Potter, La Forest (1933). *Strange Loves*. New York: The Robert Dodsley Company.

VI. CAPITALISM
AND THE GAY IDENTITY

Political-Economic Construction
of Gay Male Clone Identity

John Lauritsen, AB

New York City

SUMMARY. Social Construction is an ill-defined approach, lacking in specificity and poorly suited for solving problems of the real world. A concrete analysis of negative aspects of the Gay Clone Lifestyle, with a particular focus upon the premier gay clone drug, "poppers" (or nitrite inhalants), is contrasted to the desultory verbalizing characteristic of most social constructionist writing. The central point: Many features of the gay clone lifestyle were not created by or in the interests of gay men at all, but instead were economically constructed. The gay subculture largely evolved according to the profit-logic of an expanding sex industry.

Over a dozen years ago, the sidewalks of my neighborhood, New York City's Lower East Side, were spray painted with the slogan, "CLONES GO HOME!" This was not an act of antigay bigotry. Gay men themselves had done the spray painting. Living in the

John Lauritsen, AB Harvard 1963, is a survey research analyst. His books include *Poison By Prescription: The AZT Story* (New York 1990) and (coauthor) *The Early Homosexual Rights Movement (1864-1935)* (New York 1974). Correspondence may be addressed: 26 St. Mark's Place, New York, NY 10003.

Lower East Side–New York's traditional "melting pot"–these men had a way of life they wished to preserve from the encroachment of the "Gay Clone" lifestyle.[1]

Gay Lower East Siders considered themselves part of a diverse and vital community. They looked upon the newly emerging Gay Clone lifestyle as the product of a ghettoized mentality, an embodiment of commercialism, conformism, and vacuity. Living in a tough neighborhood, they were not impressed by leather queens with expensive wardrobes, nor by ersatz cowboys, nor by make-believe lumberjacks. They despised disco as an uninteresting species of submusic, referring to it as "Mafia Muzak."

Nevertheless, the clone lifestyle came to prevail all over the world, so that an entire generation of gay men defined their own identities in terms of adherence to clonism: little mustaches; very short haircuts; plaid flannel shirts, boots, denim or leather jackets; a particular repertoire of movements, sounds, facial expressions, drug taking, and sexual practices. By the mid-70s there was a phrase in Frankfurt, "ein falscher Amerikaner" ("a fake American"), to describe a German gay man who had adopted the lifestyle of the American clone. At present, the clone lifestyle seems to be on the way out, though no doubt there are those who will carry it with them, as *their* identity, to the very end.

The purpose of this paper is to evaluate the strengths and weaknesses of social construction theory for understanding the clone episode in gay male history. I am particularly interested in the issues of continuity and specificity.

MY APPROACH: AN INTERDISCIPLINARY FOCUS ON MALE LOVE

From my own academic training I favor an interdisciplinary approach, and regard intellectual compartmentalization, or an excessive attachment to any particular schema or dichotomy, as a sign of provincialism. Every gay scholar has the right and the obligation to define the scope of his or her inquiries, and my choice has been to focus upon all-male relationships. Benedict Friedlaender (1904) asserted that love, sex, and friendship were different aspects of one and the same phenomenon, for which he used such terms as "Uranian Eros," "Platonic Love," and "male-male love." I agree. My preferred term is "male love," whose linguistic heritage goes back to classical antiquity.

BASICS OF SOCIAL CONSTRUCTION

Social constructionists have devoted much analysis to conceptual changes that occurred in the latter part of the 19th century. Beginning in the 1870s, medical thinkers grouped both all-male relationships and all-female relationships under a single rubric: "homosexuality." [2] This new term denoted a presumably abnormal *condition* of being attracted to one's own sex, not being attracted to the opposite sex, or both. Sometimes this was confounded by additional psychological or physiological issues ("masculinity," etc.). Corresponding substantives such as "the homosexual," "a homosexual," "homosexuals" referred to individuals who were defined by their homosexuality, who were set apart as "different from others." Social constructionists correctly criticize these 19th century notions for assuming that "homosexuals" in the medically constructed sense had always existed, that these labels reflected universal truths about human sexuality.

In historical perspective, these 19th century medical views were based upon false premises. It is a pity that social constructionists seldom go back much further than the 19th century, for historical evidence is still the most powerful refutation of medical constructionist (or essentialist) fallacies. On the one hand, the great civilizations of classical antiquity had no categorical condemnation of same-sex eroticism. Male love occupied a place of honor in ancient Greece. On the other hand, the condemnation of sex between males is "theologically constructed." Roughly 2500 years ago, the Levites, the priestly class of the tribe of Judah, formulated a taboo on all-male sex, as part of their *Holiness Code.* This taboo, carried forward by Jew and Christian alike, evolved into the concepts of sin, crime (sodomy), sickness, and deviance.

The above argument is not new. John Addington Symonds a century ago rebutted 19th century medical views by asserting the antiquity and nobility of "masculine love" and placing the blame for unhappiness upon the circumstances surrounding this "type of passion" in modern times:

> What has to be faced is that a certain type of passion flourished under the light of day and bore good fruits for society in Hellas; that the same type of passion flourishes in the shade and is the source of misery and shame in Europe. The passion has not altered; but the way of regarding it morally and legally is changed. (Symonds 1983)

Criticisms of the use of the word "homosexual" as a substantive–a noun describing a type of person, rather than an adjective describing a type of activity–are not new either. Among others, such criticisms were made effectively by Alfred Kinsey (1948, 1953) and by Wainwright Churchill:

> Whatever convenience there may be in the habitual use of this word as a substantive is offset by the confusion and abuse to which such a habit inevitably leads. Talk about the "homosexual" encourages generalizations that usually cannot be substantiated by reality, and one is never sure to whom this substantive really refers. (Churchill 1967)

Regrettably, the social constructionists, having perceived the fallacies inherent in the terms "homosexuality" and "homosexuals," frequently use them without qualification, as if they were oblivious to their own analyses.[3]

PROBLEM AREAS IN SOCIAL CONSTRUCTION

In the long run, social construction will be judged according to its accomplishments: whether it leads to the acquisition of specific historical or other information, or whether it increases our understanding of the information we already have. Compared to the formidable scholarly achievements during the first decade (1897-1907) of the homosexual rights movement in Germany (as documented in the *Jahrbuch für sexuelle Zwischenstufen),* the record of the social constructionists has not been very weighty (Lauritsen and Thorstad 1974).

Social construction seems to languish in a bog of desultory verbalism, withdrawn from practical endeavors. It too often falls into what C. Wright Mills termed "Grand Theory"–"an elaborate and arid formalism in which the splitting of Concepts and their endless rearrangement becomes the central endeavor." According to Mills, both "Grand Theory" and its counterpart, "Abstracted Empiricism," are abdications of classical social science, which lead away from the solution of concrete problems:

> As practices, they may be understood as insuring that we do not learn too much about man and society–the first [Grand Theory] by formal and cloudy obscurantism, the second [Abstracted Empiricism] by formal and empty ingenuity. (Mills 1959)

There is nothing profound in the dichotomy: "essentialism-constructivism." "Social construction" is ill-defined, and I'm sure many of us would be grateful if the proponents of social construction could provide us with a clear and concise definition of their concept. The meaning of "essentialism" is not clear, and I cannot help expecting its opposite to be "existentialism," the murky philosophy that was fashionable in the 1950s. In recent polemics, feminists have attacked "essentialism" in the same ways that they used to attack "nature" or "biology," and I suspect they regard these words as almost synonymous. Behind the "essentialism-constructivism" opposition I sense the ghosts of earlier dichotomies ("nature-nurture," "heredity-environment"). If this is the case, then the attack on "essentialism" is naive, for nearly all human phenomena result from an interaction of *both* heredity and environment.

If the attack on essentialism means simply a rejection of transhistorical "universals," then rejecting essentialism is simply affirming the millennia-old dictum of materialist philosophy: "The only absolute is change itself." However, I don't think this is what social constructionists have in mind.[4]

The question of "continuity" is raised, with essentialism apparently implying a maximum of historical continuity, and constructionism, a minimum. This echoes the nature-nurture dichotomy. Here I would argue for specificity. If we consider male love as a *phenomenon*, as a *type of experience*, or as a *"type of passion,"* then it is as old as humanity. The heritage of male love, its traditions and literature, is ancient. Male love may have manifested itself differently and been received differently from one society to another, but it is *real*, not just a socially constructed concept.[5] In addition, I am convinced that the erotic attraction of human males for each other is biologically inherent, and therefore, a product of evolution. But that is another topic.

One might expect social construction, with its roots in labelling theory, to be useful in understanding how individuals define themselves and are defined by others as being "gay," and in understanding how a gay subculture develops. Here again is a need for historical specificity. Some aspects of the gay male subculture–certain words, gestures, rituals, even certain meeting places–may be centuries old. Other things, like the clone mustache or disco, are recent and presumably ephemeral.

THE GAY CLONE LIFESTYLE (1974-1982)

It may be generally agreed that the gay clone lifestyle came into being and flourished in the years following the Stonewall Rebellion of 1969 and that it began to wither during the troubles of the 1980s. The above dates are admittedly arbitrary. Nineteen seventy-four is the year that poppers and disco became common features of the gay male lifestyle; 1982, when the Centers for Disease Control (CDC) formulated its first surveillance definition for the Acquired Immune Deficiency Syndrome (AIDS).

In his thoughtful essay, "Male dominance and the gay world" (Plummer 1981), Gregg Blachford identifies the Leitmotiv of the clone lifestyle as a "celebration of masculinity." Sometimes Blachford gives the impression that gay men are voluntarily constructing a culture to meet their own needs and desires. At the same time, he emphasizes a dilemma in which: "The sub-culture itself, through its own actions, cannot alleviate the conditions that led to these problems" (Plummer 1981).

I shall argue that many features of the gay clone lifestyle were not created by or in the interests of gay men at all, but instead were *economically constructed,* that the gay subculture largely evolved according to the profit-logic of an expanding sex industry.

Gay men who came out in the 1970s encountered a subculture that seemed almost too good to be true. Neophyte clones became avid consumers of "gay" clothes, grooming styles, music, and drugs. Forming their new gay identities and relating to each other largely on the basis of these things, they embraced a lifestyle of "commodity fetishism" with its inherent alienation.

To be sure, the creation of the clone lifestyle was a complicated process and not all aspects of clonism stemmed directly from business interests. Shirt manufacturers had no vested interest in plaids versus stripes, and barbers made no more money from cutting hair short, rather than long or in-between. And most clones took care of their little mustaches all by themselves. However, a case could be made that the clone look was itself a commodity–that, for example, the dress codes, of the legendary Mine Shaft or the more fashionable discos, were essential features of what was being purveyed by these establishments.

Sexuality itself became reified. Sex was reduced to frenetically fleeting encounters in baths or back rooms. In the latter environment, sexual partners were not even seen, let alone confronted as complete human beings. Some clones came to define their sexual identity in terms of an unseemly repertoire of *acts*–without learning the ABC's of making love, they became adept at performing skin piercing, "tit jobs," "rimming," enemas, "golden showers" and "scat," and other such acts which they had been taught by hard-core porn or S&M/leather publications.[6]

With the appearance of AIDS in the 1980s, the euphoria of the previous decade dissipated, and it became urgently necessary to determine whether the gay male lifestyle, either in whole or in part, might be *toxic.*

THE IMMUNOSUPPRESSIVE LIFESTYLE

Viewed without rose-colored spectacles, the clone subculture was in many ways an Immunosuppressive Lifestyle. With the gay bar as the primary meeting place, some men became alcoholics. Excessively loud barroom jukeboxes prevented socializing through the oldest of barroom diversions, conversation. At gay discos, regular and prolonged exposure to pain-threshold noise posed serious health hazards (stress, immunosuppression, and premature deafness). Promiscuity led to frequent infection and re-infection with a wide spectrum of venereal diseases, including syphilis, gonorrhea, amoebiasis, chlamydia, hepatitis, CMV, etc. Not only were frequent treatments with antibiotics necessary, but some men began taking them prophylactically: they would swallow a handful before going to the baths.[7] Inadequate sleep, malnutrition, and feelings of alienation, loneliness, and low self-esteem were concomitants of the lifestyle.

Epidemiological studies have indicated that virtually all of the gay male AIDS patients were regular and heavy users of such "recreational" drugs as the nitrite inhalants ("poppers"), marijuana, amphetamines, cocaine, LSD, quaaludes, ethyl chloride, barbiturates, MDA, Eve, Ecstasy, and heroin. In one study, 58% of the gay male AIDS cases used five or more different "street drugs" (Lauritsen 1990). With the possible exception of marijuana, all of these drugs are known to be dangerous.[8]

POPPERS: THE PREMIER GAY DRUG

The poppers industry represents an extreme case in which the gay male subculture was constructed according to profit-logic, rather than the needs of gay men (Lauritsen and Wilson 1986).

Almost all gay men, but few other people, know what poppers are: little bottles containing a liquid mixture of isobutyl nitrite and other chemicals. When inhaled just before orgasm, poppers seem to enhance and prolong the sensation. When used by the passive partner in anal intercourse, poppers facilitate things by relaxing the smooth muscle of the rectum and the sphincter muscle, deadening the sense of pain. With regular use poppers become a sexual crutch. Some gay men are unable to have sex, even with themselves, without the aid of poppers.

The original poppers were little glass ampules enclosed in mesh, which were "popped" under the nose and inhaled. They contained amyl nitrite manufactured by a pharmaceutical company and were intended for emergency relief of angina pectoris, a heart condition afflicting mostly elderly people. Amyl nitrite was a controlled substance until 1960 when the prescription requirement was eliminated by the Food and Drug Administration (FDA). From 1961 to 1969 some gay men, especially those who were into S&M, began using amyl nitrite as a "recreational" drug. At the request of the pharmaceutical industry, the prescription requirement was reinstated by the FDA in 1969.

In 1970 a new industry stepped into the breach, marketing commercial brands of butyl and isobutyl nitrite. By 1974 the poppers craze was in full swing and by 1977 poppers were in every corner of gay life.

At its peak, the poppers industry was the biggest money-maker in the gay business world, grossing upwards of $50 million per year. Gay publications were delighted to run full-page, four-color ads for the various brands of poppers, with revenues running into many tens of thousands of dollars. One poppers manufacturer boasted he was the "largest advertiser in the Gay press."

Every time a gay man picked up a gay publication he was confronted with vivid ads persuading him that the act of inhaling noxious chemical fumes was butch and sexy, an essential ingredient in the "celebration of masculinity."[9] One brand, Rush, had a brilliant red and yellow label which was so distinctive that a successful gay political candidate in San Francisco used the color scheme on his campaign posters as a subliminal reinforcement.

Accessories were marketed: for leather queens there were little metal inhalers on leather thongs, a proper part of an evening's wardrobe. One magazine had a comic strip entitled "Poppers": its hero, Billy, is a child-like but sexy blond who just simply loves sex and poppers.

In 1981 Hank Wilson, a gay activist in San Francisco, noticed that many of his popper-using friends were developing swollen lymph nodes. After reading medical literature on the nitrite inhalants, which was extensive even then, he founded the Committee to Monitor Poppers.

In 1983, after reviewing the literature on AIDS, I realized that environmental factors necessarily had to be responsible for the syndrome's being compartmentalized and that poppers were high on the list of suspects. I contacted Hank Wilson and we started collaborating. Since we have written a book on poppers (Lauritsen and Wilson 1986) I will give only the barest summary here.

Poppers are hazardous to the health in many different ways. They are immunosuppressive, reduce the ability of blood to carry oxygen, cause anemia (Heinz body hemolytic anemia and methemoglobinemia), cause cellular changes, are mutagenic (i.e., damage chromosomes), and have the potential to cause cancer by producing deadly N-nitroso compounds.

There are strong epidemiological links between the use of poppers and the development of AIDS, especially Kaposi's sarcoma. Obviously poppers are not *the* cause of AIDS. But, in light of their toxic effects, they are likely to be a major co-factor.

WHOSE GAY COMMUNITY? CUI BONO?

Often we speak of the "gay community," the "gay press," etc., as though it were self-evident that it is to us, gay people, that these things belong. But maybe not. I have talked to gay men who were incredulous when I described the known toxicity of poppers. They were sure that if poppers were really harmful they would have read about it in the gay press. How naive they were! Beginning in 1981 Hank Wilson regularly sent out packets of medical reports to the gay press. These were ignored. In 1982 a research scientist sent a letter to the *Advocate*. She urged the editor to publish it so gay men would know that "persons using nitrite inhalants may be at risk for development of AIDS." She was informed, "We're not interested." In 1983, at the request of a poppers manufacturer, the *Advocate* ran a series of advertisements ("Blueprint For Health") which falsely claimed that government studies had exonerated poppers from any connection to AIDS (Lauritsen and Wilson 1986). For some of the gay press advertising dollars were more important than the lives of gay men.

Although poppers are now illegal in the U.S. they are easily obtained on the black market. Articles claiming that the ban on poppers is a denial of civil liberties, and that the drug is really innocuous, have recently appeared in the gay press.

More could be said about poppers, but the point is made: to a large extent the "gay community" is constructed around profits, not the welfare of gay men.

POLITICAL CONSTRUCTION

One might also analyze how the gay male subculture is *politically constructed*. On one level politics and economics are intertwined. Politics is money and the poppers industry knows how to use its political "influence." The FDA and other government agencies have accepted the ridiculous claim that poppers are a "room odorizer" rather than a drug. The poppers industry, which has a full-time lobbyist in Washington, has demonstrated in practice that it can "influence" academics, gay leaders, gay doctors, state representatives, and even a U.S. senator.

On another level, it is noteworthy that, during the present health crisis nearly all of the gay press and AIDS groups in the U.S. have followed the government's lead. No critical thinker would believe what the U.S. government says about Southeast Asia, South America, Grenada, or the Middle East. Yet the gay media, with the notable exception of the *New York Native,* has endorsed the Public Health Service's untenable etiological hypotheses,[10] its statistical prevarications, its incompetent epidemiological research, its hysteria-mongering, and now its unconscionable promotion of AZT, a toxic drug which causes cancer and destroys bone marrow, whose alleged benefits derive from incompetent and/or dishonest research, and whose speedy approval resulted from improper and illegal collusion between its manufacturer and branches of the U.S. Public Health Service (Lauritsen 1990).

SUMMING UP

The best intellectual approach at this point is one that will enable us to buckle down to the tasks at hand, for there is a lot to be done. We are living in a time of crisis, fighting a war on many fronts against unrecognized enemies. The outcome is uncertain. If we survive, we shall have to do a ruthlessly honest reappraisal of our environment, our identities, and the ways that we live.

NOTES

1. Two groups were responsible for the spray painting: Faggots Against Gays (FAG) and Faggots Against Facial Hair (FAFH).
2. In historical perspective, the forced grouping together of gay men and lesbians is questionable, a consequence of the "social construction of the homosexual." As men, gay men have more in common with all men, gay or straight, than with women, lesbian or otherwise. At any rate, the concept "straight man" is extremely problematical and deserving of close analytical scrutiny.

Further, a case could be made that gay men have more in common with women who love men, as they do, than with women who do not. Gay men must fight to reclaim the right to be fathers of families, as well as to experience and practice male love–to be full male human beings, as the men of ancient Greece were. Their need is for women who will love them and bear their children, not women who reject them.
3. Observe, for example, the wildly indiscriminate uses of these words in the social constructionist bible, *Making of the Modern Homosexual* (Plummer 1981).
4. It is not essentialism, but rather constructionism (obsessed with nebulous concepts of consciousness, identities, lifestyles, etc.) that tends to the idealist end of the philosophical spectrum. In contrast, a materialist approach would

concentrate upon more fundamental and specific phenomena: practice, the concrete circumstances in which gay men find themselves, the political and economic underpinnings of those circumstances.

5. John Boswell (1982) has provided an intelligent analysis of the essentialism-constructionism (or "realism-nominalism") debate.

6. *Totalitarian tolerance* seems to be a tenet of clonism. In 1983, during a meeting of the New York Safer Sex Committee at which scatology and "golden showers" were being discussed, I commented, "A civilized human being does not repudiate his childhood toilet training." I was immediately rebuked and told that I had no right to be judgmental towards another's lifestyle.

7. One New York City bath house (now closed) sold black market tetracycline on the second floor, along with "recreational drugs" of all kinds.

8. In New York City the main gay discos and bathhouses were, among other things, drug distribution centers.

9. Two muscular guys, leaning against gasoline pumps, are lecherously looking over a third guy, also very muscular and stripped to the waist, who is on a motorcycle. The caption says: "New from the makers of RUSH. HEAVY DUTY BOLT LIQUID INCENSE."

10. The HIV-AIDS hypothesis has been elegantly and powerfully refuted by the eminent molecular biologist, Peter Duesberg (Duesberg 1989, 1990; Duesberg and Ellison 1990)

REFERENCES

Boswell, J. (1982), "Revolutions, Universals and Sexual Categories," *Salmagundi*, no. 58-59, pp. 89-113.

Churchill, W. (1967), *Homosexual Behavior Among Males: A Cross Cultural and Cross-Species Investigation*, New York: Hawthorne.

Duesberg, P. (1989), "Human Immunodeficiency Virus and Acquired Immunodeficiency Syndrome: Correlation But Not Causation," *Proceedings of the National Academy of Sciences*, Vol. 86, February 1989.

Duesberg, P. (1990), "AIDS: Non-Infectious Deficiencies Acquired By Drug Consumption And Other Risk Factors," *Research in Immunology*, Vol. 141.

Duesberg, P. and Ellison, B. (1990), "Is the AIDS Virus a Science Fiction?" *Policy Review*, Summer 1990 (Followed by intense and voluminous correspondence in the Fall 1990 issue).

Friedlaender, B. (1904), *Renaissance des Eros Uranios: Die physiologische Freundschaft, ein normaler Grundtrieb des Menschen und eine Frage der männlichen Gesellungsfreiheit*, Schmargendorf-Berlin: Renaissance (Otto Lehmann); reprint 1975, New York: Arno.

Kinsey, A.C. et al. (1948), *Sexual Behavior in the Human Male*, Philadelphia: W.B. Saunders.

Kinsey, A.C. et al. (1953), *Sexual Behavior in the Human Female*, Philadelphia: W.B. Saunders.

Lauritsen, J. (1990), *Poison By Prescription: The AZT Story*, New York: Pagan.

Lauritsen, J. and Thorstad, D. (1974), *The Early Homosexual Rights Movement (1864-1935)*, New York: Times Change.

Lauritsen, J. and Wilson, H. (1986), *Death Rush: Poppers & AIDS*, New York: Pagan.

Mills, C.W. (1959), *The Sociological Imagination*, New York: Oxford.

Plummer, K., editor (1981), *The Making of the Modern Homosexual*, New Jersey: Barnes & Noble.

Symonds, J.A. (1983), *Male Love: A Problem in Greek Ethics and Other Writings*, New York: Pagan.

The Mineshaft:
A Retrospective Ethnography

Joel I. Brodsky, PhD

Lincoln, Nebraska

SUMMARY. The Mineshaft, a male sex club, is described from the patron's perspective, in retrospect, and in the context of gay male urban life in circa-1980 North America. It is suggested that the Mineshaft functioned to provide, on a for-profit basis, a relatively safe environment for liminal erotic behaviors, and did so in response to a variety of sociocultural conditions. The latter include the lack of institutionalized anticipatory socialization for intramale sexual relations, and the tension between S&M and non-S&M gay male styles. The Mineshaft occupied marginal niches in terms of its physical location, its hours of operation, and its legal status. Access was ritualized, social structure was simplified, social control was informal but adequate. The setting was amenable to a wide range of fantasy, eroticization and erotic role playing.

The Mineshaft was a bar and sex club which operated for a number of years in New York's meatpacking district on the lower West Side of Manhattan. This bar gained great notoriety among gay men, was discussed in the gay press, and used as the setting for pornographic stories. Late in 1985, in an atmosphere of lurid headlines, right wing agitation, and panic over AIDS in the public school system, it was closed by order of New York State authorities for clearly political reasons (see Rist, 1985). In what follows I try to describe the Mineshaft in such a way as to ground it in sociological and anthropological theory.

Dr. Joel I. Brodsky received his PhD in Sociology at the University of Nebraska-Lincoln. He is grateful to Barry D. Adam, Mary Jo Deegan, Helen A. Moore, and Stephen O. Murray for comments, and to former patrons of the Mineshaft for an encouraging and critical interest. Correspondence may be addressed: 5840 Locust Street, Lincoln, NE 68516.

Specifically, I present an overall ethnography of the Mineshaft in its cultural and institutional context. My aim is to suggest some answers to the question "what did going to the Mineshaft do for those who went there?" While it is obvious, if not tautological, that customers in a sex club ordinarily obtain, or hope to obtain, sexual gratification by their participation, the question arises why in one such place and not another? Indeed, why in a sex club, as opposed to the privacy and intimacy of a monogamous relationship at home? And if in a sex club, why in ways quite so contradictory of dominant cultural standards (as were some common Mineshaft practices such as handballing, micturition, and S&M)? My contention is that the Mineshaft performed a variety of integrative social and cultural functions for gay men at the communal level, and that these functions were manifest in its physical and social structure and setting.

My analysis begins with a brief review of the literature on male recreational S&M which I believe offers a key to understanding the Mineshaft's cultural base. Then, after a brief note on my methodology and its limitations, I present my retrospective data and findings.

MALE RECREATIONAL S&M: FETISH AND FANTASY IN AMERICA

The Mineshaft was, by reputation, an "S&M" bar, and a well-known site to gay men of the late 1970s whom Mains (1984) would have described as "leathermen." Its customers evinced a hypermasculine style of dress and an ethos which posited sexual excitement as a self-justified basis for meaningful human relationships. In contrast to the dominant culture's requirement that eroticism be linked to gender relations, and thus that "real men" only desire women, the Mineshaft articulated the principle that "real men" not only can and do desire other "real men," but that "real men" can be *exclusively* homosexual. In order to examine this relationship between a gay male "S&M" bar and changes in the gender system, it is important to clarify what "S&M" means to gay men.

In the 1970s gay men found themselves strongly at odds with the dominant system of erotic norms. While the dominant system continued to be heterosexist, rationalized, materialist, power-oriented, and erotophobic, a counterculture prevailed among gay men which was in many respects Dionysian (see Maffesoli, 1983). So, for example, while both of these systems could have been described as "phallocentric," phalli themselves remained invisible, kept secret and taboo in the imagery of the dominant system; while the counterculture, itself denied visibility, encouraged playfulness with and admiration of phalli. It has been claimed that a majority of American males experience homoerotic arousal, and perhaps half experience orgasm while engaged in homosexual behavior at some point in their lives. Yet male homoeroticism in the United States is legitimated with only extreme difficulty, and most men try to forget their pubescent sexual experimentation.

A significant contrast with many pre-capitalist societies concerns societal norms for rites of passage into adult male roles. Rather than being normatively initiated into a male *communitas* (see Turner, 1969), American males are normatively inducted into patriarchal, heterosocial bureaucratic structures. In fact, there is a dearth of universalized sacred rites of passage in American society. All of these characteristics can be viewed (e.g., by some gay men) as alienating and oppressive defects in the American system. My argument is that the Mineshaft functioned for some participants to address these defects, with partial success. Insofar as it did succeed, it took on meaning within the gay male community as a place of transformative experience and possibly awesome rituals.

"S&M" can be interpreted as "sadomasochism" or "Slave/Master" (Townsend: 1983:14-17). The latter meaning suggests two aspects of S&M, (1) Since slavery was abolished in the United States in 1863 it is not surprising that researchers have discovered that S&M is a kind of playacting or game; and (2) though a game, it is concerned with some of the more profound sociocultural contradictions in American culture.[1] Responding to the first meaning ("sadism" and "masochism," as per Krafft-Ebing, 1965) the literature discusses "recreational S&M," which it sharply distinguishes from popular and medicalized usages of "sadistic" and "masochistic" to refer to, respectively, cruel brutality and pathological self-destructiveness. Masochism of the latter sort is common among oppressed people in the form of "guilt-expiation rituals," and is often manifested among gay men appearing before psychiatrists (Adam, 1978:101), for whom psychiatric treatment is such a ritual. Empirical sociological studies of male recreational S&M (see Spengler, 1983/1977) have been rare and hermeneutic, but are more than adequate to discredit Krafft-Ebing's pathologizing concept of an inevitable progression of disease from "atavistic manifestations" to "the most monstrous acts of destruction." S&M is posited as a "career" which some gay men will follow and which begins with an early disenchantment with the gay world (Kamel, 1983a:75). It is critical for initiates firstly to come to view "leathersex" as a process in which psychosexual fulfillment is mutual and can only be achieved interdependently, and secondly to develop their acting skills (ibid., p. 77). For this reason, supposedly, novices prefer submissive roles in which the script is seemingly prescribed. At some later point the initiate is likely to become a dominant partner himself (ibid.). Catalogs of paraphiliac activities which constitute the discursive universe of S&M have also been elaborated (Kamel, 1983a; Weinberg, 1983/1978), and include: pain, bondage, humiliation, domination, and watersports. Featured are analyses of dyadic relationships such as "master/slave." In Kamel's (1983b) scenario leathersex uses restraint (either physical or psychological) to establish dyadic roles, humiliation to carry them out, and fear to maintain them. Prior to erotic interaction participants use costume to signal desires to prospective partners and often verbally negotiate the question "what-do-you-like-to-do?" Frequently S&M sexual activity "culminates in masculine gentleness, warmth, and affection" (ibid., p. 171).

The final stage described by Kamel (1983a) in the development of the S&M career is a stage he calls "limiting," a period of deliberate experimentation with activities during which the experimenter establishes the boundaries of "his S&M tastes." This concept points directly to Lee's notion of socially organized risk reduction (discussed below), and Kamel claims that many of the implicit rules of the leather world revolve around this notion of limits. For example, a sadist's reputation hinges on his ability to decode and abide by a partner's limits. Individuals experimenting with "limiting" would clearly benefit from an environment where liminality, in the sense of threshold experience, particularly sensory threshold experience, could be engaged in while experienced persons willing and able to assist were present. It will be clear that the Mineshaft provided such an environment.[2]

At the community level, Lee (1983) and Weinberg (1983/1978) are concerned with the sociology of risk. They argue that sadomasochism is theater, invoking Goffman's concept of the "theatrical frame." What ideally occurs in the S&M world, says Weinberg (1983:106) quoting Goffman, is that participants "play the world backwards" and "the individual can arrange to script what is to come, unwinding his own reel." Through appropriate social organization the S&M world functions to reduce actual risks. Dyads and sex clubs are viewed as desirable means of creating and maintaining social support networks among participants.

Murray (1984:42) points out that the theatrical realization of fantasies and the reality of behavioral risk-taking may often coincide in S&M, and that not all participants in S&M scenes may "maintain role distance" as well as "adepts." Yet he agrees that S&M is theater, and argues on this basis, that the emergence of S&M in the 1970s may be part of a transition "from Mother Camp to Father Camp." In this respect he sees "a continuity between female and male drag in the common focus on costuming and in choreographing near-caricatures of gender."

But who is the audience for this theater? Is it the hostile, oppressive heterosexual world, or is it the gay world itself? And Murray's own question remains unanswered: Why does this shift emerge at this particular time in this particular way?

Goffman argues (1963) the possibility of a minority within a minority being created, a community of deviants within a deviant community. The "shift" Murray describes is an emergence into *gay* discourse of an S&M controversy. It occurs about the time the Mineshaft opened in the mid 70s. At this time, in response to the new aspirations and conditions of greater tolerance created by the Gay Liberation movement, the traditionally closed S&M world was becoming more open and accessible to "non-adept" gay men. As it did so, the hypermasculine S&M style of dress and eroticism increasingly challenged the stereotypical equation of open gay identity and gender reversal (see Newton, 1972:24). S&M styles became at least a widely understood means of signaling desire for other men. But this change also brought to light an elaborate subculture available to gay men which systematically violated taboos against a wide range of sexual behaviors in addition to those against male homosexual relations. This was a time when gay bars were beginning to drop their traditional practices of hiding in remote locations behind blacked out windows, and becoming more visible. In this context of increasingly conceivable legitimacy for some as yet undefined gay male role in American society the new style appeared to some as a politically liable display of dirty linen. Indeed, if the Mineshaft exaggeratedly caricatured anything, it was a camp version of the gay past.[3]

If the Mineshaft is to be understood as an embodiment of "Father Camp," then the process by which "camp" itself becomes meaningful must be sought within the gay male world. I would suggest that camp has an interior, deadly serious side: perhaps an unnamed side associated with the neglected socialization needs of gay men.[4] The serious side of "Father Camp" might be the lack of institutionalized anticipatory socialization for male erotic relationships in American society. Behind S&M as theater might be a genuine compensation for this lack.

Murray also criticizes the view that S&M emerges more distinctly with diversification of the gay community, as implying that there is a "reservoir" of repressed S&M eroticism waiting to fill the expanding capacity. In effect, his criticism is that this is an essentialist argument.

Yet, as even Krafft-Ebing acknowledges, there may be a physiological basis for S&M which is inherent and normal in human sexual response. It seems to be the case cross-culturally that any adrenal arousal brings human beings physiologically closer to sexual arousal. If so, the view that S&M emerges more distinctly with diversification of the gay community is not an essentialist claim, but emphasizes the role of culture in shaping and differentiating erotic from violent behavior. It emphasizes the cultural distinctiveness of patterns of life in the gay world: a sociocultural world which has, in dramatic contrast to the hegemonic "Rambo" culture of the contemporary United States, preferred the eroticization of adrenalin to the adrenalization of eros.

METHOD

What follows is retrospectively based on numerous observations and conversations in the Mineshaft between the spring of 1979 and winter of 1982, and recent conversations with a small number of friends who also observed the Mineshaft. All of these observations were made from the perspective of participants in the role of customers, rather than employees or managers of the Mineshaft. The Mineshaft was, however, a consumer-oriented business which functioned in a capitalist social context. These observations thus reflect an experiential impression that was "managed" with the intent of attracting and pleasing customers. The observations extend to a variety of customer sub-roles, including non-club member and club member; weekday night "regular," and weekend night "tourist"; and "novice" or "initiate." In short, some observations were made on weekends, during periods of employment in the "straight" world; while others were made during periods of unemployment when the Mineshaft served as an important communal focus for the researcher.

The observations are retrospective, and may suffer from the fallibility of memory, as opposed to systematic observation; they are selective, and are certainly not representative or random. As an ethnography, this study is rather incomplete. Since the data do not exist, I do not attempt to analyze the details of interaction in the Mineshaft; the glances, gestures, movements, and language(s). Since the site is closed, more systematic research and analysis will not be possible.

THE INSTITUTIONAL CONTEXT
OF A COMMERCIAL ANTI-STRUCTURE

The Mineshaft operated in a highly developed market economy which provided services to gay men.[5] It began operation as an "after-hours" "leather" bar in the "Triangle" district, three terms whose explanation below will clarify the bar's market position. But more than a service, the Mineshaft was a focal point for symbolic ritual activity among gay men, and itself eventually acquired symbolic and political/media significance. For example, the movie *Cruising* began shooting on location in several S&M bars in New York, and a version of the interior of the Mineshaft was featured prominently in one vivid scene. While permission to shoot the movie had been granted the director, Stanley Freidkin, by various bar owners, the expectations that were raised in the gay male community that a "quality"' movie would feature their lifestyle turned to rage when the nature of the script became known. This script recreated several actual sex-related Greenwich Village murders of gay men and implied that such violence was inherent in the world of leather and S&M, and indeed, in gay community life (Russo, 1981:236). Such distortions implicitly legitimated anti-gay violence as beyond the control of rational political authority (while the actual murders remained unsolved). The gay male community's anti-*Cruising* rage produced in 1979 the most severe gay/police confrontations in New York between the Stonewall riots of 1969 and the Liberty Centennial riots of 1986. (The latter protested the Burger court's antigay decision in the Hardwick vs. Georgia case.) It did not, however, prevent *Cruising*'s dissemination of exploitative and homophobic images of gay male life, in the established Hollywood tradition (see Russo, 1981).

Given Friedkin's history as the director of the much despised *Boys in the Band*, the trust exhibited by the bar owners in retrospect seems naive, at best. But Russo notes (ibid, p. 233) that gay men working in the film wrote an article at the time in the popular magazine *Mandate* explaining that their participation in the film was intended to project a new, masculine, gay image to the American public. In other words, some gay men perceived the Mineshaft and its world as symbolic manifestations of their own carefully constructed masculinity. Some believed that a deeply homophobic culture would attribute the same positive meaning to the Mineshaft that these actors did. Perhaps the community's rage would more appropriately have been directed at the culture that rejected their lifestyle than at the film's portrayal of it. It is clear, in any case, that from the perspective of that dominant culture, the Mineshaft was a convenient, if hazily perceived, confirmation of homophobic stereotypes of sexual evil and violence.

The "triangle" was a small triangular shaped block formed by an odd intersection in Manhattan's meatpacking district along the Hudson River just north of the West Village, and just southwest of the Chelsea district. Few lived in the triangle district, and the city's repeated efforts to run a major expressway through it lowered its commercial value, as meatpacking plants nervously sought to relocate just across the river in New Jersey. At night this anomalous urban landscape of nineteenth century meat packing plants with their covered sidewalks was silent and deserted. At the same time it was geographically convenient to a variety of gay districts. It proved an ideal location for a series of after hours clubs and bars devoted to sexual/legal marginality. For example, the "Anvil" featured a large stage where those not engaging in other sexual or social activity could watch paid performers engage in extraordinary feats, on occasion with members of the audience.

It is likely that the floorshow at the Anvil popularized previously limited sexual practices such as "fisting," or handballing. During the period of observation informants made recurrent references to a legendary performance at the Anvil during which an adult female member of a family prominent in national politics allegedly got up from the audience and "fisted" an onstage performer. As this story implies, the Anvil (and the Mineshaft) had pretensions to attract members of the American elite. Whether this was at all the case, is not clear, but both bars often had long lines to get in, not a few limousines at their entrances, and long lines of taxis outside when people were leaving. Other bars in the triangle were less glamorous. The Mineshaft did not feature staged performances so much as a large space and multifunctional facilities for a full complement of sexual activities which ranged from "vanilla" sex to fisting, whipping, and the use of hot candle wax.

"After-hours" bars were bars that operated after the legal closing hours of the "regular" bars. They began to proliferate in the early 1970s, benefitting from a hands-off political attitude that characterized municipal government at that time (probably maintained through graft), and from the relative safety they offered to those who had been for many years engaging in so-called "anonymous" sexual encounters in a variety of increasingly dangerous open air sites in Greenwich Village along or close to the Hudson River. They survived the test of a raid by federal agents of nine such bars on the evening of July 17, 1971 (Weinberg and Williams, 1974:40-41). So, too, did the Mafia links that the raid was ostensibly intended to thwart. During the period of observation the Mineshaft itself was closed down for several weeks of the busy winter season. One rumor suggested that this was because of its lack of a liquor license. Another said that the Gay Men's Health Crisis, a community group, had discovered amoebas, the protozoans responsible for amebiasis, growing on the walls. At any event, it was much cleaner when it reopened and smelled less fetid.

Different after-hours bars attracted different crowds, had different entrance requirements, and featured different atmospheres and activities. A common feature of after-hours bars was their "backroom" function, that is the sheltering of sexual activity. After the "regular" bars closed, their remaining patrons would migrate to the after-hours bars where they could be assured of sexual activity.[6] Employees of the regular bars would also go to the after-hours bars to relax after work. These bars were thus complementary in their market functioning to the regular bars, encouraging customers to stay until closing and reducing social pressures to meet and arrange sexual encounters. At the same time they competed for customers with other late night or all-night establishments which sheltered sexual activity such as the bath-houses and discos. In competing with the bath-houses and discos they generally offered lower admission costs and the availability of alcoholic beverages. The Mineshaft, in the rather thin guise of being a "private club," provided alcoholic beverages to patrons in exchange for "donations," and the $5.00 admission for a non-member would include use of the coat-check room and a "free" beer. Bathhouses and discos cost more, forbade alcohol, and offered greater prestige as places to go in some gay circles.

"Leather" bars were foci for the S&M world, and I have suggested that this world intersected the gay male world in such a way as to provide a measure of "in-group deviance" (Goffman, 1963:145) in relation to the latter. The S&M world has its own institutions, which include: dyads and social networks, specialty bars and clubs (which may or may not be "after hours"), publications, political organizations, and motorcycle clubs. Kamel (1983b) describes the cultural outlook of "leathermen" as distinct from both heterosexual S&M participants and other gay men who have not developed an "S&M career." Kamel claims that "leathermen" are devoted to "the ultimate in man-to-man interaction." That gay male S&M is not universally so perceived among gay men is fairly obvious. In the traditional "Mother Camp" slang among gay men in the ghetto, the term "leather queen," not "leatherman" was used. Such usage included a complex set of pejorative meanings: (1) There is an implication that S&M is a sexual specialty or fetish like any other and available to any gay man so inclined, since the formula noun + queen (Dynes, 1985: 119) implies an extreme of sexual specialization; e.g., "I thought he was just an ordinary queen, I didn't know he was a leather queen." (2) There is an implication that S&Mers' claims to ultramasculinity and more meaningful sexual experience are suspect, since the term "queen" has semantic roots which imply an "impudent woman, jade, or hussy" (ibid.). In a variant usage, leathermen were referred to as "leather girls," a word play on the British movie *The Leather Boys*, which is about the unrequited love of a gay male biker for a heterosexual biker. The pejorative connotations of these usages could have expressed a wish among many gay men to distinguish themselves categorically from S&M gay men, to cognitively bound gay S&M, and may have disguised a latent fear and insecurity about S&M. Or, on the contrary, as Stephen Murray suggests (personal communication), shown a familiarity-bred contempt for and skepticism of the leathermen's own distancing. At any rate, in spite of the ideological boundary between the leather and non-leather worlds, it is clear that "leathermen" and "normal gays" were highly interdependent components of the gay male ghetto. From the literature one would expect that the S&M world received a sizeable complement of initiates from the gay world at large. Indeed, in comparatively observing crowds in S&M and "normal" gay bars, one would be struck by the relatively larger proportion of older men in the former.

INSIDE THE MINESHAFT:
LAYOUT, RULES, STAGES, PROPS, ACTS

The Mineshaft could be approached with a sense of abandon, reverence, anxious dread (typically the first time), but usually evoked some sense of excitement, however mild. On weekends few arrived before 2:00 A.M. and the crowd was dense until at least 5:00 A.M., but on weekday nights customers came in earlier and left earlier. The Mineshaft was laid out on two windowless floors: the front entrance led to a blackwalled flight of stairs on which one waited on line, with one's eyes at the level of the small of the back of the person in front. At the top of the stairs stood a bouncer and an assistant manager behind a small lectern where one showed identification and paid admission. "Members" paid a lower rate than "non-members," but "non-members" were given a "temporary membership pass" which advised them of the Mineshaft's rules of admittance and decorum. These included a dress code which expressly forbade designer clothes of any kind, suits and ties and dress shoes, "drag," and cologne. It also applauded clothes associated in American culture with working class masculinity: levis and leather, t-shirts, boots, lumber jackets and uniforms, and "just plain sweat." In practice, one would be refused admission for inappropriate dress, and in some cases the exclusion criteria were extended on the basis of unwritten rules by the employee at the door to judgements of appearance, deportment or reputation as well. For example, attempts were made to exclude pickpockets. In general, it appeared that the exclusion criteria were applied fairly consistently to those wearing forbidden articles. If one was not a member, there was a greater chance of being refused admission. Memberships were sold at a variety of rates (for example $10.00 for three months) and entitled one to receive discount admission for the period in question. Membership meant one's name was put on a membership list, and a glossy black plastic membership card, the size of a credit card, was issued in that name. Members also recorded their "alias" or "code-name" while signing up for membership. These were typically masculine and informal such as "Butch," "Skipper," "Johnny Boy," or "Dick." This combination Boys' Club and pseudorationalized bureaucratic ritual may well have cosmeticized a genuine gatekeeping function defined by the need to circumvent legal authority.

The first room one entered after being admitted was the "front room." This was a large space, with spotlit pool tables, a long bar which was the most brightly lit area in the Mineshaft, a coat check area, and a few benches in the shadows along the far wall. The walls were mostly unvarnished planks and there was sawdust on the floor, as there was throughout the upper floor. Near the front entrance was the entrance to a red lit restroom which contained a number of stalls, urinals, and a small single sink which allowed water to splash onto the floor. At the coatcheck a sign offered a 5-cent discount to anyone who was "uncut and could prove it." Coatcheck employees were friendly and would without question check any and all articles of clothing a customer wished. This allowed some imagination to be used in devising appropriate costumes, since customers could check their street clothes and don something more exotic. One evening, for example, I was startled to realize that the man standing silently next to me in the shadows was wearing a New York City policeman's uniform. When I could speak, I whispered "I think it's a raid," and was informed by someone nearby "Huh? Oh. No, he always does that." On crowded evenings, a coatcheck line would form during peak entry hours, and again at closing. The coatcheck thus represented a second transition zone, one where minus the uncertainty of admission one could get into costume, or look around and stake out the territory. The front room was the most convivial area of the Mineshaft, as it was the only area where "talking out loud" was not frowned upon. It was a place to "get in the mood" for further activity, or to "relax" prior to returning to the outside world. People spending time in the front room were often willing to have friendly conversations, but the front room was also a favored place for initiating sexual contact. Scenarios that used verbal scripts to develop erotic momentum found a place here. Occasionally it became the scene for a variety of simple activities that used the pool table or the bar as props: people would bend over a pool table, sit astride it, or stand at the bar, while their partners would penetrate or fellate them. It was especially appropriate for those who enjoyed a sense of public spectacle, exhibition, or humiliation. Activities at the bar were somewhat constrained by the expectation that those standing there would order drinks. A sign over the bar listed the suggested "donations" of $1.00 for beer and $2.50 for liquor. If erotic activity began close by people whose conversation was unrelated to the activity, the talkers might move away slightly so as not to be in the way, they might ignore it, or, rarely, they might lower their voices and watch. The front room set a tone of non-competitive respect for and indulgent nonchalance about sexual activity that became the rule throughout the Mineshaft.

Activities begun in the front room might also move into an adjacent area. The red lit restrooms were often the site of watersports. A more dramatic transition was the darkened archway that led to the blackwalled "playground." The playground had its own set of rules which were spelled out on the temporary membership pass: no talking, no laughing, no dishing in the playground. Above the entrance another sign gave the more practical advice: No winter coats in the playground. The playground (and the entire lower floor when it was in use) were usually maintained at a higher temperature than the front room. It was much dimmer than the front room, contained a small bar, a table, some wooden stalls, two recesses which contained slings, and featured a spotlit wooden frame in the center with a sling about six feet off the ground. The slings were used to suspend men who wished to be fisted, and the bartender at the small bar would provide paper mayonnaise cups of crisco and handfuls of paper towels to those doing the fisting. The wooden stalls could be used by those wishing to exclude others, but also had "glory-holes" to allow both voyeurism and pseudo-anonymous fellatio. The table was moved about from time to time and used variously. One evening I observed a man lying on it while another stood over him dripping hot wax from a red candle on his nipples. The playground also had its own small restroom.

The lower level could only be reached through the playground, and was only open during the weekend crush. In effect, then, it was an extension of the playground belowstairs. Two flights of stairs went down. One, reached through a door, was a standard, wide, steel-inforced stairway that presumably conformed to fire regulations. The other, spotlit and situated just behind the central fisting frame, was a ramshackle, single-width, barely navigable wooden staircase, which presumably looked appropriate to an abandoned mine. Customers did not appear to have any preference between the two stairways. The lower level was more extensive than the upper but was internally divided by concrete walls, which were painted black throughout. The first part of the lower level was virtually a maze. The floor was not level, and the area was difficult to navigate, pitch-black in some corners. Most of the darkened corners were the setting for ordinary fellatio or intercourse, between pairs or in groups. Beneath the wooden stairway were several more wooden stalls with glory-holes. In one section, kept especially warm, were several bathtubs. Men would sit in the bathtubs, usually naked, but occasionally clothed, waiting for others to urinate on them. The silence of this activity was occasionally broken by whispered encouragement. In another room was a stage, but I never observed it used for a performance. The last room on the lower floor contained a large bar, which was overshadowed by an enormous mirror in which one could observe the room as if from a bird's eye view. This room was used primarily for "backroom" style sex, that is, whatever activity people wanted to engage in with those adjacent to them in the crowd.

The Mineshaft was equipped with a sophisticated sound system which was used to play original tapes. The tapes were eclectic, but favored avant-garde, punk, and classical music. The sound system operated at a lower volume in the front room than in the playground areas.

ROLE SYSTEMS AND RITUAL DRAMA

In spite of the complexity of the institutional, cultural, and psychological forces which appear to have been at play in the Mineshaft on a typical Saturday night, it nevertheless appeared that socially structured roles in the formal sense were rather simple. Since, at least from the customer's view point, the meaning of a Mineshaft experience was a highly personal one, it was necessary for individuals to feel free to develop their own fantasies and create their own roles to match. Such personal improvisation was a form of self-education, and I would hypothesize, unlike Sambian initiation, was largely self-directed. I would suggest, however, that two simple role systems operated independently of individual fantasy. These can be described as the distinction between employees and customers, and between members and non-members.

The former corresponds to the capitalist political economy which created and sheltered the Mineshaft. From this perspective the Mineshaft was part of the American entertainment industry, and its employees provided a service. The distinction between employees and customers exists in any commercial organization. Like most employees in the ghetto, Mineshaft employees were workers in the secondary labor market, and dependent on tips.[7] They dressed like customers, fraternized freely with customers, and in some cases might become customers during their free time. This apparently vague line between the two roles was characteristic of ghetto employment, but was especially vague at the Mineshaft. This might have been partly a result of the relatively high complement of ghetto workers among the Mineshaft's clientele, whose expertise would make them demanding; and partly due to the Mineshaft's marginal legal status, which would make management wary of any overt conflict with customers. Since the municipal police were probably paid off to ignore the Mineshaft's existence, they could hardly be called in to deal with any altercation. Along with their manifest duties, employees would look out for the welfare of customers, who might, for example, require medical attention. They would eject pickpockets. On one occasion, I observed someone who had passed out being carried up the stairs.

The line between members and non-members was less formal than it sounds, and I have already suggested that it could be operationalized in a variety of ways, such as weekend versus weekday night attendance, or newcomers versus old hands. It has been described in a romantic short story about the Mineshaft (Preston, 1984:80) as, in effect, the difference between "The Committed" and the presumably not-so committed. The significant variation was one of degree of socialization.

Of course, the normative standards of membership in the Mineshaft did not assume any single definition of masculine erotic reality. Indeed, the ability of the Mineshaft experience to accommodate the individual homo-erotic realities of hundreds, if not thousands of gay men, was its most interesting feature. While each participant performed his own ritual with his own meanings, the Mineshaft functioned somehow to hook up all these performances with a common set of facilities, rules, symbols, and emotions. It suggests on the one hand, the possibility of non-violent community in a fragmented, specialized, and culturally atomized society; or forces one to "consider the dionysian as an archetypal aspect inherent in every society" (Maffesoli, 1983). Thus, in contrast to the two simple, socially imposed role systems just described, ritual dramatic roles at the Mineshaft were flexible and complex. Nothing prevented an individual who so desired from assuming a variety of roles in any number of different activities, even during the course of a single evening. The lighting was dim, there was no reason to speak aloud, and one could change costume. Men who were tired of playing erotic subjects could find a way to be erotic objects, and vice versa. Some ritual activities, especially those involving more than two participants, were far more complex than simple dyads. Indeed, spontaneous orgiastic combinations centered on fellatio, masturbation, and anal intercourse were quite liminal. Even clearly defined active/passive dyads in the context of the Mineshaft were often transformed into group experiences, and informants have described their experiences in the Mineshaft as having had a religious meaning. For example, consider the following description of a playground whipping from Preston's romance:

> The men who crowded us couldn't help but try to touch him. Even while my belt thudded on his back their hands would reach out and worshipfully attempt to feel some part of him. They were awesomely silent. It was as though a new, precious icon had appeared in this house where men were venerated. (1984:82-83)

In this story the narrator decides that the man he is whipping does not really want these others around, that "it broke the finely tuned communication between us." So after an interaction wherein "he kissed me just a little," the restored dyad "go back to the front." "People followed us from room to room hoping that the ritual this man and I were performing would be repeated," reports the obviously boastful narrator.

As in this example, the main problem of social control in the Mineshaft centered on this tension among the tremendous variety of erotic fantasies people might be acting out in any given encounter. This tension was usually contained by an extraordinarily fine-tuned etiquette of glances, gestures, movements, and whispered encouragements or "dirty talk." During the entire period of observation I only witnessed one incident involving actual rage or violence, an exception which revealed the rule of ritualized social control. This took place on an especially crowded weekend evening on the lower floor in the superheated area near the bathtubs. A man called out very loudly "I said STOP THAT!" and apparently struck another man. The crowd was stunned, and in Goffman's terminology, the frame was obviously broken–no one knew what to do. All sound but the disco tapes ceased. People all around stopped what they were doing and stood frozen as if in a tableau. The man continued to shout and struck out several more times. It appeared to me that he struck out at random, and may have injured more than one person. Someone called out "Hey, no fighting!" One injured man left the area. Finally people close to the assailant began to take action appropriate to the situation, taking hold of the man and talking to him. The assailant was maneuvered away, while some of those who had witnessed the incident edged out of the area, clearly disturbed. Meanwhile newcomers moved in, and the frame was re-established within a few minutes.

CONCLUSION

What then do we know about the Mineshaft?

Decoding the language of social control used in the Mineshaft would need systematic study of a similar site. Such a study would need to include such symbolic languages as costume, pose, and choreography. The boundary between the front room and the playground suggests Mead's discussion of the relation between games and play (1962:151-163). The Mineshaft fostered both intense play, where one took on a single role and played it, and the greater complexity of the game, where knowledge of other roles (and the roles of others) was also required. The Mineshaft needed to accommodate different levels of understanding of every language it used. If an initiate was unable to articulate his needs through costume, or moving in a certain way, or standing in a certain position, he might still be able to stumble upon fulfillment in the dark, or just stand still until someone with clever hands decoded his secret. The complex and ill-lit layout necessitated slow, stage-like movement, even when crowds were not present, and simultaneously facilitated fantasy.

But analysis must move beyond the symbolic; it must also examine touch, smell, taste, and non-verbal sound as non-symbolic avenues of culturally meaningful experience. In a highly verbal culture, where words and mass-produced images dominate socially constructed reality, the dim lighting and primarily non-verbal communication of the playground eerily emphasized the openness of touch, smell, taste, and non-verbal sound as avenues of experience. These zones were as much a vacant niche in the psychocultural landscape of America as the meatpacking district in which the Mineshaft was located was a vacant niche in the political economy of the urban landscape. The playground especially was devoted to the way things literally *felt* to participants. It was a place where cultural inhibitions were displaced, rather than discussed; that is, an arena of critical practice, rather than critical discourse.

The Mineshaft may have addressed unarticulated and neglected desires of gay men for social sanctioning by allowing individuals to act out their fantasies and "unwind their reels" in a group setting. If so, how deeply did these experiences affect people? How did they interpret what was going on around them? How well did their experiences match the diversity of their fantasies?

The Mineshaft probably functioned to socially organize risk reduction at the nexus of the S&M and larger gay male communities by maintaining an environment in which limiting experimentation could be carried on in the presence of experienced persons. Relative to less organized alternatives such as the streets and dockside, it was a safe place for initiates into the S&M world to meet those with developed S&M identities. It was at times a site of awesome and liminal rituals of initiation which the culture in which it was situated maintained in secrecy and considered taboo. As was also true in the Sambian rituals, humiliation and fear were linked with affection and mutual erotic satisfaction.

At the same time the Mineshaft was not under the control of the homo-erotic male community. It was clearly the creation of secondary labor market capitalism and maintained through traditional forms of political corruption. Its owners allowed its use as a vehicle for media exploitation of gay men.

Nevertheless, nightly, it clearly demonstrated the power of culture and social organization to transform sensation and physiological response into erotic experience.

NOTES

1. Such as those between, on the one hand, normative ideals of "equality" and "freedom," and on the other hand, the realities of inequities of power and constraints on opportunity.

2. Liminality, and its relationship to *communitas,* is a central concern for Turner (1969). In a *rite de passage,* the individual or group undergoing the rite is first separated from social structure or cultural givens before becoming liminal, i.e., not subject to social definition, "neither here nor there" (op.cit.:94-95). *Communitas* is the relatively unstructured society which emerges in the liminal phase. As will be shown, the Mineshaft could well have provided its customers with such experiences.

As a more classical example of ritual liminality it is interesting to note Herdt's (1982, 1987) discussions of Sambian initiation. The initiation experience, as Herdt describes it, is "deeply awesome" (1982:68) if not terrifying, rather than "fun," although for the older participants it seems enjoyable enough. This difference between the experience of the initiates and that of the older males seems due primarily to the secrecy which is maintained about the rites, as a result of which the initiates have no clear expectation of what will happen to them.

During the ceremony, violence and joking hostility are exercised by the older males on the initiates, and a homoerotic norm is successfully introduced and established in most cases. This norm involves an explicit association between fellatio and flute playing, whereby the flutes are eroticized. The young boys are taught that performing fellatio on older males is necessary in order to become men themselves. They ultimately learn to enjoy this activity and enter into various libidinal liaisons with older men to whom they are attracted. The initiation also prepares them for their subsequent role as older participants in such relations.

A startling surface similarity between the Sambia and the United States lies in the secrecy attached to homoerotic socialization. However, the secrecy attached to the Sambian rites is hegemonic within the tribe, secret knowledge which is a source of power for its practitioners. In the United States the secrecy attached to homoeroticism is resistive, a result of domination.

3. The Mineshaft's decor, for example, was in some ways suggestive of a late evening at some of those outdoor sites in its vicinity at which many patrons would have erotic experiences under conditions of considerably greater personal danger of, among other things, being mugged. Certainly, as will be discussed below, the Mineshaft's location was as out-of-the-way and its admission policies as elaborate as anything necessitated by police surveillance during the early 1960s.

4. For example, the need to develop stigma management skills, or overcome internalized negative stereotypes of gay identity. This has improved somewhat in that there are now books available on how to come out to one's parents or maintain a long-term relationship with another man, and in large cities psychotherapists willing to help one develop a positive gay identity. But where does a 15-year-old go to find true love, or failing that, to practice sexual risk reduction techniques, with other young men?

5. A service economy centered in Greenwich Village had emerged with extraordinary vitality from the underground during the previous decade. During the early 1960s as few as five packed gay bars might be serving the entire metropolitan New York area at a given moment, and these were subject to Mafia administration and police pay-off, and of course, raids. Even private gay parties were subject to raids. The "Stonewall Rebellion" of June, 1969, was essentially a communal response to a bar raid, but marked the beginning of a new era of relative governmental indifference to non-political group activities of gay men.

6. As Barry Adam has reminded me, there were also back rooms in some bars in operation during regular hours.

7. Secondary, relative to primary labor market employment, is characterized by low pay, low status, short or non-existent career ladders, lack of benefits, non-unionization, job insecurity, and transience

REFERENCES

Adam, B. D. (1978). *The survival of domination.* New York: Elsevier.

Dynes, W. (1985). *Homolexis: A historical and cultural lexicon of homosexuality.* New York: Gai Saber.

Goffman, E. (1963). *Stigma: The management of spoiled identity.* Englewood Cliffs, NJ: Prentice-Hall Inc.

Herdt, G. H. (1982). Fetish and fantasy in Sambia initiation. In G. H. Herdt (Ed.), *Rituals of manhood: Male initiation in Papua New Guinea.* (pp. 44-98). Berkeley: University of California.

Herdt, G. H. (1987). *The Sambia: Ritual and gender in New Guinea.* New York: Holt, Rinehart and Winston.

Kamel, G. W. L. (1983a). The leather career: On becoming a sadomasochist. In T. Weinberg & G. W. L. Kamel (Eds.), *S and M: Studies in sadomasochism* (pp. 73-79). Buffalo, New York: Prometheus.

Kamel, G. W. L. (1983b). Leathersex: Meaningful aspects of gay sadomasochism. In T. Weinberg & G. W. L. Kamel (Eds.), *S and M: Studies in sadomasochism* (pp. 162-174). Buffalo, New York: Prometheus.

Krafft-Ebing, R. (1965). *Psychopathia sexualis* (F. S. Klaf, Trans.). New York: Bell.

Lee, J. A. (1983). The Social Organization of Sexual Risk. In T. Weinberg & G. W. L. Kamel (Eds.), *S and M: Studies in sadomasochism* (pp. 175-193). Buffalo, New York: Prometheus.

Maffesoli, M. (1983, June). *The orgiastic as an agent of socialization.* Handout at the conference *Among men, among women: Sociological and historical recognition of homosocial arrangements,* Universiteit van Amsterdam.

Mains, G. (1984). *Urban aboriginals.* San Francisco: Gay Sunshine.

Mead, G. H. (1962). *Mind, self, and society,* (C. Morris, Ed.). Chicago: University of Chicago. (Original work published 1934.)

Murray, S. O. (1984). *Social theory, homosexual realities.* New York: Gai Saber.

Newton, E. (1972). *Mother camp: Female impersonators in America.* Chicago: University of Chicago.

Preston, J. (1984). Interludes. In Preston, J., *I once had a master* (pp. 80-89). Boston: Alyson.

Rist, D. Y. (1985, November 26). Policing the libido. *The Village Voice.* pp. 17-18, 20-21.

Russo, V. (1981). *The celluloid closet: Homosexuality in the movies.* New York: Harper & Row, Pub. Inc.

Spengler, A. (1983). Manifest sadomasochism of males: Results of an empirical study. In T. Weinberg & G. W. L. Kamel (Eds.), *S and M: Studies in sadomasochism* (pp. 57-72). Buffalo, New York: Prometheus. (Reprinted from *Archives of Sexual Behavior,* 1977, 6, 441-456.)

Townsend, L. (1983). *The leatherman's handbook II* (4th printing). New York: Modernismo.

Turner, V. W. (1969). *The ritual process: Structure and anti-structure.* New York: Aldine.

Weinberg, M. S. & Williams, C. J. (1974). *Male homosexuals: Their problems and adaptations.* New York: Oxford University.

Weinberg, T. S. (1983). Sadism and masochism: Sociological perspectives. In T. Weinberg & G. W. L. Kamel (Eds.), *S and M: Studies in sadomasochism* (pp. 99-112). Buffalo, New York: Prometheus. (Reprinted from *The Bulletin of the American Academy of Psychiatry and the Law,* 1978, 6, 284-295.)

Index

accommodation, in "coming out" 103

acquired immune deficiency syndrome (AIDS)
 Centers for Disease Control's recognition of 226
 ethical reactionism and 29-30
 homophobia and 30
 illicit drug use and 227
 in Nicaragua 178
 nitrite inhalants and 228-229

Action for Lesbian Parents 31

activo 23-24,174,175,179,196

adolescents, homosexual behavior of, in ancient Greece 60-61,62

adoption, by homosexual and lesbian couples 32,112

adultery 120

Advocate (newspaper) 229

Africa, lesbianism in 149, *see also* Lesbianism, among Black women

aggression, as heterosexual male trait 18

alcoholism, gay bars and 227

Allgemeinen handrecht 80,86-87

altruism 7,18

American Indians, berdaches of 44

AMNLAE 176

amphetamines 227

amyl nitrite 227-228, *see also* nitrite inhalants

anal intercourse
 in ancient Greece 61
 with boys 10, *see also* man/boy love

forensic diagnosis of 82,83
 as male initiation rite 9
 nitrite inhalant use during 227

androgynism 78

animals, reproductive strategies of 58

Anvil bar 240

aphilia 128

Archivos de Psiquiatria y Criminologia 193

Argentina
 feminist movement in 188
 police harassment of homosexuals in 205
 sexual inversion construction in 24,184,192-208
  homosexuals' resistance to 198,199-204
  of sexual-invert subculture 204-208
  stereotypes of 197-199

arousal
 homoerotic 235
 S&M-related 237-238

artificial insemination 29,31

Ashanti, lesbianism in 149

Athens, *see also* Greece, ancient
 social gender allocation in 60-62

Austria Penal Code 87-88

autobiographies, of sexual inverts 199-202,203,206-207

AZT 230

Baal religion 117

barbiturates 227

Barricada (newspaper) 178

Because of the force of Freudianism for ego, these ppl even make "repressions" a reality so that they even (super) transit - it is their reality.

P7 - in this sense SC is the same (is that bad) as the others because they don't see their own basis as constructs or rather, they assume the existence of the distinctions between nature/nurture. ---

How can SC not give importance to biology?